ABSTRACTS

OF

WILL BOOK I
NASH COUNTY,
NORTH CAROLINA

1778-1868

by
RUTH SMITH WILLIAMS
and
MARGARETTE GLENN GRIFFIN

Southern Historical Press, Inc.
Greenville, South Carolina

Please direct all correspondence and book orders to:
SOUTHERN HISTORICAL PRESS, Inc.
PO Box 1267
Greenville, SC   29602-1267

Originally printed: Rocky Mounty, NC 1967
ISBN #978-1-63914-128-9
Printed in the United States of America

INTRODUCTION

Will Book I, as found in the Nash County Court
House, Nashville, North Carolina, is in reality, a typed
and bound copy of the original Will Books I, II, III,
and IV.

No personal property is included in these
abstracts. However, when description of land was avail-
able, those records appear.

Williams and Griffin

FOREWORD

The origin of Nash County, formerly a part of early Edgecombe, North Carolina, was brought about by an Act of the North Carolina Assembly, April 8, 1777. The County was named for General Francis Nash, who lost his life in the American Revolution, and Nashville was made the County Seat.

This Abstract of Wills of Nash County complements the Early Edgecombe Records by Ruth Smith Williams and Margarette Glenn Griffin:

Abstract of Wills of Edgecombe   1733-1856
1956

Marriages of Early Edgecombe   1733-1868
1958

Bible Records of Early Edgecombe
1958

Tombstone and Census Records of Early Edgecombe
1959

ADAMS, SACKFIELD
     P. 11. May 1, 1779 - April Ct. 1780. Wife:
SUSANNAH. Sons: 1. WILLIAM, 2. ROBERT. No ex. Wit:
SAMUEL MILLER, ROB'T. CLARK.

ADKINS, BENJAMIN
     P. 55. Mar. 22, 1789 - May Ct. 1789. Wife and
EXTX: PENELOPE. Dau: RACHEL. Ex: JOHN POWELL. Wit:
ALANSAN POWELL, HENRY SCREWS.

ALLEN, ARTHUR of ELIZABETH PARISH
     P. 40. Dec. 14, 1784 - May Ct. 1785. Sons:
1. THOMAS - 400 A. whereon he lives and 3 A. orchard;
2. ARTHUR - all land whereon I live, below Mouth of Fall
Branch adjoining THOMAS ALLEN; Daus: EASE ALLEN - 180 A.
bought of JOSEPH HARWOOD on east side Marsh Branch;
RHODEA ALLEN - 150 A. adjoining THOMAS ALLEN; ELIZABETH
ALLEN - 150 A. adjoining RHODEA ALLEN; SARAH ALLEN. Ex:
sons THOMAS AND ARTHUR ALLEN. Wit: DAVID PRIDGEN,
BRITTON WHITLEY, NANCY BAKER.

ANDERSON, PETER
     P. 141. June 30, 1801 - Nov. Ct. 1801. Wife: ANN.
Sons: 1. JOHN, 2. HARDY - 243 A. at mother's death,
3. HENRY - 210 A. purchased of WILLIAM ARRINGTON, 4.
WILLIAM, 5. NATHAN, 6. JAMES, 7. HOWELL. Daus: 1. SUSANA
HAYES, 2. MARY, 3. ANNEY. Ex: JOSEPH ARRINGTON, JOHN
ARRINGTON. Wit: JOHN HARRISON, JOHN GREEN, JAS. BRADEY.

ANDERSON, SARAH
     P. 546. Jan. 19, 1849 - Aug. Ct. 1855. Daus:
1. MARTHA EMILY, wife of JOHN Q. A. DRAKE, 2. SARAH ANN,
wife of HOLMAN ARRINGTON, dec'd, 3. ANN ELIZABETH, wife
of LEMUEL WHELESS, 4. MARY ELIZA, wife of RICHARD
WHITAKER. Ex: THOMAS W. WRIGHT (friend and relative).
Wit: NATH. H. MURPHY, BENJ. A. DOZIER. Clerk's notes:
THOMAS W. WRIGHT renounced his right to administer as
executor, and RICHARD M. WHITAKER was appointed administrator with HENRY WHITAKER and BENJ. A. HOLLMAN as sureties.

ARCHBELL, NATHAN B.
    P. 556. Sept. 5, 1852. Nov. Ct. 1857. Wife:
SOPHIA. Son: JOHN, estate to be settled when he,
JOHN, the youngest son comes of age. Ex: ISIAH
RESPASS. Wit: WILLIAM T. WRIGHT, AJMES T. RESPASS.

ARRINGTON, ARCHIBALD H.
    P. 614. May 6, 1872 - July 29, 1872. Sons: 1.
JOHN P., 2. THOMAS M., 3. ARCHIBALD H., 4. SAMUEL L.,
5. ROBERT W., 6. GEORGE W., 7. JOSEPH C., Dau: 1.
MARY. Ex: Bro. SAMUEL L. ARRINGTON of Alabama to
serve in that state; THOS. J. A. COOPER and BENJ. L.
ARRINGTON, along with all his sons to serve as Ex's.
in Nash Co., N. C. All sons are minors except JOHN,
and are to be allowed to serve as Ex, anytime after
reaching 18 yrs. of age, with the provision that they
take the proper precaution for and interest in my
estate. Codicil, July 14, 1872. I direct that 60 A.
adjoining THOS. J. A. COOPER and Dr. JOHN G. F. DRAKE
be laid off and conveyed to a colored boy, ALEXANDER
ARRINGTON, who is bound to me until 21 yrs. of age,
with provision that in the event of my death, he shall
remain with my children and discharge his duties until
he reaches 21 yrs. of age. Wit: SAM L. ARRINGTON,
JNO. ARRINGTON.

ARRINGTON, ARTHUR
    P. 102. May 23, 1795 - Nov. Ct. 1795. Wife:
MARY. Sons: 1. HENRY, 2. RICHARD, 3. ARTHUR - all
land, 4. JOSEPH, 5. WILLIAM, 6. PETER. Daus: 1.
ELIZABETH VICK - 2 negroes bought of JOHN BATTLE,
now in possession of HENRY VICK: 2. POLLY HUNTER,
3. ANN ARRINGTON. Gr. daus: MARY and ELIZABETH
BATTLE. Ex: wife MARY and sons JOSEPH, JOHN, and
WILLIAM ARRINGTON. Wit: WILLIAM LEWIS, JAMES
SANDERFORD.

ARRINGTON, ARTHUR
    P. 140. April 1, 1779 - Aug. Ct. 1801. Wife:
MARY. Sons: 1. ARTHUR, 2. BENJAMIN, 3. JAMES.

2

Daus: 1. ELIZABETH DREWRY, 2. MARY WHITEHEAD, 3. ANN
DRAKE. Gr. Son: ARTHUR ARRINGTON. Ex: Sons JOSEPH
and JAMES ARRINGTON. Wit: WM. HALL, JETHRO DENSON,
FANNIE ROSE.

ARRINGTON, ARTHUR
    P. 607. Feb. Ct. 1868. Son & Ex: THOMAS C.
ARRINGTON all land and tools. Remainder of estate to
be divided among "all my children" (unnamed). Wit:
N. W. COOPER, JOHN ARRINGTON.

ARRINGTON, BARBARA
    P. 510. Jan. 13, 1848 - Feb. Ct. 1848. Bro:
FRANCIS HEIGHT. Daus: 1. MARY I., wife of ARCHIBALD
H. ARRINGTON, 2. BARBARA S., wife of WILLIAM K. A.
WILLIAMS. Ex: Son-in-law ARCHIBALD H. ARRINGTON.
Wit: JNO. ARRINGTON, THOS. C. ARRINGTON.

ARRINGTON, HENRY
    P. 423. Dec. 23, 1837 - May Ct. 1838. Wife:
REBECCA. Sons: 1. ROBERT, 2. JOHN L., 3. HOLMAN, the
Cooper tract, 4. HENRY. Dau: 1. ELIZABETH WARD, wife
of JOHN WARD, decs. Reversion of land whereon I dwell.
Chil. of ELIZABETH WARD: MARY, REBECCA AND JOHN WARD.
The Conight land in Halifax Co., adjoining AFRED MOORE,
JAMES MOORE AND DR. YELLOWBY to be sold. Ex: Son,
JOHN L. ARRINGTON. Wit: JAMES S. BRYAN, ARCHIBALD H.
ARRINGTON, RICHARD ARRINGTON.

ARRINGTON, HOLMAN
    P. 508. Aug. 31, 1846 - Nov. Ct. 1847. Wife:
SARAH ANN. Sons: 1. HENRY, 2. HARDY, 3. JOHN DOUGLAS,
4. ROBERT ARTHUR, 5. HOLMAN THOMAS, 6. PETER WATSON
ARRINGTON. Ex: N. W. ARRINGTON. Wit: WM. F. DRAKE,
TEMPERANCE G. ARRINGTON.

ARRINGTON, JOHN
    P. 463. June 10, 1830 - Nov. Ct. 1845. Sons:
1. SAMUEL L. - has his land, 2. ARCHIBALD - land whereon
I dwell. Dau: 1. ELIZABETH ANN WILLIAMS - 400 A. N.
side Swift Crk. Ex: SAMUEL L. ARRINGTON, HENRY G.
WILLIAMS, ARCHIBALD ARRINGTON. Wit: WM. BURT, Wm.
DRAKE, GEO. CLANTON.

3

ARRINGTON, JOSEPH, SR.
P. 300. Nov. 12, 1818. Feb. Ct. 1819. Wife:
MARTHA. Sons: two youngest sons, CRAFFORD and JAMES
HENRY to have land whereon I live, at death of their
mother; 3. JOSEPH, 4. CARTER. Daus: 1. ELIZABETH
CRAFFORD, wife of JOHN NICHOLSON; 2. MARTHA, wife of
THOMAS ARRINGTON, 3. ANN, 4. LEAH, wife of ARTHUR
ARRINGTON. Ex: sons, CARTER and JOSEPH. Wit: JETHRO
DENSON, JAMES WHITEHEAD.

ARRINGTON, JOSEPH, SR.
P. 413. Mar. 8, 1836. May Ct. 1836. A debt
to be paid to THOMAS MAYFIELD and JESSE PERSON.
Daus: MARY, wife of PRESLY C. PERSON, RHODA, wife of
CARTER ARRINGTON, TEMPERANCE, wife of NATHANIEL MASON.
Wit: JOHN ARRINGTON, ARCHIBALD H. ARRINGTON.

ARRINGTON, JOSEPH W.
P. 571. May 31, 1860. Nov. Ct. 1860. Bro:
1. JOLLY B. ARRINGTON, 2. WILLIAM T. Nephew: JAMES
J. ARRINGTON. Wit: Sam'l. L. ARRINGTON, JNO. B.
SMITH, JAMES N. ARRINGTON. Clerk's Notes: JOSEPH
W. ARRINGTON, a citizen of Montgomery Co., Ala., whose
will had been authenticated in Ala. - WM. T. ARRINGTON
appt'd. admin. for estate in Nash Co.

ARRINGTON, LEW
P. 568. April 27, 1857. Aug. Ct. 1860. Sons:
1. BENJAMIN L. - the land I live on, known as the
WM. MANN tract, on Sandy Crk.; tract lying on Redbud Crk., called Viny Collins land or Marsh tract,
the tract known as Pitts land or Webb land, also one
on Redbud called the ELIJAH BODDIE tract, being part
of WM. BRIDGERS land tract. 2. GEROGE W. - the land
where he lives in Franklin Co., called the PETER
ARRINGTON tract. 3. WILLIAM HENRY - two tracts lying
on the north side Sandy Crk., known as the JOHN and BENJ.
MANN tracts. Daus: 1. SALLY ANN TAYLOR - the ZILPHA
WILLIAMS tract, the JESSE BRASWELL tract, part of the
JOHN MANN LAND, the DEMPSEY and MARY BRASWELL land,
and the JOHN EARLS tract; 2. MARY E. SUMNER - wife of
DANIEL E. SUMNER: Ex: Son BENJAMIN L. ARRINGTON.

Wit: ARTHUR ARRINGTON, JOHN ARRINGTON, SEN.

ARRINGTON, MARY
    P. 288. Sept. 3, 1816 - Nov. Ct. 1816. Sons:
1. THOMAS BATTLE, 2. LAWRENCE BATTLE, 3. WILLIAM BATTLE,
4. FREDERICK BATTLE - 213 A. which I inherited from my
father, 5. LARKIN BATTLE, 6. ALFORD BATTLE, 7. NICHOLAS
ARRINGTON. Daus: 1. ELIZABETH BATTLE, 2. MARTHA BATTLE,
3. MARY ANN BATTLE, 4. NANCY ARRINGTON. Step-dau:
MARTHA BATTLE, wife of LAWRENCE BATTLE (could this be
dau-in-law?) Ex: Friend MICHAEL COLLINS. Wit: A.
(ATHELSTON) ANDERSON, BENJAMIN BLOUNT.

ARRINGTON, MARY
    P. 154. Dec. 2, 1804 - Feb. Ct. 1805. Sons:
1. JOSEPH, 2. JOHN, 3. WILLIAM, 4. PETER, 5. HENRY,
6. RICHARD. Daus: 1. ELIZABETH VICK, 2. MARY HUNTER,
3. NANCY SANDEFORD. Gr. daus: MARY BATTLE, ELIZABETH
BATTLE. Ex: Sons JOSEPH, JOHN, WILLIAM ARRINGTON.
Wit: D. (DANIEL) B. POTTER, JOHN BORLAND.

ARRINGTON, NICHOLAS
    P. 595. Mar. 16, 1863 - Aug. Ct. 1865. Wife:
TEMPERANCE - home plantation with reversion to JOHN G.
and JOSEPHINE, youngest dau. Sons: 1. JOHN G.,
2. NICHOLAS W., my poor, unfortunate son. Daus:
1. TEMPY ANN HARRIS - the Culpepper place where N. M.
HARRIS lives, 2. MARY WILLIAM ARRINGTON and 3. CELESTIA
C. ARRINGTON - to share the Bynum place, mill, etc.,
4. JOSEPHINE, 5. ELIZABETH, wife of W. T. WRIGHT, has
already been provided for. Trustee: W. M. CONYERS,
ESQ., - to guard property for chil. Ex: Nephews L.N.B.
BATTLE, L. F. BATTLE. This will disposes of much
wealth, in both real and personal property. Wit: J.J.
COLLINS, L. N. B. BATTLE.

ARRINGTON, PETER
    P. 441. June 8, 1837 - Aug. Ct. 1837. Wife:
BARBARA. Sons: 1. ARTHUR, 2. LEWELIN, 3. JOHN,
4. PETER. Daus: 1. MARY JONES ARRINGTON - reversion of
plantation whereon I live together with lands adjoining

FED BATTLE, JOHN DERING, and others, 2. BARBARA
SANDERFORD ARRINGTON - 1500 A. with mill in Franklin
Co., N. C. Gr. chil: ELIZA HARRIS - a bond against
AMOS HARRIS, MOURNING SCREWS, MARY T. DRAKE, HARRIETT
ADELINE DRAKE, RICHARD ARMSTRONG DRAKE, THOMAS I. A.
COOPER, WILLIAM COOPER, GEORGE COOPER, NEVERSON COOPER,
NANCY BUNN, the last named five, chil. of my dau.,
ELIZABETH COOPER desc. Their property now held by George
Cooper. Ex: Sons ARTHUR AND JOHN ARRINGTON. Wit:
RICH. ARRINGTON, A. L. BATTLE. Ordered recorded by
Nov. Ct. 1840.

ARRINGTON, PETER
        P. 530. Sept. 24, 1851 - Nov. Ct. 1852. Wife:
SARAH ANN - to have land where I reside, along with all
tools, household and kitchen furniture, in fact, everything on the plantation including all Negroes that
belong to me in this state, until her death or remarriage,
upon condition she is to make no charge against any one
of my children for board or necessaries furnished them
until they marry or come of age. Chil: 1. SUSAN ANN,
2. HARRIETT ELIZA, 3. PETER, 4. WILLIAM BURT, 5. KEARNEY
WILLIAMS, 6. LUCY JONES. Tract of land known as the
Eben Nelms tract in Franklin Co. to be sold. Ex:
Nephew DR. THOMAS E. ARRINGTON. Wit: ROBERT D. HART,
ARCHIBALD H. ARRINGTON.

ARRINGTON, PETER
        P. 538. Sept. 24, 1851 - May Ct. 1854. Wife:
SARAH ANN. Sons: 1. PETER, 2. WILLIAM BURT. Daus:
1. SUSAN ANN, 2. HARRIET ELIZA, 3. KEARNEY WILLIAMS,
4. LUCY JONES. Ex: Nephew DR. THOMAS C. ARRINGTON.
Wit: ROB'T. C. HART, ARCH. H. ARRINGTON. This will was
offered for probate at Nov. Ct. 1852, and is again pro-
pounded and duly proven by the witnesses and ordered to
be recorded. G. W. WARD, C.C.C.

ARRINGTON, RICHARD
        P. 432. Nov. 17, 1838 - Feb. Ct. 1839. Wife:
TEMPERANCE G. Son: 1. RICHARD W. ARRINGTON. Daus:
1. MARY L. ARRINGTON, 2. MARTHA E., 3. SUSAN L.,

6

4. TEMPERANCE B. Ex: Friends ARCHIBALD H. ARRINGTON, DR. JOHN ARRINGTON. Wit: HOLLMAN ARRINGTON, JOHN A. WHITEHEAD.

ARRINGTON, SARAH
P. 337. Oct. 11, 1826 - Nov. Ct. 1826. Son:
1. HOALMAN GARDNER. "All my chil." unnamed. Ex: JOHN DERRING. Wit: JOHN ARRINGTON, ARCH. ARRINGTON.

ARRINGTON, TEMPERANCE G.
P. 587. Jan. 3, 1864 - Feb. Ct. 1864. Son:
1. RICHARD W. (Ex) and TEMP. to share 160 A. where I live. Daus: 1. TEMPERANCE, 2. ELIZA, wife of GEORGE W. POWELL. Ex: GEORGE W. POWELL. Wit: H. G. WILLIAMS, D. E. SUMNER.

ARRINGTON, WILLIAM
P. 254. Sept. 17, 1812 - Feb. Ct. 1813. Dau:
1. MARY. "Other children" not named. No Ex. Wit: WOOD TUCKER, PHIL BENNETT, JOHN H. HARRISON.

ARRINGTON, WILLIAM T.
P. 582. May 26, 1860 - Aug. Ct. 1862. "Being about to take a journey of considerable duration and extent, do publish and declare this to be last will and testament". Wife: REBECCA E. - to have entire estate. At her death to be divided among "all my chil." Ex: Wife REBECCA and WILLIAM W. BODDIE. Wit: ARCHL'D H. ARRINGTON, WM. T. WILLIAMS. "Archl'd H. Arrington proved handwriting of Wm. T. Williams, who is absent in the army." W. W. Boddie renounced executorship. Rebecca E. Arrington qualified as Admin.

ATKINSON, ELIJAH
P. 285. Nov. 27, 1816 - Feb. Ct. 1817. Wife: ELIZABETH - 560 A. (the Tisdal land) with reversion to daus. Son: 1. BENNETT - 572 A. whereon I live. Daus: 1. TEMPERANCE GANDY, 2. ANNE ATKINSON, 3. MOURNING ATKINSON. Ex: Bros. JOHN ATKINSON, THOMAS ATKINSON. Wit: JESSE JOINER, JOHN S. BOTTOMS, SHEROD WILLIAMS.

ATKINSON, HENRY

P. 287. Mar. 9, 1816 - Feb. Ct. 1817. Sons:
1. BENJAMIN, 2. HENRY, 3. WILLIAM, 4. JACOB, 5. THOMAS.
Gr. son: ALSEY MOORE ATKINSON, son of HENRY - 100 A.
and mill on Sappony Crk. Gr. dau: SALLY, dau. of my
son THOMAS. Dau: 1. TEMPERANCE HARRISON. Ex: Son-
in-law WILLIAM HARRISON. Wit: JOHN VICK, HOPKINS RICE,
HARDY PRIDGEN.

ATKINSON, JAMES

P. 33. Dec. 21, 1779 - Apr. Ct. 1783. Wife:
MARGARET. Sons: BURWELL and EPHRAIM to share all land.
Indicates other children, but does not name them. Ex:
Wife MARGARET, son BURWELL. Wit: NATHAN BODDIE,
BENNETT BODDIE.

AVERETT, JEDUTHAM

P. 118. Feb. Ct. 1798. Wife: REBECCA. Dau:
SUSANNAH DRAKE. Other children unnamed. No Ex. Test:
NANCY AVERETT, HARDY AVERETT.

BAILEY, JOHN

P. 14. June 12, 1781 - Oct. Ct. 1781. Wife:
JUDITH. Sons: 1. HENRY, 2. JOHN - land whereon I live,
3. LEVY - land in Johnston Co., bought of HENRY FINCH
and HARDY BLACKWELL. Daus: 1. DREWSELLER O'NEAL,
2. PRISCILLA CARTER, 3. CHRISCHANEY, 4. RUTH, 5. CELIA,
6. UNITY. Ex: Wife JUDITH and son HENRY. Wit: HENRY
FINCH, DAVID BALEY, ISHAM FINCH.

BAILEY, SAMUEL

P. 65. Dec. 15, 1789 - Feb. Ct. 1790. Son: HENRY.
Daus: 1. CARRON HAPPOCK JOYNER, 2. ELIZABETH WHITLEY,
3. MILLEY JOYNER. Ex: Son-in-law JACOB JOYNER. Wit:
EDWARD NICHOLSON, JOHN SHEPPARD, W. M. BAKER.

BAILEY, SAMUEL

P. 382. Feb. 11, 1831 - Feb. Ct. 1832. Legatee:
SAMUEL JACKSON ARRINGTON, son of GEN. JOSEPH ARRINGTON.
Ex: GEN. JOSEPH ARRINGTON. Wit: JOHN DERING,
THOMPKINS ROSE.

8

BAILEY, WILSON

P. 584. Feb. 23, 1863 - May Ct. 1863. Wife unnamed.
"All my chil." unnamed. Ex: Friend KINCHEN BAILEY. Wit:
CHARLES H. HARRIS, A. F. LEWIS.

BAKER, DUNCAN

P. 574. June 7, 1861 - Aug. Ct. 1861. Wife: ZILPHA.
Sons: 1. CALVIN H., 2. ALEXANDER, 3. JOSIAH. Daus:
1. ADALINA BAKER, 2. ROENY BOON. Ex: GEORGE W. COOPER.
Wit: JOINER LANGLEY, JOHN BONE.

BAKER, WILLIAM SR.

P. 320. Jan. 1, 1820 - Feb. Ct. 1824. Sons:
1. WILLIAM, JR., 2. ALLEN, 3. ARCHIBALD, 4. ELISAH
(ELISHA?), 5. JOHN - 287 A. whereon I live, purchased of
ELISAH (ELISHA?) ELLIS. Daus: 1. NANNEY BAKER,
2. ELIZABETH LANGLEY, 3. MARY WELLS. Gr. dau: SALLEY
BAKER. Ex: Friend JOHN BAKER, DREWRY PRIDGEN. Wit:
JOINER LANGLEY, FOSTER GANDY, SHERROD WILLIAMS.

BALL, WILLIAM

P. 483. Mar. 24, 1842 - Nov. Ct. 1845. Wife:
MILLY. Son: WILLIAM KINCHEN BALL - all land. Dau:
PRISCILLA LAWRENCE WALKER. Son-in-law: BOLING WALKER.
Gr. chil: JOHN B. WALKER, ELICK H. WALKER, REBECCA H.
WALKER. Ex: JOHN F. BELLAMY. Wit: JOSEPH S. BATTLE,
DENNIS SOREY.

BALLARD, WILLIAM

P. 264. Sept. 23, 1814 - Feb. Ct. 1815. Wife:
ANNA. Dau: PHEREBY - whole estate after sale of land
bought of my bro. Ex: ELIJAH ATKINSON. Wit: FANNY
BABB. Proven by oath of WILLIAM LINDSEY and JESSE
JOINER who proved handwriting of WILLIAM BALLARD.

BALLENTINE, WILLIAM

P. 583. Nov. 9, 1860 - May Ct. 1863. Wife:
LINNY (Ex). Son: JOHN. "All my chil." Wit: J. M.
TAYLOR, H. D. LEWIS.

9

BARNES, BARSHEBA
    P. 438. Nov. 20, 1836 - May Ct. 1840. Father:
WILLIAM JOINEk. Sis: MORNING JOINER. Dau: ELIZA D.
JOINER, wife of CALVIN JOINER. Gr. dau: JACKY ANN
FRANCES ELIZABETH HILL JOINER. Ex: Son-in-law CALVIN
JOINER. Wit: EXUM S. CURL, JORDAN JOINER.

BARNES, BENJAMIN
    P. 91. Aug. 29, 1794 - Nov. Ct. 1794. Wife:
CHARITY. Sons: 1. DEMPSEY - land on N. side Great
Branch and lines of WILLIE BUNN, 2. EDWIN, 3. BENJAMIN-
remaining land. Daus: 1. RHODA, 2. MORNING, 3. RACHEL,
4. DELILAH. Ex: Wife CHARITY, Bro. WILLIAM BARNES.
Wit: REDMUN BUNN, SAMUEL SKINNER, JAMES MULLINS.

BARNES, BENNETT
    P. 561. April 26, 1856 - May Ct. 1859. Sis: MARY
RICKS - to have use of land and stock at RUFFIN H.
RICKS' for her lifetime. Son: ROBERT BARNES (Ex). Dau:
MARY ANN E. WILLIFORD - these two to share remaining
estate. Wit: EXUM L. CURL, FRANCIS M. B. CURL. Codicil, Sept. 15, 1858. In case I should have to pay the
note due WM. S. BATTLE from JOSIAH B. WILLIFORD, husband
of MARY ANN E. WILLIFORD, for which I am security, that
amount shall be deducted from her inheritance. Wit:
T. P. WESTRAY, HENRY VICK.

BARNES, CHARITY
    P. 161. Sept. 19, 1805 - Nov. Ct. 1805. Daus:
1. MORNING, 2. RACHEL, 3. DELILAH, 4. RHODA HUNT (Desc?).
Heirs of RHODA HUNT: 1. ANSLE, 2. BRITTAIN, 3. BENJAMIN.
Ex: REDMUN BUNN, son-in-law HENRY JOYNER. Wit: REDMUN
BUNN, CHARITY BUNN.

BARNES, ELIZABETH
    P. 360. June 28, 1828 - Aug. Ct. 1828. Nephews:
BINEL (?) BARNES, VINCENT BARNES. Bro. & Ex: JACOB
BARNES. Wit: BENNETT ATKINSON, BASHABA BARNES.

BARNES, JACOB
    P. 21. Jan. 25, 1780 - Oct. Ct. 1781. Wife:
ELIZABETH. Sons: 1. JOHN, 2. JACOB - 100 A. whereon I
live north of Tar River, 3. WILLIAM, 4. JAMES,
5. BENJAMIN. Daus: 1. SALLY JOINER, 2. ANN JONES. Gr.
son: JONAS BARNES WHITLEY. Ex: Wife ELIZABETH and
son BENJAMIN. Wit: DUNCAN LAMON, ARCH. LAMON, JOHN
GORDON.

BARNES, JACOB
    P. 487. Aug. 16, 1845 - Feb. Ct. 1846. Wife:
MORNING. Sons: 1. BURRELL - land where he lives,
2. JODIN - 112 A. where he lives, 3. JOHN, 4. CASWELL
H. - 60 A. where he lives, 5. VINSON, 6. JOEL. Daus:
1. PRIMMY BARNES, 2. ELIZABETH BARNES. PRIMMY, ELIZABETH
and VINSON share land whereon I live at mother's death.
Ex: Sons JOHN and JOEL BARNES. Wit: ELIZABETH H.
COCKRELL, PIETY H. VICK.

BARNES, JAMES SR.
    P. 333. Oct. 1, 1817 - Feb. Ct. 1826. Wife: POLLEY.
Sons & Ex: BENNETT and JAMES - all my land. Daus:
1. DRUCILLA McDADE, 2. POLLY BARNES. Gr. sons: JOSEPH
JAMES BARNES, THEOPHILUS BARNES. Wit: SAM SMITH,(ORREN) O.
D. BARNES, DAVID DANIEL.

BARNES, JAMES T.
    p. 622. Aug. 27, 1859 - Feb. Ct. 1866. Wife: MARY-
whole estate. Son & Ex: JOSEPH T. BARNES. Dau: AMANDA
BUNN and her heirs - 225 A. where she lives.

BARNES, JOHN
    P. 358. June 17, 1828 - Aug. Ct. 1828. Wife:
BERSHEBA - 160 A. whereon I live - reversion to dau.
ELIZA. Dau: ELIZA D. BARNES. Sis: 1. ELIZABETH BARNES,
2. NANCY BARNES. Legatees: UNITY JOINER, dau. of HARDY
JOINER, also - chil. of Bro. JACOB BARNES. Nephews:
JORDAN, JOHN, JOEL and JACOB BARNES. Ex: Bro. JACOB
BARNES. Wit: WILLIE BUNN, JOHN BUNN, EATON GAY.

BARNES, MARY
     P. 172. Dec. 8, 1805 - Aug. Ct. 1807.   Sons:
1. JOHN, 2. JACOB. Daus: 1. ELIZABETH, 2. MOLLY,
3. NANCY.   Ex: Son JOHN.   Wit: DRUERY JOYNER.

BARNES, MARY (wid. of JAMES T. BARNES)
     P. 609. Nov. 11, 1867 - May 20, 1871. Sons:
1. JOSHUA B. BARNES, 2. JOSEPH J. BARNES. Daus:
1. ELIZA C. or LOUISA C. BARNES - 60 A. adjoining
JOSEPH J. BARNES and T. P. WESTRAY, 2. FRANCES J.
MERTON, wife of JOHN MERTON, 3. MARY E. T. BARNES,
wife of ROBERT BARNES. Remaining land to be divided
among all chil. except (ELIZA OR LOUISA?) BARNES. Ex:
JOSEPH J. BARNES. Wit: REDMUN BUNN, D. TREVATHAN.

BARNES, PIETY
     P. 461. Feb. 20, 1843 - Feb. Ct. 1844. Dau:
MARTHA ANN BARNES. Bros. & Ex: WILLIAM JOYNER, ALFRED
JOYNER. Wit: EXUM S. CURL, WILLIAM JOYNER, ALFRED
JOINER.

BARNES, POLLY
     P. 270. Sept. 23, 1823 - Nov. Ct. 1815. Nephew:
BURWELL BARNES - money, etc. Brother: JACOB BARNES'
children to have remainder of my estate divided between
all of them except BURWELL BARNES. Ex: Bro. JACOB
BARNES. Wit: WILLIE BUNN, JAMES PERMUNTER (PERMENTER?),
NANCY BARNES.

BARNES, WILLIAM
     P. 334. Nov. 17, 1825 - May Ct. 1826. Sons:
1. SAMUEL BARNES, 2. ORRIN D. BARNES. Daus: 1. LUCRETIA
HARRELL, 2. LURANY READING, 3. TEMPERANCE FERRELL. Gr.
son: WILLIAM JOEL TOLLIVER FERRELL, son of TIMOTHY
FERRELL. Ex: Son ORRIN D. BARNES, son-in-law TIMOTHY
FERRELL. Wit: ISHAM DANIEL, ALFRED BUNN, JEREMIAH
BRASWELL.

BARRETT, DAVIS G.
     P. 613. Jan. 31, 1868 - May 6, 1872. Sis. and Extx:
SUSAN WINBORN - all estate. Wit: H.B.BARRETT, J.E.BARRETT.
12

BARRETT, NANCY
    P. 563. May 11, 1859 - Nov. Ct. 1859. Son:
1. DAVIS G. BARRETT - 83 A. land. Daus: 1. JANE
BARRETT, 2. MARTHA J. BARNES, 3. SARAH E. EDWARDS,
4. SUSAN WINBOURN - 83 A. land. Ex: Son DAVIS G.
BARRETT, son-in-law BENJAMIN EDWARDS. Wit: DAVID B.
RICKS, J. W. W. WOODRUFF.

BARRON, BARNABY
    P. 81. June 7, 1792 - Aug. Ct. 1793. Gr. chil:
BARNABY LEE - 300 A., which is the Lee place and where
JOHN GAY lives, BUD LEE - 300 A. known as Pope field,
TALTON LEE - 250 A. between Pope field and my homeplace,
WILLIAM LEE - 200 A. whereon I live, ELIZABETH LEE -
300 A. on Meadow Branch, NANCY LEE - 487 A. in Edgecombe
Co. Son-in-law: WILLIAM LEE. Ex: Friends JOHN RICE,
JAMES BARRON, BARNABY BARRON. Wit: ROBERT RUTHERFORD,
DAVID BISSETT, WILSON TAYLOR.

BASS, ABRAHAM
    P. 157. June 17, 1803 - Aug. Ct. 1805. Legatees:
(no relationship given) 1. ANN ROSE, wife of THOMAS
ROSE, 2. ANN MOORE, wife of COLLUM MOORE, 3. CHARITY
ROGERS, dau. of ROBERT ROGERS, 4. MOURNING ROGERS, dau.
of ROBERT ROGERS, 5. ZONA ROGERS, dau. of ROBERT ROGERS,
6. THOMAS HAMILTON. Grandson: JORDAN BASS. Dau:
ELIZABETH BRIDGERS. Heirs of SION BASS and JOHN BASS
are: JORDAN BASS, POLLY PARKER, QUINNE BASS, ALDIN BASS,
KINCHEN BASS, JOHN BASS AND MOURNING FLOYD, wife of FED
FLOYD. Ex: WILLIAM BRIDGERS, JESSE BASS, GEORGE BODDIE.
Wit: D. SILLS, LUCY BODDIE.

BASS, ISAAC
    P. 136. Dec. 27, 1800 - Feb. Ct. 1801. Wife: NANCY.
Sons: 1. JETHRO - 150 A. on lines of CHARLES, BROWN,
WHITEHEAD, and BENSON PEN BRANCH, 2. JESSE, 3. ISAAC -
Beech Swampland, 4. JOHN, 5. AUGUSTIN - reversion of his
mother's land, also mill. Daus: 1. NISE ROGERS,
2. LEVICY LAWRENCE. Gr. sons: ISAAC, son of JESSE, JOHN
DAVENPORT. Ex: Sons JETHRO and JESSE BASS. Wit: JOHN
RICHARDSON, GEORGE RICHARDSON.

BASS, JESSE

P. 323. May 6, 1822 - May Ct. 1822. Wife:
FRANCES - lend land adjoining MANNING, PRIM, GEORGE
BODDIE and BUNTING. Sons: 1. COFFIELD, 2. COUNCEL -
½ mill and adjoining land, and part of land bought of
AUGUSTIN BASS,desc., 3. GOODMAN - other half the mill
and adjoining land and 100 A. purchased of AUGUSTIN BASS
heirs, 4. SION - the cherryland, 5. JORDAN - the Cooper
land, Joiner land and Prim land, 6. GIDEON, 7. EDWIN -
upper part of the Britain land, also 72 additional A.,
8. ISAAC - balance of Brittain land, 9. EDMON, 10. JESSE.
Daus: 1. FRANCES BASS, 2. PENELOPE WILHIGHT,
3. ELIZABETH BASS, 4. LOUZANY BASS. Friend: MORNING
SIKES. Ex: RICHARD HOLLAND. Wit: LITTLE B. WHITE,
J. J. BOWDEN, ELIZABETH WHITE.

BASS, LUCY

P. 613. Aug. 24, 1868 - Mar. 23, 1872. Son: GIDEON
R. BASS - 100 A. land in Arkansas, a part of 400 A. which
descended to me by the death of my son, JAMES WILLIE
MOORE. Dau: CHARITY ANN, wife of J. D. MANNING - 175 A.
adjoining VAN B. BATCHELOR and WM. WEAVER, from the
division of the dower of late MOURNING HOLLAND (her
mother?) Gr. dau: MOURNING FRANCES MANNING. No Ex.
Wit: G. W. WARD, J. D. BARNES.

BASS, MILDRED

P. 473. Mar. 23, 1843 - Feb. Ct. 1845. Sons:
1. EMBRO, 2. WILLIAM T. Daus: ELIZABETH EDWARDS, wife
of EATON H. EDWARDS. Gr. dau: AQUILLA, dau. of EMBRO
BASS. Ex: AUGUSTIN BASS. Wit: MADISON SIKES, EDMUND
SIKES.

BASS, NANCY

P. 224. May 22, 1811 - Feb. Ct. 1812. Daus:
1. DINISHA ROGERS, 2. LEVECY LAWRENCE. Gr. son: JOHN
DAVENPORT. Ex: WILLIAM BODDIE. Wit: WILLIAM W. BODDIE,
WILLIAM WOODRUFF.

BATCHELOR, CHARLOTTE

P. 612. July 25, 1867 - Mar. 12, 1872. Dau: MARTHA W. SIKES, wife of MADISON SIKES. Ex: CALVIN WARD. Wit: A. THOMAS, A. H. WESTER.

BATCHELOR, CULLEN

P. 515. April 10, 1849 - May Ct. 1849. Wife: CYNTHIA. Son: STARLING JONES BATCHELOR. Daus: 1. BETSY ANN MANNING, 2. TEMPERANCE COLLINS, 3. MARIAH BATCHELOR. Ex: DR. JOHN H. DRAKE. Wit: WM. H. SMITH, JOHN G. MATHEWS.

BATCHELOR, DRURY

P. 589. April 10, 1863 - Nov. Ct. 1864. Wife unnamed. Son & Ex: MERRITT. Daus: 1. DELANY BOWDEN, 2. REBECCA BATCHELOR, 3. ELIZABETH BATCHELOR, 4. ? COPPEDGE. Gr. dau: ANN ELIZA COPPEDGE. Sis-in-law: LUCY SAVEDGE (SAVAGE?). Wit: JOSIAH COLLINS, RICHMOND UPCHURCH.

BATCHELOR, JOHN

P. 517. Sept. 30, 1848 - Aug. Ct. 1849. Wife unnamed. Sons: 1. HENRY I. BATCHELOR, 2. WRIGHT, 3. BERRY. Daus: 1. EDY VICK, wife of HENRY VICK, 2. ? WILSON, 3. NICEY BONE, 4. SALLY WILDER, 5. MOURNING WILLIAMS. Gr. chil: LUCINDA, dau. of HENRY and EDY VICK; LUCINDA WILSON; JOSEPH, son of JOHN VICK; MARY, dau. of BERRY BATCHELOR; PENNY, dau. of MOURNING WILLIAMS. Ex: Son WRIGHT BATCHELOR. Wit: WM. H. J. SMITH, JNO. H. DRAKE, JR. A codicil dated May 1, 1847 states that his wife has since died - has same witnesses. I cannot understand dates. M.G.G.

BATCHELOR, SAMUEL

P. 347. Jan. 19, 1818 - Aug. Ct. 1827. Sons: 1. WRIGHT STEPHEN BATCHELOR - all land, 2. JOHN, 3. WILLIAM, 4. WILLIS, 5. WILSON. Daus: 1. EDITH WHITFIELD, 2. ELIZABETH GLOVER. Ex: Sons JAMES and WRIGHT STEPHEN BATCHELOR. Wit: ABIJAH PRIDGEN, JOSIAH MELTON, DREWRY BATCHELOR.

BATCHELOR, SAMUEL
    P. 599. May 25, 1866 - Nov. Ct. 1866. Son and
Ex: JAMES S. BATCHELOR - to have entire estate. Wit:
DAVID BONE, ABRAHAM SMITH.

BATCHELOR, SAMUEL Mc.
    P. 590. Dec. 24, 1860 - Feb. Ct. 1865. Wife:
CHARLOTTE - my mother's land where I live with reversion
to son and Ex: JORDAN E. BATCHELOR, who is to have
remaining land. Dau: MARTHA, wife of MADISON SIKES.
Ex: Son-in-law MADISON SIKES. Wit: B. H. SORSBY, JOHN
T. BRASWELL.

BATCHELOR, STEPHEN
    P. 165. Feb. 26, 1796 - Feb. Ct. 1806. Wife and
Extx: MARGARET. Son and Ex: DANIEL - 140 A. Heirs
(Gr. chil.?): WILLIAM BATCHELOR, STEPHEN BATCHELOR,
SAMUEL BATCHELOR, SOLOMON BATCHELOR, MARY PRIDGEN,
JOSEPH BATCHELOR, MARGET WARD, ELIZABETH CREEKMORE,
SARAH PRIDGEN, BARSHEBA CREEKMORE, NANNY CREEKMORE.
Wit: DAVID PRIDGEN, ABIJAH PRIDGEN, MARY PRIDGEN.

BATCHELOR, WILLIAM
    P. 153. July 30, 1803 - Feb. Ct. 1805. Son:
WILLIAM JOHN BATCHELOR. ? son or gr. son: WILLIAM JOHN
BATCHELOR HARPER. Dau (apparently): MARY MANNING, wife
of PRIDGEN MANNING. Gr. son: JOHN BATCHELOR MANNING.
Ex: Friends JESSE PRIDGEN, PRIDGEN MANNING. Wit: WM.
TISDAL, AHIJAH PRIDGEN, ACHSE PRIDGEN.

BATCHELOR, WILLIAM J. B.
    P. 593. May 18, 1863 - Aug. Ct. 1865. Sis: QUILLY
BATCHELOR. Nieces: QUILLY LAMON BATCHELOR; LEITHA ANN
BATCHELOR, chil. of sister QUILLY BATCHELOR, are to
receive whole estate provided they do not marry contrary
to the will and consent of my - friend and Ex: B. H.
SORSBY. Nephew: WILLIAM MORGAN, son of WM. MORGAN, to
have estate in case nieces do not marry with consent of
my Ex. B. H. SORSBY. Wit: T. H. SCOTT, R. B. GRIFFIN.

BATCHELOR, WRIGHT STEPHEN
    P. 493. Aug. 5, 1845 - Nov. Ct. 1845. Wife: CHARITY.
Sons: 1. ABEL - ½ tract where NATHAN lives, 2. JAMES,
3. NATHAN WRIGHT - ½ tract where he lives, 4. ANNANIPAS,
5. HARDY DAVIS BATCHELOR - reversion of land whereon I
live. Daus: 1. SUSAN PERRY'S chil., 2. POLLY CONE'S
chil. Ex: Sons ABEL and HARDY DAVIS BATCHELOR. Wit:
MERRITT MANNING, WILLIAM R. RACKLEY, PRIDGEN MANNING.

BATTLE, BENJAMIN D.
    P. 557. Oct. 12, 1844 - Feb. Ct. 1858. Wife:
HENRIETTA T. H. BATTLE. He speaks of "mills, cotton fac-
tory, etc. situated in Nash and Edgecombe Counties, at the
Falls of the Tar River." Whole estate to wid. and chil.
as the law directs. Ex: Bros. WILLIAM H. BATTLE and
RICHARD H. BATTLE. Wit: A. J. BATTLE, THOMAS NEWBY.
This will offered for probate on the testimony of AMOS J.
BATTLE, one of the subscribing witnesses. He states he
saw THOMAS NEWBY (now dead) sign the will at the request
of said B(ENJAMIN) D. BATTLE. WILLIAM T. DORTCH appeared
in Court with power of attorney from the widow HENRIETTA
T. BATTLE to file her dissent to the will, and she was
allowed to file a petition for a year's provision. The
will ordered probated.

BATTLE, JAMES
    P. 255. Apr. 7, 1803 - Nov. Ct. 1803. Wife: ABIAH.
Sons: 1. THOMAS, 2. JAMES, 3. JOHN - sons to have all
land. Daus: 1. MARY, 2. ELIZABETH, 3. TEMPE. Admin:
wife ABIAH. Ex: NATHAN WHITEHEAD. Wit: JOHN NICHOLSON,
ARTHUR WHITEHEAD, MATHEW DRAKE.

BATTLE, WILLIAM L.
    P. 562. Nov. 13, 1858 - Aug. Ct. 1859.   Mother
unnamed. Bros: N. L. B. BATTLE (Ex), ALEX W. BATTLE (Ex)
LAW(RENCE) F. BATTLE, CURAN (CULLEN?) BATTLE.   Sis:
AMARIAH FREEMAN - $50. I give this small amount for
causes best known to myself and well calculated to justify
my action; MARY E. SCOTT - $3000 for education of her
chil. with request that she never again live with DR. T.
H. SCOTT. I direct the Court to appoint her a trustee -
her own choice. MITTY and LOVEY BATTLE, two eldest daus.
of Bro. CURAN BATTLE, to share my interest in the Flewellin
Negroes in Georgia that were given my father's chil. by

17

MRS. E. FLEWELLIN, and I direct the courts of law of
Georgia to appoint CURAN (CULLEN?) BATTLE their guardian
under surety for safe keeping until they come of age.
Wit: JOHN H. RENFROW, JAMES I. HARRIS.

BECKWITH, AMOS
    P. 297. May 20, 1818 - Aug. Ct. 1818. Wife: RODAH.
Sons: 1. HENRY, 2. JAMES, 3. THOMAS, 4. WILLIS, 5. SION,
6. DEMPSEY. Daus: 1. SALLEY FLOYD, 2. POLLEY BRASWELL,
3. MOURNING SNEED, 4. RODAH HUNT. Ex: Son DEMPSEY.
Wit: LOD. F. ELLEN (FLEWELLEN), HENRY EDWARDS.

BECKWITH, DEMPSEY
    P. 540. Aug. 13, 1854 - Aug. Ct. 1854. Wife and
Extx: MARTHA. Wit: W. T. ARRINGTON, CHARLES GAY, JAMES
B. ELLIN.

BECKWITH, HENRY
    P. 109. Dec. 18, 1789 - Aug. Ct. 1796. Sons and
Exs: 1. AMOS - all land, 2. THOMAS, 3. BOLLEN. Wit:
LEWIS VICK, HOWELL ELLEN, DAVID MELTON.

BECKWITH, THOMAS SR.
    P. 336. May 9, 1826 - Nov. Ct. 1826. Gr. chil:
1. BENJAMIN BECKWITH, 2. SION BECKWITH and wife NANCY,
3. MARY WOODARD, wife of COLEMAN WOODARD, 4. THOMAS
WRIGHT BECKWITH, 5. CLINTON BECKWITH, 6. DAWSON
BECKWITH - 50 A. on E. side Tar River adjoining his own
land, 7. MAHALAH MOORE. Ex: WILLIAM DRAKE. Wit: SION
WHITLEY, WILLIAM H. HALL (HALE?).

BELL, ARTHUR
    P. 5 Sept. 13, 1778 - Apr. Ct. 1779. Wife:
ELIZABETH - 250 A. where I live, with reversion to sons
BENJ. and WM. Sons: 1. BENJAMIN, 2. WILLIAM, 3. JAMES,
4. THOMAS, 5. GREEN, 6. ARTHUR. JAMES, THOMAS, and
GREEN are to have 200 A. conveyed to me by JOSEPH
PASSMORE, also land entered by ELIAS BELL. Daus:
1. SARAH BECK, 2. ELVILAH (ELVIRA?) STATTER (SLATTER?).
Ex: Wife ELIZABETH and son GREEN. Wit: W. S. MEARNS,
WM. SANDEFORD, HARDY GRIFFIN.

BELLAMY, JOHN F.
P. 485. Dec. 31, 1845 - Feb. Ct. 1846. Sons:
1. JOHN T. N. - a minor - all my land adj. his land,
inherited from his mother, 2. JOSEPH CLINCH BELLAMY -
a minor - land on which I live on Beech Run. Daus:
1. ANN W. S. N. HUNTER - all my land adj. her land,
inherited from her mother. Legatees: ELIZABETH W.
COFFIELD, MARTHA C. COFFIELD, and SARAH S. COFFIELD are
given personal property which was their mother's. However, the devisor desires that "my son JOSEPH C.
BELLAMY remain with his sister, MARTHA C. COFFIELD."
So it appears that the COFFIELD heirs may be children
of his late wife by a former marriage. Ex and guardian:
Son-in-law DR. WILLIAM HUNTER. Wit: JOHN PARIS, WM.
BELLAMY.

BELLAMY, WILLIAM
P. 494. No date - Nov. Ct. 1846. Desc. wife and
daughter unnamed. Sons: 1. EDWARD C., 2. WILLIAM,
3. ALEXANDER A., desc., 4. SAMUEL C. Sons of ALEXANDER
A., desc., unnamed. Ex: BENJAMIN HUNTER of Halifax Co.,
N. C. Wit: S. S. JUDGE (Clerk: J. J. JUDGE), J. B.
WHITAKER.

BERGERON, WILLIAM B.
P. 607. Oct. 18, 1870 - Nov. 28, 1870. Wife:
DEMARIS. "All my children" unnamed. Ex: WESLEY
PRIVETTE. Wit: GREEN B. BRANTLEY, JAMES R. WHITLEY.
On April 19, 1871, DEMARIS BERGERON, widow of WM. B.
BERGERON, dec'd, entered her dissent to the will of sd.
WM. B. BERGERON, dec'd., requesting a year's allowance
and a dower allotted to her.

BILBRO, BERRYMAN
P. 283. Apr. 22, 1815 - Aug. Ct. 1816. Wife: BETTY.
Sons: 1. WILLIAM - all land, 2. BERRY, 3. THOMAS,
4. JOSEPH, 5. BENJAMIN. Daus: 1. BETTY HILSMON
(HILLMAN?) - her legacy to be divided between her chil.
WILLIAM and NANCY when he becomes of age; 2. DIANA
McFARLAND and her heirs; 3. NANCY WHITEONE(?) and her
heirs; 4. SALLEY BILBRO; 5. REBECCA BILBRO; 6. MERIAH
BILBRO. Ex: Friend NATHANIEL BILBRO, son WILLIAM BILBRO.
Wit: ROGER REESE, THOMAS SAVAGE, JOHN LEWIS.

BIRD, WILEY
    P. 393. Mar. 13, 1833 - May Ct. 1833. Mother:
KISIAH BIRD. Father: JAMES BIRD. No Ex. Wit: PATSEY
BIRD, ABSALOM B. BAINES.

BISSETT, DAVID
    P. 166. Feb. 28, 1806 - May Ct. 1806. Wife and
Extx unnamed. Sons: 1. LODRICK, 2. JOHN, 3. DAVID,
4. JOSEPH - all land. Ex: Son JOHN. Wit: CHARLES
HOGG, WILLIAM SELLARS.

BISSETT, JOHN
    P. 431. Aug. 18, 1838 - Nov. Ct. 1838. Wife: DELIA.
Legatee: JOHN HENDERSON BISSETT, son of JOSEPH BISSETT.
Ex: JOSIAH VICK. Wit: GERMAN D. LANGLEY, MATHEW JOYNER.

BISSETT, JUDITH
    P. 343. June 17, 1826 - Feb. Ct. 1827. Friend PENNY
SHERROD - all estate including a note from JOHN SHERROD
for $50.45. Ex: MATHEW JOINER. Wit: AMOS GANDY,
MATHEW JOINER.

BLACKWELL, NATHAN
    P. 479. Jan. 24, 1845 - Aug. Ct. 1846. Sons:
1. JOSIAH, 2. NATHAN. May be other children. Ex: ASBERRY
BLACKWELL. Wit: JAMES F. MERCER, THOMAS MERCER.

BODDIE, GEORGE
    P. 465. Oct. 9, 1841 - Feb. Ct. 1843. Wife: LUCY.
Sons: 1. WILLIE W. BODDIE - 600 or 700 A. on Back Swamp
called Allen's, where SAUL lives, adjoining HENRY MITCHELL
and WILLIE W. BODDIE, also sawmill N. side Peachtree Crk.,
also 640 A. on lines of EATON EDWARDS; 2. NICHOLAS W.
BODDIE - all remaining land both sides Peachtree Crk.,
also grist mills; 3. VANVAN SALAIR BODDIE - the BYNUM and
SORSBY tracts. Daus: 1. LUCY MOORE, 2. TEMPERANCE ANN
YANCY, 3. CATHARINE BELL. Ex: Son-in-law BAT (BARTHOLOMEW
F. MOORE, ESQ., of Halifax Co. Wit: H. BLOUNT, SAM BROWN
Handwriting of H. BLOUNT desc. proved by oath of THOS. A.
COOPER.

BODDIE, NATHAN
    P. 117. April 2, 1797 - no prob. date.   Sons:

20

1. BENNETT - all lands in Wake Co., on Neuse R.; 2. GEORGE.
Daus: 1. TEMPERANCE, 2. MARY, 3. BETTEY, 4. MOURNING. Gr.
son: ELIJAH BODDIE - 350 A. bought of SAMPSON POWELL. Ex:
Son GEORGE. Wit: PENELOPE MANNING, PEGGY COLLINS, WM.
BODDIE. Codicil wit. by REBECCA FOSTER, MARY HILL, WM.
BODDIE, Dec. 5, 1797.

BODDIE, PATTIE
     P. 436. Nov. 25, 1834 - Nov. Ct. 1839. Son and Ex:
WILLIAM W. BODDIE. Dau: TEMPERANCE ARRINGTON. Gr. chil:
JOHN L., WILLIAM W., and JAMES B. H. BODDIE. May be other
daus. Wit: GEORGE BODDIE.

BODDIE, WILLIAM
     P. 286. No date - Feb. Ct. 1817. Wife: PATTY. Son
and Ex: WILLIAM WILLIS BODDIE. Daus: 1. ELIZABETH,
2. MARTHA ANN. Wit: HENRY DANCE, RHODA DANCE.

BODDIE, W. W.
     P. 460. Dec. 29, 1840 - Nov. Ct. 1843. Sons: 1. JOHN
S. (unmarried), 2. WILLIAM W. (unmarried), 3. JAMES B. H. -
a minor, 4. THOMAS JEFFERSON - oldest. Daus: 1. ELVIRA
CORNELIA, 2. SARAH T., 3. PENELOPE JONES BODDIE. Estate
divided equally. Ex: GEORGE BODDIE (relative), sons JOHN
S. BODDIE and W. W. BODDIE. Wit: JOHN L. B. WOODARD,
JOHN A. WHITEHEAD, WILSON COLLINS.

BODDIE, W. W.
     P. 606. Sept. 25, 1870 - Oct. 25, 1870. App't GEORGE
RICKS, D. A. T. RICKS, JOHN RICKS, W. W. BODDIE, and JAMES
B. H. BODDIE my Exr's.....and request them to draw off a
suitable will in accordance with the many mortgages I hold,
and I wish estate to remain as it is as long as my son
WILLIS BODDIE is capable of managing it, and my children
can agree. I wish all my children to have an equal share
of my estate. Wit: THOS. J. BODDIE, J. S. BODDIE, JOSEPH
A. DRAKE.

BONE, JOHN
     P. 362. Jan. 8, 1824 - Feb. Ct. 1829. Wife: ELIZABETH.
Sons: 1. WILLIE - 100 A. E. side Jacob Swamp, whereon I
live, after death of his mother; 2. NELSON - 215 A. W. side
Jacob Swamp. Daus: 1. NANCY VICK - 115 A. bought of REUBEN

and SIMON JACKSON; 2. FEREBA BAKER; 3. MARY POLEN. Ex: Son NELSON. Wit: MATHEW JOINER, SPARLING B. LEWIS, NATHAN JOINER.

BOON, RAIFORD
P. 537. Mar. 16, 1854 - May Ct. 1854. Son: PHILIMON - 40 A. Daus: 1. ELIZABETH, wife of WILLIS WESTRAY; 2. CATHERINE, wife of EDWIN EDWARDS; 3. MARY BOON; 4. MARTHA BOON. Gr. dau: HARRIET WESTRAY. Ex: ARCHIBALD N. ARRINGTON. Wit: JOSEPH A. DRAKE, WM. T. ARRINGTON.

BOTTOMS, SAMUEL L.
P. 98. Feb. 3, 1795 - May Ct. 1796. Wife: ALLAMINTA S. Son: MICAJAH S. Dau: ALLEVENE S. Estate belonging to me in Granville Co. to be sold. Ex: WM. S. BOTTOMS, JORDAN SHERROD, ELIZAH? ATKINS. Wit: EDW. NICHOLSON, LUCY E. BOTTOMS.

BOTTOMS, SARAH LONG
P. 156. Jan. 19, 1805 - Feb. Ct. 1805. Sis: 1. FORTEN (FORTUNE)WHIDDON, 2. OLIVE PITMAN. Bros: 1. WILLIAM LINDSEY, 2. JOHN PITMAN. Ex: WILLIAM LINDSEY. Wit: JESSE JOINER, LUCY L. BOTTOMS.

BOWDEN, HIRAM
P. 584. April 20, 1861 - May Ct. 1863. Wife: MARTHA. Sons: 1. MALCUS (Ex), 2. HARRY - sons to have land. Dau: ELIZABETH H. JOHNSON. Wit: GEO. N. LEWIS, E. C. LEWIS. Clerk's notes: "G. N. LEWIS, absent in the army, handwriting proved by E. H. MORGAN."

BOYKIN, HARDY
P. 419. Aug. 8, 1837 - Nov. Ct. 1837. Wife: POLLY- 200 A. given me by my father, 100 A. bought of ROBERT EATMAN and 50 A. adjoining HILLIARD BOYKIN. Sons: 1. RICHMOND - mother's land; 2. HARDY W. BOYKIN - land bought of JOSEPH PEALE; 3. COUNCIL BOYKIN - land bought of OWEN SULLAVENT and IRVIN BOYKIN and my mill; 4. ALSEY; 5. HILLIARD BOYKIN; 6. ALFRED BOYKIN; 7. COUNCIL. Daus: 1. CLARREY RENFROW; 2. LINSEY BOYKIN. Ex: Sons HILLIARD and ALFRED BOYKIN. Wit: JESSE FULGUM, EDWIN FULGUM.

BOYKIN, JONATHAN
    P. 383. Jan. 13, 1832 - May Ct. 1832. Sons:
1. STEVEN, 2. THOMAS, 3. IRVIN, 4. JONATHAN - land
whereon I live. Daus: 1. CLARY SIMPSON, 2. NEALY
FLOWERS, 3. TEMPY, 4. EADY. Ex: Friend STEPHEN
BOYKIN. Wit: JOS. WILLIAMSON, HILLIARD BOYKIN.

BRADLEY, JAMES
    P. 54. Jan. 30, 1789 - Feb. Ct. 1789. Cousins:
offsprings of ROBERT ROGERS, unnamed - 100 A. whereon
I live; Cousin JOHN ROGERS. No Ex. Wit: JESSE DENSON,
JAMES MOORE.

BRANTLEY, JOHN
    P. 41. June 18, 1785 - May Ct. 1786. Wife:
ELIZABETH. Sons: JACOB - 112 A. on south side SAPONY
CREEK. Remainder estate divided among "all my children."
Ex: Son JACOB BRANTLEY, WILLIAM LONG BOTTOMS. Wit:
JESSE JOINER, JOHN JOINER.

BRASWELL, BENJAMIN
    P. 344. Jan. 23, 1827 - Feb. Ct. 1827. Wife: CHLOE-
180 A. south side Tar R., purchased of WILLIAM BRASWELL,
adjoining SIMON WILLIAMS. Sons: 1. ORREN D.(ORRENDATUS);
2. WILLIAM - land to hold until his son NORFLEET BRASWELL
comes of age; 3. REUBEN; 4. DAWSON. Daus: 1. MARY BASS,
2. BETSEY FREEMAN, 3. MILLY MELTON, 4. ELIZABETH THANEY
STONE, 5. SUSAN LINCH BRASWELL, 6. ROEANY BRASWELL.
886 A. to DAWSON, SUSAN and ROEANY, to be rented until
they come of age. Ex: GIDEON BASS, ISAAC BASS. Wit:
THOMAS BRYANT, SIMON WILLIAMS.

BRASWELL, JACOB
    P. 313. Aug. 22, 1815 - Aug. Ct. 1823. Sons:
1. JACOB, 2. WILLIAM, 3. BRITTAIN, 4. JESSE - land whereon
I live, also land bought of DENY BRASWELL. Note: He does
not mention son NATHAN who moved to Bladen Co., N. C.
before 1800. M.G.G. Daus: 1. CLOAH (CHLOE) SELLARS,
2. CHARITY HEDGEPETH, 3. SELAH EVANS, 4. MARY JONES,
5. PATIENCE THOMPSON, 6. PATSEY ATKINSON, 7. LUCRETIA
PITTMAN. Gr. daus: NANCY, PATSEY and HARTY JONES,
SUSANNA, TEMPERANCE, RHODA and NANCY ATKINSON. Gr. son:
JOHN ATKINSON. Ex: WILLIAM BODDIE, GEORGE BODDIE. Wit:

WILLIAM BRASWELL, ELIAS BASS, BENJAMIN BRASWELL, JOHN
BRASWELL.

BRASWELL, JEREMIAH
    P. 554. May 26, 1856 - May Ct. 1857. Wife unnamed.
Nephew: NICHOLAS C. BRASWELL. Ex: E. B. HILLIARD.
Wit: THOS. J. A. COOPER, RICHARD F. DRAKE.

BRASWELL, JESSE
    P. 592. April 14, 1859 - Feb. Ct. 1865. Wife:
MARY ANN (Extx). Sons: 1. NICHOLAS dec'd, 2. JOHN,
3. EDWARD, 4. MADISON, 5. JEFFERSON. Daus: 1. LUCY,
2. LOUISIANA N. B. Gr. chil: MARY ANN and WILLIAM,
chil. of son NICHOLAS; ADDIE, dau. of son JOHN BRASWELL.
Wit: A. D. WESTER, THOMAS DAVIS, BENJ. L. ARRINGTON.

BRASWELL, JOHN
    P. 621. Sept. 4, 1857 - May Ct. 1860. Wife: SARAH-
land on which I live on Beachtree Crk. and to Ward's line.
Legatee: FRANCIS HEDGEPETH - $400 to be equally divided
between the chil. of my brother WILLIAM BRASWELL, by his
first wife, to wit: 1. JOE, 2. CHARITY, 3. LUCY,
4. HARRIETT. Ex: Nephew JOHN T. BRASWELL. Wit: GEORGE
N. LEWIS, C. W. WARD.

BRASWELL, SAMUEL
    P. 94. Nov. 30, 1794 - Feb. Ct. 1795. Wife: SARAH -
plantation whereon I dwell and the land where my father
lived and died - the two parcels containing 296 A. were
given me by my father with reversion to my son MICAJAH.
Sons: 1. MICAJAH, 2. SAMPSON - 300 A. land, 3. WILSON -
remainder of land. Daus: 1. ELIZABETH WOODARD,
2. MARGARETT, 3. QUINNY, 4. SALLY. Ex: HOWELL ELLEN,
FREDERICK HINES. Wit: JAMES WILLIAMS, JESSE HUNT, MARTHA
THOMAS.

BRASWELL, WILLIAM JR.
    P. 6. Nov. 30, 1778 - Jan. Ct. 1779. Wife: MARTHA.
Sons: 1. ROBIN - 740 A. on north side Little Creek,
2. DEMPSEY - 710 A. south side Little Creek, when they
come of age. Daus: 1. JUDAH HUNT, 2. LUCRECY WILLIAMS,
3. PRISCILLA EXUM, 4. RHODA POWELL, 5. MOURNING BRASWELL.

Gr. son: ALEXANDER HUNT. Gr. Dau: NANCY HUNT. Son-in-law: THOMAS BECKWITH. Ex: WILLIAM WILLIAMS, JOSEPH EXUM, JESSE POWELL. Wit: WILSON VICK, JAMES DANIEL, WILLIAM BRASWELL.

BRASWELL, WILLIAM
    P. 104. April 2, 1794 - May Ct. 1796. Wife: MILLEY. Sons: 1. BENJAMIN; 2. WILLIAM - all my land south of Tar R.; 3. JOHN - 286 A. north side of Tar R. on TANNER'S line. Daus: 1. SARAH, 2. PHEREBY, 3. MILLY, 4. ELIZABETH, 5. PENELOPY, 6. RHODA, 7. CLOE, 8. LEAH, 9. PIETY, 10. BERSHEBY. Ex: Friends BENJAMIN MANNEN, SOLOMON BATCHELOR, BENJAMIN WILLIAMS. Wit: JAMES MOORE, JOSEPH RITCHESON, JUDAH MOORE.

BRIDGERS, WILLIAM
    P. 162. Sept. 22, 1804 - Nov. Ct. 1805. Wife and Ex: ELIZABETH. Sons: 1. JOHN; 2. HENRY - reversion in land south side Swift Crk. Guardians for JOHN and HENRY: JOHN DRAKE and MICA (MICAJAH) BRIDGERS; 3. SAM-land on north side Swift Crk.; 4. MICAJAH. Wit: BENJAMIN BRIDGERS, WILLIAM ROSE.

BRITTON, CHARLES
    P. 124. April 28, 1791 - Nov. Ct. 1793. Wife and Extx: MARTHA. JESSE BRITTON (no relation given) Sis: NANNY BRITTON. Ex: Friend DANIEL TAYLOR. Wit: JOSEPH PARROTT, WRIGHT TAYLOR, CORBAN TUCKER.

BROWN, JEREMIAH
    P. 39. Wife: MARY. Sons: 1. JOHN, 2. JOSEPH. Estate to be divided between all my children at death of wife, MARY. Ex: Wife MARY, JAMES MORPHIS (?). Wit: E. W. MOORE, JAMES BIRD, CHARLES CARTER.

BROWN, JOHN
    P. 532. July 29, 1852 - Nov. Ct. 1852. Wife: MARTHA - land where I live, also small tract on Little Peachtree Crk., in all 107 A. Chil: 1. WILLIAM, 2. REBECCA, 3. ELIZABETH, 4. MARY WESTER, dec'd - her children to receive one share. Ex: JAMES HARRISON. Wit: W. H. EDWARDS, R. H. LANIER.

BRYANT, SAMUEL
   P. 236. Feb. 18, 1791 - no probate date. Wife:
MARY. Sons: 1. WILLIAM, 2. ROBERT - 100 A. on Wolf
Branch, 3. THOMAS, 4. SAMUEL - the last two to have all
remaining land. Daus: 1. ALEY?, 2. ELIZABETH,
3. SARAH, 4. MARY, 5. MILBERRY. Gr. chil: MARY HOBS,
BRYANT WILLIAMS. Ex: Friends WILLIAM LANCASTER, JOHN
SUMNER. Wit: ELIAS ATKINSON, SARAH ING, EDWARD TURNER.

BRYANT, THOMAS
   P. 531. June 7, 1848 - 1852. Legatee: ELIZABETH
BRYANT, wid. of WM. F. BRYANT, dec'd - 100 A. where she
now lives, with reversion to the heirs of JAMES RANSON
by his wife SALLY. The same heirs of JAMES and SALLY
RANSON to have all remaining estate. Ex: A. B. BAINES,
JR. Wit: WM. B. BRYANT, JOHN B. RICE.

BRYANT, SUSAN
   P. 593. April 10, 1863. Sons: 1. GIDEON,
2. THOMAS N., 3. WILLIAM T., 4. EVAN N. Daus:
1. MOURNING, wife of NICHOLAS RICE; 2. POLLY, wife of
HENDERSON RICE. Ex: BENNET GAY. Wit: JOS. B. MANN,
JNO. B. RICE. Clerk's notes: Both witnesses were dead;
and BENNET GAY renounced his executorship. Adm. granted
HENRY H. BRYANT, (son of the dec'd SUSAN BRYANT) with
N. N. RICE, G. B. BRYANT and W. T. BRYANT sureties.

BRYANT, WILLIAM SR.
   P. 340. Aug. 26, 1826 - Nov. Ct. 1826. Wife: POLLY.
Sons: 1. WILLIAM - land where he lives on Sappony Swamp,
2. EVANS - remaining land. Daus: 1. PATSEY RICE,
2. SALLY STRICKLAND, 3. RHODY WILHITE, 4. SUSAN UPCHURCH,
5. ELIZABETH RICE, dec'd, 6. JENCY (JENEY, JINY) BRYANT,
7. DELANY BRYANT. Gr. chil: JOHN, JINEY, NICHOLSON,
BERRY, and BOYKIN RICE, chil. of ELIZABETH RICE, desc.
Sons-in-law: BENJAMIN RICE, JOSIAH VICK. Ex: GIDEON
BASS, son WILLIAM BRYANT. Wit: RICHARD DOZIER, JAMES
T. DOZIER.

BRYANT, WILLIAM B.
   P. 571. Oct. 6, 1860 - Feb. Ct. 1861. Wife: SUSAN.
Sons: 1. JOHN W. and his wife, WILLIAM JANE; 2. HENRY

26

H.; 3. WILLIAM T.; 4. EVAN N.; 5. GIDEON B.; 6. THOMAS N.
Daus: 1. MOURNING, wife of N. N. RICE; 2. MARY M., wife
of HENDERSON RICE. Gr. son: WILLIAM, son of HENRY H.
BRYANT. Ex: Son JOHN W. BRYANT. Wit: GEORGE N.
LEWIS, THOMAS CREEKMORE. A complicated division of real
and personal property.

BRYANT, WILLIAM JANE
     P. 616. Aug. 9, 1872 - Oct. 7, 1872. Sons:
1. JOHN - 105 A., 2. ROBERT (minor) - 100 A. Daus:
1. MEDORA DEANS - 50 A., 2. ELLEN (minor) - 100 A. A
tract of land to be sold to T. A. JOHNSON. Ex: Kins-
man GEORGE N. LEWIS. Wit: D. M. JOHNSON, W. F. EDWARDS.
"Should my executor ever collect from the United States
the money due my husband for taking the last Census in
Nash County, he shall apply same for the purpose of edu-
cating my children: ROBERT and ELLEN."

BUNN, BENJ.
     P. 155. Sept. 5, 1801 - Feb. Ct. 1805. Sons and
Ex: 1. JOEL - 989 A.; 2. BURWELL; 3. WILLIE. Daus:
1. SARAH BATTLE (dec'd); 2. MARGARET LAMON. Wit: J. G.
LAMON, ROGER REESE, ORRENDATUS LAMON.

BUNN, BENJAMIN
     P. 263. June 11, 1814 - Feb. Ct. 1815. Wife:
PRISCILLA. Son: BENNETT - land whereon I live, also
all lands N. side Stoney Crk. Gr. son: REDMUN BUNN.
Daus: 1. MILLEY, 2. SALLY. Ex: Son BENNETT. Wit:
REDMUN BUNN, CHASEY CARRELL.

BUNN, DAVID SR.
     P. 28. Nov. 27, 1784 - Feb. Ct. 1785. Sons:
1. DAVID - 402 A. where I live, 2. REDMUND, 3. BENJAMIN.
Daus: 1. ANN, 2. SARAH, 3. ELIZABETH, 4. RACHEL,
5. SELETER, 6. CREASY. Ex: BENJAMIN BUNN, SR., JOSIAH
BUNN, JOHN BUNN.

BUNN, JOEL
     P. 185. Dec. 28, 1807 - Feb. Ct. 1808. Sister:
MARGARET BATTLE. Legatees: ELISHA BATTLE, SR., PIETY,
WM., HENRY and JEREMIAH, orphans of BURWELL BUNN, dec'd.,

DR. JEREMIAH BATTLE, JESSE BATTLE. Ex: Bro. WILLIE
BUNN. Wit: ROGER REESE, NATHAN GILBERT, WILLIE
BUNTING.

BUNN, JOEL D.
    P. 509. Sept. 22, 1847 - Feb. Ct. 1848. Bro and
Ex: JOHN I. BUNN. Wit: EATON GAY, JONATHAN JOINER.

BUNN, RACHEL
    P. 447. Mar. 14, 1835 - May Ct. 1837. Sons and
Exs: 1. JOHN J. BUNN, 2. JOEL DAVIS BUNN. Wit: JOEL
WELLS, MOSES JOINER, EATON GAY. Ordered recorded Nov.
Ct. 1840.

BUNN, REDMUN
    P. 337. Feb. 9, 1822 - Nov. Ct. 1826. Wife:
DRUCILLA. Nephews: 1. WILLIE BUNN - 534 A. at the
death of my wife; 2. ALFRED BUNN (ALFORD?); 3. DAVID
BUNN; 4. WILLIE BUNN, JR. Niece: 1. CHARITY BUNN.
Friend: JORDAN SHERROD. Legatee: JOEL WELLS. Ex:
WILLIE BUNN, ESQ., BENNET BUNN, ISAAC RICKS. Wit:
ELISHA BATTLE, JOEL BATTLE, GEORGE COOPER. Codicil to
will of REDMUN BUNN May 26, 1825: Revoke bequest made
to nephew WILLIE BUNN, as he is now dead and hereby
devise the same to nephew BENNET H. BUNN. Sister:
CRESEY FORT. Nephews: WILLIE RICKS, ALFORD BUNN,
DAVID BUNN. Wit: SAM. W. M. VICK, TIMOTHY FERRELL.

BUNN, WILLIE
    P. 377. Mar. 5, 1831 - Nov. Ct. 1831. Wife and
Extx: RACHEL. Sons and Exs: 1. JOHN JOLLY BUNN,
2. JOEL DAVIS BUNN. Daus: 1. POLLY BATTLE - her share
given her during her first husband's lifetime, 2. SALLY
ARRINGTON, 3. PEGGY VICK. Wit: REDMUN BUNN, ROBERT
SORY, BYRD B. TUNNELL.

BUNTING, B. B. (Clerk's notes: BENJAMIN BUNTING) p. 509.
April 12, 1847 - Nov. Ct. 1847. Wife and Extx: SARAH.
Father, mother and brother unnamed. Sis: SUSAN. Wit:
None. Proven by the oaths of RICH. DOZIER, REUBEN
STRICKLAND, JNO. BRASWELL, JNO. E. MATHEWS, JNO. PITTMAN,
BURTIS CONE, JOHN FARMER, GUILFORD POLAND, WILLIAM
COOPER, KINCHEN TAYLOR, JACOB STRICKLAND, ELIAS BARIL(?).

BUNTING, SALLY

P. 569. Aug. 7, 1860 - Nov. Ct. 1860. Nephew: JOHN H. HARRIS (Ex). Estate to be divided between my three chil: 1. SALLY E., 2. JOHN W. B., 3. THOS. B. B. Wit: T. SHRADER, WILLIAM T. GRIFFIN.

BUNTING, WILLIAM

P. 405. May 6, 1828 - Feb. Ct. 1835. Wife: PENELOPE. Sons: 1. DAVID, 2. WILLIE, 2. WILLIAM - the BUNN and WALL tracts, 3. VINCENT - the PEARCE tract, 4. JAMES. Dau: 1. SUSANNAH MANNING. Gr. chil: PENELOPE and CAROLINE, daus. of son JAMES BUNTING. Ex: Son WILLIE BUNTING. Wit: H. G. BLOUNT, JOHN G. BLOUNT, A. WATSON.

BURT, ELIZABETH

P. 531. Jan. 10, 1850 - Nov. Ct. 1852. Sis and Ex: ANN L. BURT - land where we live, also my interest in a tract in Halifax Co., adjoining LITTLETON ARRINGTON and others. Chil: 1. SOLOMON, 2. LANE, 3. LUCINDA, 4. CUFFY(?), 5. WILLIAM. Legatees: LUCRETIA A. GARRETT for L. A. GARRETT, HARRIETT M. C. LEWIS, MARY A. BURT, HARRIETT C. BURT, SAMUEL B. GARRETT, JOHN W. B. GARRETT, PETER ARRINGTON, SALUMITH and LUCY, daus. of WM. BURT, deceased, CASSANDRA BURT, LEONARD L. SIMMS. Wit: MARK P. PERRY, A. ARRINGTON, HENRY SIMS.

CARTER, MARY

P. 417. Aug. 11, 1828 - Nov. Ct. 1837. Friend and Extx: NANCY STEPHENS, MERRITT STEPHENS. Wit: Z. B. BILBRO, WRIGHT TAYLOR.

CHADWICK, NOAH

P. 19. July 9, 1781 - no probate date. Wife and Extx: MARTHA. Son: NOAH - all land. Daus: 1. FRANCES, 2. MARTHA. Ex: EPHRAIM ATKINSON. Wit: THOS. MORRIS, EPHRAIM ATKINSON, VALLEY SCOULES.

CLINCH, EDWARD

P. 7. Nov. 23, 1778 - July Ct. 1779. Wife unnamed. Sons: 1. CHRISTOPHER MOORE CLINCH - all land on Turkey Crk., 2. HORATIO GATES CLINCH - all land on Tar R. Dau: 1. HANNAH. Ex: DUNKIN LAMON, ESQ., JOS. JOHN CLINCH, and "my wife."   Wit: EDWARD NICHOLSON, ETHELRED DANCE, EDWARD MOORE.

CLINCH, JOSEPH D.
     P. 100. June 12, 1794 - Aug. Ct. 1795.   Sons:
1. EDWARD CLINCH, 2. DUNCAN LAMON CLINCH, 3. JOSEPH JOHN
CLINCH - sons to have all land.   Daus: 1. ELIZABETH,
2. MARY.   Ex: WILLIAM BELLAMY, JOHN LAMON.   Wit:
THOMAS PILLSON, THOMAS EZELE, HORATION G. CLINCH.

COCKRELL, JACOB
     P. 80. Aug. 22, 1792 - Nov. Ct. 1792. Wife unnamed.
Sons: 1. JONATHAN, 2. NATHAN, 3. WILLIAM HAYWOOD
COCKRELL - 100 A. on Juniper at death of mother.   Ex:
JOHN EATMAN.   Wit: JOHN COCKRELL, JOHN VICKS.

COCKRELL, JOHN
     P. 199. Mar. 20, 1809 - Aug. Ct. 1809. Wife: ANNE.
Sons: 1. JOSEPH; 2. JOHN and 3. SAMUEL - to share all
land on north side Tar R. on lines of JOHN POULAN, DAVID
PRIDGEN and WELLS; 4. VINCENT and 5. BALDY - to share
plantation whereon I live at their mother's death.   Daus:
1. BETSEY, 2. NANCY.   Ex: Friend JOHN VICK, ESQ.   Wit:
JOS. VICK, WILLIAM HORN, EVERARD EATMAN.

CONE, GUILFORD
     P. 548. May 29, 1855 - Feb. Ct. 1856.   Wife:
PENELOPE.   Gr. son and Ex: WILLIAM W. BRYANT - to hold
estate after death of my wife for the benefit of: SIMON
BRYANT, GUSTON BRYANT, MARTHA BRYANT, and PENNY BRYANT.
Wit: HENRY G. LEONARD, WILLIE BUNTING.

CONE, WILLIAM
     P. 522. April 20, 1850 - Aug. Ct. 1850.   Wife:
BEEDY - whole estate including 200 A. of land and also
all Negroes that justly belong to me at NANCY MORGAN'S
decease, if my wife is still living. At the death of the
last survivor all property to be divided among my 9
chil: 1. HARRIET, 2. ALSEY MAY, 3. HENRY RICHARDSON,
4. JAMES, 5. JOHN TURNER, 6. CATHERINE, 7. SUSAN,
8. WILLIAM and 9. ELIZABETH GREEN.   Ex: REUBEN MURRAY.
Wit: J. M. TAYLOR, WM. B. BRIDGERS.

COOK, LAZARUS
   P. 538. Jan. 8, 1849 - May Ct. 1854. Wife: SALLY.
Son and Ex: ANDREW G. COOK. Daus: 1. LUCY, 2. MARY,
3. MARTHA, 4. LAVINIA, 5. NANCY, 6. CELIA. Gr. chil:
EDWIN and MARTHENIA COOK. Wit: JAMES F. MERCER,
THOMAS MERCER.

COOPER, ELIZABETH
   P. 348. Oct. 22, 1827 - Nov. Ct. 1827. Sons:
1. ISHAM - desc., 2. JAMES, 3. JOHN. Daus: ELIZABETH
BATCHELOR - all land. Gr. chil: ALFRED, NANCY, LUCY,
ELIZABETH and ISHAM COOPER; GEORGE WASHINGTON BATCHELOR.
Dau-in-law: POLLY, wid. of ISHAM COOPER. Ex: Son
JAMES COOPER. Wit: GIDEON BASS, WILLIAM PARROT,
LITTLE B. WHITE.

COOPER, JOHN
   P. 33. Dec. 28, 1784 - Feb. Ct. 1785. Wife:
PENELOPE. Sons: 1. CANNON COOPER - 100 A. on lines of
ELIZABETH BELL, JOHN HUNT and Swift Creek; 2. REUBEN
COOPER - 100 A. on lines of GRIFFIN, JOHN HUNT and Haw
Br.; 3. JOHN COOPER; 4. JOEL COOPER - these two to share
land whereon I live; 5. EDWARD COOPER; 6. WILLIAM COOPER;
7. JAMES COOPER; 8. MARK COOPER;   Daus: 1. SARAH DEEN;
2.AMY COOPER; 3. MARY COOPER; 4. MOURNING COOPER;
5. PENELOPE COOPER. Ex: Wife PENELOPE, sons EDWARD,
REUBEN and CANNON COOPER. Wit: HARDY GRIFFIN,
ARCHIBALD GRIFFIN, W. S. MEARNS.

COOPER, JOHN
   P. 119. Sept. 6, 1798 - Nov. Ct. 1798. Bros:
1. MARK - 100 A. whereon I dwell, 2. JOEL. Sis: MARY
GREEN. No relationship given: MOURNING WILLIAMS. Ex:
Friend WILLIAM S. MEARNS. Wit: JOHN ARRINGTON, ALEX
W. HINES.

COOPER, MARCUM
   P. 215. Aug. 30, 1809 - May Ct. 1811. Wife: SARAH.
Sons: 1. VINSON, 2. HARDY, 3. DAVID, 4. JOHN - 500 A.
purchased of BRINLY (BRINKLEY?) GANDY on Stoney Branch,
5. GEORGE - land purchased of SAMUEL SMITH between Red
Point Branch and Hicks Branch, 6. WILLIAM - remainder of

land including home plantation. Daus: 1. RHODA DEANS,
2. MARY COOPER. Legatee: (may be dau.) ELIZABETH
TUCKER. Ex: Sons JOHN, GEORGE and WILLIAM. Wit:
JAMES WILLIAMS, TIMOTHY FERRELL, JOEL PRIDGEN.

COOPER, WILLIAM
     P. 520. Aug. 11, 1849 - May Ct. 1850. Wife:
MARGARET - lands on lines of DAVID JOYNER and Sappony
Swamp, with reversion to son DAVID COOPER. Sons:
1. WILLIAM, 2. WILLIE H.(WILEY?), 3. CALVIN, 4. ASHLEY
G. H., 5. DAVID, 6. GEORGE H., 7. VINCENT, 8. LITTLE
I. B. COOPER, dead. Left no heirs. Daus: 1. ROSA
BARNES, 2. MARGARET COOPER, 3. PRIMMY FINCH, 4. RHODA
REDDING. Ex: Sons WILLIE H. COOPER, ASHLEY G. H.
COOPER. Wit: N. W. COOPER, GEO. W. COOPER, T. H.
SCOTT.

COPPEDGE, JESSE
     P. 604. Aug. 30, 1867 - no prob. date. Wife unnamed:
All my lands, with reversion of the home tract to any
unmarried daus., at death of wife. "All my children"
unnamed. Ex: Sons JORDAN COPPEDGE, WILLIAM B. COPPEDGE.
Wit: J. T. WEBB, JAMES E. WARD, WILLIAM F. EDWARDS.

COUNSEL, CLARISSA
     P. 518. Aug. 15, 1846 - Aug. Ct. 1849. No relation-
ship to legatees. SUSANNAH HUNTER'S chil. to have all my
land: DAVID HUNTER, RICHARD HUNTER, PETER H. HUNTER. Ex:
Friend JESSE H. DRAKE. Wit: TEMPY COOPER, MOURNING
DRAKE.

CREEKMORE, FRANCES
     P. 541. Mar. 9, 1854 - no prob. date. Husband:
THOMAS CREEKMORE - land where I live. Sis: 1. NANCY
MANNING'S heirs, 2. SUSAN BOON'S heirs. If any of above
heirs marry into the family of WILLIS WARREN, they shall
receive no part of my estate. Nephew: WILLIS E. MANNING.
Niece: FRANCES B. MANNING. Bro: WARREN ? Friend: JOHN
W. BRYANT. Ex: BENJAMIN BILBRO. Wit: TIMOTHY A.
JOHNSON, NATHAN BATCHELOR.

CREEKMORE, TIMOTHY
P. 400. Nov. 15, 1832 - May Ct. 1834. Wife: NANNA.
Sons: 1. TIMOTHY TERRY, 2. SOLOMON C., 3. THOMAS F.
Daus: 1. SALLY, 2. NANCY D., 3. ANNAS. Gr. dau:ARKADDAR
(ARCADIA?) EXUM. Ex: WILLIAM W. BODDIE. Wit: HENRY
DANCE, JESSE RICKSON. Codicil wit. by H. MITCHELL, GEORGE
BODDIE.

CROWELL, JAMES B.
P. 543. July 17, 1848 - Feb. Ct. 1855. Sons:
1. WILLIAMS D., 2. JONAS W. Daus: 1. ISLEY WILLIAMS,
2. SUSAN BARBEE. Gr. chil: FRANCES JANE BARBEE; JONAS
CROWELL - the HOLLAND land. Ex: J. J. TAYLOR. Wit:
WILLIAM H. JOYNER, MATHEW JOYNER.

CROWELL, JOSEPH
P. 44. Aug. 31, 1787 - Nov. Ct. 1787. Wife and
Extx: MARTHA. Sons: 1. JOHN, 2. JAMES BARNES,
3. EDWARD. Dau: 1. BETSY LUTON? CROWELL. Ex: Friends
JAMES BARNES, LEWIS ABLEWIS LAMKIN. Wit: DUN. LAMON,
LEWIS ABLEWIS LAMKIN, MARY PRIDGEON.

CRUMPLER, BENJAMIN
P. 331. Jan. 18, 1825 - Nov. Ct. 1825. Dau: POLLY
POLAND. Gr. chil: WILLIAM and MARTHA CRUMPLER - 201 A.
where I live. Legatee: JAMES FLEMING - 150 A. in
Edgecombe Co. on Town Creek. Ex: DAVID WINSTEAD.
Wit: JOHN RICE, JR., JOHN FLEMING.

CULPEPPER, ELIZABETH
P. 56. Feb. 12, 1788 - May Ct. 1789. Daus:
1. RAHAB WHITEHEAD, 2. ELIZABETH WHITEHEAD, 3. MARTHA
MANNING. Gr. chil: JOHN CULPEPPER, HENRY WHITEHEAD,
NATHAN WHITEHEAD, MARY DANIEL, ABIAH WHITEHEAD, MARTHA
MANNING. Relationship not given: P. J. CULPEPPER,
NATUS CULPEPPER. Ex: RAHAB WHITEHEAD, SION DANIEL.
Wit: JOHN SMEDLEY, MARTHA SMEDLEY, CHERRY POWELL.

CULPEPPER, JAMES
P. 127. Aug. 20, 1799 - Nov. Ct. 1799. Wife and
Extx: ELIZABETH. Sons: 1. CHRISTOPHER, 2. JEREMIAH,
3. JAMES, 4. HENRY - these 4 sons to share 416 A. Daus:
1. ELIZABETH, 2. SELAH, 3. SALLEY. Ex: Son CHRISTOPHER

CULPEPPER. Wit: DANIEL TAYLOR, JAMES BRUICE, WRIGHT TAYLOR.

CULPEPPER, JEREMIAH
P. 137. Jan. 28, 1800 (1801 in another place) - Feb. Ct. 1801. Wife: PASHIONS (PATIENCE?). "All my children" unnamed. Ex: ABRAHAM HEDGEPETH. Wit: JORDAN BASS, JOHN EDWARDS, ABRAHAM HEDGEPETH, E. EDWARDS.

CULPEPPER, WILLIAM
P. 611. Sept. 22, 1868 - Nov. 20, 1871. Sons: 1. HENRY H. CULPEPPER - 25 A. adjoining his land, 2. JOHN J. CULPEPPER - residue of land. Daus: 1. MARIAH ELIZABETH ROSE, 2. MARY LIZA JOYNER, 3.FRANCES R. JOYNER. Ex: Son JOHN J. CULPEPPER. Wit: G. D. LANGLEY, W. A. J. LANGLEY, LIZEBETH CULPEPPER. Codicil attached - no date, no wit.

CURL, SOPHIA
P. 266. Mar. 18, 1814 - May Ct. 1815. Sons: 1. SAMUEL VICK, 2. AXIUM L. CURL (EXUM?). Bro: SAM? Gr. daus: SALLY T. WESTRAY, KIZIAH WESTRAY, chil. of dau. MARY WESTRAY. Ex: Son SAMUEL VICK. Wit: SAMUEL WESTRAY, KATY SEALEY.

DAVENPORT, DORREL (DARREL?)
P. 34. July 13, 1784 - Aug. Ct. 1785. Wife unnamed. Sons: 1. JOHN - land whereon I live, 2. ELIAS - land bought of JOB TUCKER. Dau: 1. CARENDELLE. Ex: NATHAN BODDIE. Wit: GEORGE BODDIE, SOLOMON COLLINS, TEMPERANCE BODDIE.

DAVIS, LEWIS
P. 13. Nov. 22, 1779 - Apr. Ct. 1780. Wife: TABITHA-160 A. land purchased of WM. SMITH. Sons: 1. DIOCLESIAN-440 A. on lines of Porter, Booth, and White Oak Swamp; 2. YOUNG. Daus: 1. PRISSILA; 2. LOEZY (LOUISEY). Exrs: Wife TABITHA and son DIOCLESIAN. Wit: LUCY GAINER, ARTHUR DAVIS.

DAWSON, DEMPSEY
    P. 252. June 3, 1797 - no prob. date. Wife: MARY.
Cousin (Nephew): DEMPSEY, son of JOHN DAWSON - 456 A.
whereon I live, also 74 A. purchased of THOMAS VIVERETT
on lines of Hominy Swamp, JOSEPH BARNES and JOHN
FLOWERS. Legatees: DAVID and MILLEY DAWSON, children
of Bro. SOLOMON DAWSON; also children of JOHN DAWSON;
AILEY SMITH. Sis: MARTHA VASSER and her chil. Ex:
Wife MARY, friends JONAS WILLIAMS, ROLAND WILLIAMS,
DRURY WILLIAMS. Wit: JOSEPH BARNES, JOHN FLOWERS,
SARAH BARNES.

DEANS, JOHN
    P. 496. Oct. 31, 1846 - Feb. Ct. 1847. Wife: RHODA.
Sons: 1. DAVID M. - ½ remaining land, 2. MARCUM H. - ½
remaining land, 3. JOHN E. - home plantation and the
Creekmore land. Daus: 1. ELIZABETH WINSTEAD, 2. NANCY
DEANS, 3. MARY ATKINSON. Ex: Son DAVID M. DEANS. Wit:
THOMAS J. A. COOPER, T. H. SCOTT.

DEANS, THOMAS
    P. 114. April 23, 1797 - May Ct. 1797. Wife: LIDA.
Sons: 1. JOHN - 300 A. whereon I live, 2. WILLIAM -
200 A. whereon he lives on Long Branch. Daus:
1. ELIZABETH DEANS, 2. NANCY BOWEN, 3. DINAH EASON,
4. MARY LEWIS, 5. ANNAS JOYNER. Ex: ROBERT CREEKMORE.
Wit: WILLIAM BOWENS, RICHARD EDENS.

DEENS (DEANS), HEREMIAH
    P. 48. Feb. 19, 1788 - Nov. Ct. 1788. Wife and
Extx: MOLLEY. Son: SHERROD DEENS - all land at mother's
death. Dau: TEMPERANCE DEENS. Remainder estate
divided among all my children (unnamed). Ex: Friend
CORNELIUS TAYLOR. Wit: DANIEL TAYLOR, CORNELIUS TAYLOR,
RICHARD DEENS.

DENSON, BENJAMIN
    P. 20. Aug. 1, 1781 - Oct. Ct. 1781. Wife: MARY.
Sons: 1. JETHRO; 2. JOSEPH - 200 A., the north part of
640 A. owned by THOS. HUNTER; 3. BENJAMIN - 200 A., the
west part of same survey; 4. JOHN - 200 A., remainder of
survey; 5. JESSE - 150 A. whereon I dwell. Daus: 1. ISABELL

2. MOLLY, 3. ANN, 4. HULDA, 5. BETTY.   Exrs: Son JOSEPH
DENSON and JOHN RICKS.   Wit: WILSON VICK, MATHEW
WESTER, ARTHUR WESTER.

DENSON, MASEE (MASSEY?) (wid.?)
    P. 294. Jan. 30, 1818 - Feb. Ct. 1818.   Sons:
1. MATHEW FREEMAN, 2. HENRY FREEMAN.   Daus: 1. MARTHA
WHITLEY, 2. SALLY SCREWS, 3. REBECCA TURNER, 4. MASSEE
HACKNEY, 5. ISABEL COOPER, wife of JAMES COOPER,
6. MARY COOPER, wife of BENJ. COOPER.   Gr. chil: Chil.
of MARY and BENJ. COOPER: REBECCA, MASEE, MATHEW.   Ex:
JOSEPH ARRINGTON.   Wit: WILLIAM McGREGOR, ALLEN DRAKE.

DERRING, JOHN
    P. 500. Dec. 10, 1846 - Feb. Ct. 1847.   Wife:
MARGARET.   Sons: 1. JAMES, 2. EMELIUS - balance of
CHAMBLISS tract, 3. JOSIAH NICHOLAS DERRING - reversion
of land whereon I live and 56 A. of CHAMBLISS tract,
4. JOHN RANDOLPH DERRING - to be guardian for son JOSIAH.
Daus: 1. SOPHONIA, 2. MARY - these two to have BLOUNT
land.   Son-in-law: JOHN D. P. WILKINSON.   Ex: Son
JOHN RANDOLPH DERRING, NATHANIEL HARRISON, JOSHUA WATSON.
Wit: THOMAS W. AVENT (Clerk: M.), JOHN HARRISON.

DEW, DUNCAN
    P. 160. Dec. 3, 1803 - Feb. Ct. 1805.   Wife:
ELIZABETH.   Dau: PATSEY - the HARDY BLACKWELL land
between Toisnot and Mill Branch, also 100 A. adjacent.
If PATSEY die without heir, property shall go to the
following: BETSEY D., NANCY, RODAH and OBEDIENCE
ROBBINS; DUNCAN and LARRY BONDS (BARNES?); LARRY and
DUNCAN DEW, sons of JOHN DEW. No relationship: RODIA
CROWELL (probably daughter) - the NATHAN COBBS BLUMERY
land on south side Great Swamp. Cousin: DUNCAN DEW.
Ex: JOHN DEW, SR., JOHN ROBBINS, SR.   Wit: WILLIAM
SORSBY, MILLICENT STRICKLAND, W. R. HORN.

DEW, JOHN
    P. 71. Dec. 30, 1790 - May Ct. 1791. Son: DUNKIN
(DUNCAN).   Daus: 1. CATE ROBBINS - 300 A. lying on
Turkey Crk., loan certificates in hands of JOHN BONDS;
cattle in hands of ROBERT LANCASTER, HARTE LANCASTER
and BENJAMIN BUNN; 2. NANCY DEW - 640 A. where MATHEW

CROWELL lives; 3. ELIZABETH CONE. Ex: Son DUNKIN,
son-in-law JOHN ROBBINS. Wit: EDWARD NICHOLSON,
WILLIAM DEW, EQUILA (AQUILLA) SIRCEY.

DORTCH, JANNEY
     P. 62. May 11, 1789 - Feb. Ct. 1790. Son and Ex:
LEWIS DORTCH. Daus: 1. MOLLEY NEWSOM, 2. BETTY LONG.
Wit: BERRY MERRITT, WILLIAM WHITEHEAD, THOMAS MANNING.

DOZIER, ANN
     P. 330. Apr. 19, 1824 - Nov. Ct. 1825. Legatees-
no relationship given: (Miss) ELIZABETH BRADY, JAMES
DOZIER, JOHN DOZIER. Ex: BENJAMIN BLOUNT. Wit:
NATHAN HIGGS, ARCHILOUS HIGGS.

DOZIER, RICHARD
     P. 364. Sept. 5, 1829 - Nov. Ct. 1829. Wife:
ELIZABETH - 300 A. Sons: 1. JAMES, 2. LEONARD,
3. ZACHARIAH, 4. JOHN, 5. RICHARD. Daus: 1. MARY,
2. NANCY, 3. ELIZABETH. Ex: Sons JAMES and JOHN.
Wit: ROGER REESE, WILLIAM HENDRICKS, A. B. B. BAINES.

DOZIER, THOMAS
     P. 501. July 4, 1846 - Feb. Ct. 1847. Son:
1. WILLIAM - land north side road. Chil. to have
remaining land: 1. MARTHA SUSAN, 2. BENJAMIN A.,
3. CHARLOTTE T., 4. JULIUS. Ex: JACOB ING. Wit:
ROBERT E. DRAPER, KINCHEN C. TAYLOR.

DOZIER, WILLIAM - of Edgecombe Co.
     P. 123. Nov. 30, 1776 - April Ct. 1782. Wife:
AVERILAH (AVERILLA?). Chil: 1. JOHN, 2. WILLIAM,
3. SARAH, 4. RICHARD, 5. THOMAS, 6. MARTHA, 7. PEGGY,
8. RICHMOND. Ex: Wife AVERILAH, sons JOHN and
WILLIAM, and WILLIAM SKIPWITH MEARNS. Wit: THOMAS
WHITEHEAD, GREEN BELL, THOMAS HANKS.

DRAKE, AUGUSTIN
     P. 464. June 10, 1824 - Feb. Ct. 1842. Chil. of
HENRY MITCHELL and wife PENELOPY: 1. JOHN W., 2. ELIZABETH,
3. MARTHA ANN, 4. MARY MARCUS, 5. SYLVANIUS, 6. HENRY C.
DRAKE MITCHELL. Ex: Bro-in-law: HENRY MITCHELL. Wit:
W. W. BODDIE, WALKER MASINGALE.

DRAKE, EDMUND

P. 142. Sept. 1, 1803 - Nov. Ct. 1803. Sons:
1. EDWIN, 2. AUGUSTINE, 3. CASWELL, 4. HENRY. Daus:
1. CHLOE, 2. LOUISA, 3. SALLEY, 4. PENNY, 5. PATSY,
6. POLLEY, 7. NANCY, 8. ELIZABETH. Ex: Sons EDWIN
and CASWELL DRAKE. Wit: JOHN H. DRAKE, WILLIAM DRAKE,
JEREMIAH WILLIAMS.

DRAKE, EDWIN

P. 453. Jan. 5, 1825 - Aug. Ct. 1841. Sons:
1. ROBERT S. GLANDEN, 2. WILLIAM JACKSON GLANDEN.
Daus: 1. PATIENCE GLANDEN, 2. TEMPERANCE GLANDEN,
3. SALLY GLANDEN. The will states that the mother of
all of these children is ELIZABETH GLANDEN. Ex:
relative JESSE DRAKE - no wit. Will proven by oaths
of JACOB ING, HENRY BLOUNT, LAMON LANE and JESSE H.
DRAKE as to every part of the will being in the handwriting of EDWIN DRAKE.

DRAKE, ELIZABETH W.

P. 534. Feb. Ct. 1853. Whereas, ELIZABETH W.
DRAKE, being surprised with sudden illness......after
leaving home last Sept., not being able to return home,
was confined at the home of T. W. WRIGHT, in a few hours
of her death, she called upon JOHN J. DRAKE and SALLEY
BENNETT.....her wish was for her administrator to give
out of her estate twenty-five dollars to her gr. dau.,
ANN ELIZA WRIGHT, for attending her during her illness.
Proved by oath of JOHN J. DRAKE.

DRAKE, FRANCIS

P. 426. July 23, 1838 - Feb. Ct. 1841. Wife:
ELIZABETH. Son: WILLIAM F. Dau: DOROTHY. Other
chil. and "chil. of my dec'd son" unnamed. All my
Negroes in Georgia to be sold. Ex: Sons-in-law
NICHOLAS W. ARRINGTON and T. W. WRIGHT. Wit: WILLIAM
BURT, (DR.) J. A. DRAKE. Codicil, July 23, 1838,
leaving land where I live to wife ELIZABETH, with
reversion to all my chil. - the chil. of my deceased
son, GREEN W. DRAKE, to have his share.

DRAKE, HARRIET ADELINE

    P. 492. Oct. 5, 1846 - Nov. Ct. 1846. Sis:
1. ELIZA HARRIS, 2. MARY T. RAWLS, 3. MOURNING SCREWS.
No Ex. Wit: SARAH B. SHORT, JOHN ARRINGTON.

DRAKE, HARTWELL

    P. 109. April 25, 1796 - Aug. Ct. 1796. First
chil.: 1. FREDERICK DAVIS, 2. GOODMAN DAVIS,
3. DOLPHIN DAVIS, 4. THOMAS DAVIS, 5. ARCHIBALD DAVIS,
6. OREN DATES DAVIS, dec'd - his child POLLY DAVIS.
Dau: SALLY WARD. Chil. of second marriage: 1. JOHN
H. DRAKE, 2. BENJAMIN DRAKE. The above will (disposing of personal property) was proven before us
April 25, 1796, by the oaths of CHLOE BLANTON and SILAS
DRAKE. Signed, NATHAN BODDIE, BENJAMIN BOON. Note:
HARTWELL HODGES, dau. of BENJAMIN HODGES and wife
CONSTANCE GOODRICH, of Isle of Wight Co., Va., later
Southampton, married (1) THOMAS DAVIS of Isle of Wight.
She married (2) JAMES DRAKE of Nash Co., N. C., as his
second wife. M.G.G.

DRAKE, HINES

    P. 378. May 2, 1831 - Nov. Ct. 1831. Wife:
MOURNING - whole estate with reversion to daus:
1. TEMPERANCE, 2. ELIZABETH D., 3. MOURNING. Son and
Ex: JESSE H. DRAKE. Wit: TAYLOR THORN, ROBERT
TURNER.

DRAKE, JAMES

    P. 249. July 9, 1791 - no prob. date. Wife:
HARTWELL. Sons: 1. JAMES; 2. ALBRITTON; 3. SILAS -
land south side Swift Crk. on lines of THOMAS MANN and
BENJAMIN BOON; 4. JOHN HODGES DRAKE - 100 A. south side
Swift Crk., also land purchased of JAMES WILLIAMS and
JOHN BATTLE, also of TORMAGIN (TRIMEGIN) THOMPSON, also
land on lines of WILLIAM BRIDGERS, Buzzard's Branch,
and WILLIAMS; 5. BENJAMIN - mill and remainder of land,
including manor plantation. Daus: 1. ELIZABETH, wife
of MICHAEL COLLINS, 2. LYDA HADLEY, 3. SARAH BRIDGERS,
4. MILBREY WHELESS. Ex: Son JOHN and WILLIAM SKIPWITH
MEARNS (who wrote will). Wit: J. VAUGHAN, JACOB
VALENTINE, JOHN V. KANTZMAN. State of Virginia. This

will was signed in Richmond, Va., and was presented in Court in Richmond, Henrico Co., Va., on Mon., Aug. 1, 1791 by ADAM CRAIG, Clerk of said county, and recorded there Aug. 12, 1791. Certified Aug. 31, 1791 in Richmond by BEVERLY RANDOLPH, Gov. of Va. There is no date of the recording in Nash Co.

DRAKE, JONAS
    P. 274. Dec. 18, 1815 - Feb. Ct. 1816. Wife and Extx: CHARITY. Dau: MARTHA. Wit: ALASON POWELL.

DRAKE, MATHEW
    P. 205. Jan. 7, 1807 - May Ct. 1810. Sons: 1. MATHEW - 245 A. whereon I dwell, also part of a 400 A. survey granted by the Earl of Granville adjoining manor plantation on lines of Little Creek, Tar Trough Branch and the public road; 2. FRANCIS - 640 A. purchased of WILL HOOKS, also a note owed by CASWELL DRAKE for $104; Daus: 1. MOURNING DRAKE; 2. MARTHA NAILER PARKER - 300 A. on Little Swamp where JOHN BEDGOOD formerly lived; 3. MARY SUMNER; 4. ELIZABETH COLLINS - 444 A., a grant from the State of North Carolina adjoining SION BECKWITH, also former COOPER JONES tract; 5. TEMPERANCE DRAKE - remainder of tract left MATHEW, also a note for $43.82 owed by D. W. SUMNER and one for $30.18 owed by FRANCIS DRAKE; 6. DOROTHY DRAKE - 150 A. purchased of JOHN WILLIAMS and a note for $9 owed by MICHAEL COLLINS. Ex: Friends JOSEPH ARRINGTON, SR., JOHN H. DRAKE, MICHAEL COLLINS, ARCHIBALD GRIFFIN and son MATHEW DRAKE. Wit: JAMES DRUERY (DREWRY), LAZARUS JONES. Codicil to above will made Dec. 2, 1809 and witnessed by JAMES DREWRY ordered that MATHEW DRAKE'S son FRANCIS DRAKE be made an executor of his will.

DRAKE, MATHEW
    P. 282. Mar. 14, 1816 - May Ct. 1816. Bro. and Ex: JESSE DRAKE. Wit: TAYLOR THORN, ALEXANDER SMITH, SAM SMITH.

DRAKE, MOURNING
    P. 623. Mar., 1864 - Aug., 1867. Bro. and Ex:

JESSE H. DRAKE - whole estate. Wit: W. D. HARRISON,
J. H. HARRIS.

DRAKE, NATHANIEL
  P. 204. Nov. 20, 1809 - Feb. Ct. 1810. Mother:
DELILAH. Bros: 1. DIOCLETIAN DRAKE FLOYD, 2. ALLEN
DRAKE. Sis: 1. ELIZABETH GRIFFIN, 2. MARGARET DRAKE,
3. DELILAH DRAKE. Ex: Bro-in-law PENUEL FLOYD,
WILLIAM DRAKE. Wit: JAMES DRAKE.

DRAKE, WILLIAM
  P. 428. June 26, 1838 - Aug. Ct. 1838. Children
of my deceased nephew, GREEN W. DRAKE: 1. MARY
ELIZABETH, 2. WILLIAM GREEN, 3. LOUIZA, 4. a daughter
b. in Miss. about Mar. 12, 1837. Youngest sons of my
sis. ELIZABETH DRAKE: 1. WILLIAM F. DRAKE -the land
where I live, 2. JOSEPH JOHN DRAKE - 575 A. adjoining
THOS. W. WRIGHT, bought of JOHN SAUNDERS, 3. MATHEW
BOLIVAR DRAKE, 4. RICHARD DRAKE. Sons of my bro.
RICHARD DRAKE, dec'd: 1. JAMES W. DRAKE, 2. GEORGE
W. DRAKE. Nieces: daus. of my sister ELIZABETH DRAKE:
1. SALLY ANN ARRINGTON, 2. TEMPERANCE ARRINGTON, wife
of NICHOLAS W. ARRINGTON, 3. DOROTHY DRAKE. Niece:
ELIZABETH WRIGHT. Ex: Bro-in-law FRANCIS DRAKE,
nephew WILLIAM F. DRAKE, neighbor WILLIAM BURT, SR.
Wit: WM. BURT, JOHN ARRINGTON, E. B. HILLIARD, J. J.
M. COLLINS.

DUNN, BENJAMIN
  P. 596. Jan. 31, 1865 - Nov. Ct. 1865. Wife:
MARGARET A. - all property arising from the estate of
her deceased father WILLIE POWELL, including Negroes in
Tenn. as well as N. C. Sons: 1. WILLIAM ORRIS DUNN,
2. FRANCIS WILKINSON DUNN. Dau: 1. MARTHA SUSAN DUNN.
Friend EDWARD CONNIGLAND to be Ex. in financial matters.
Bro. LAMON S. DUNN and friend COL. F. M. PARKER to be
Ex's for remainder of estate, real and personal. "At
this critical term, and the uncertainty of everything,
should my estate be molested by the Yankees, or become
diminished in such a way as not to fill each ones
portion, I wish an equal division made between my three
children" etc. Wit: FREDERICK DOZIER, L. M. CONYERS.

EARP, JOSEPH
    P. 304. No date - Aug. Ct. 1819. Wife: SILVEY
(SYLVIA?). Sons: 1. RICHARD, 2. WILLIAM, 3. JOSEPH.
Daus: 1. HOLLEY MURRY, 2. HANEY EARP, 3. LIZE EARP,
4. POLLEY EARP, 5. TEMPY EARP. Ex: JESSE HAMMOND.
Wit: JESSE HAMMOND, WILLIAM MURRY, RICHARD EARP.
(RACHEL in Clerk's notes.)

EASON, DEMPSEY
    P. 10. Dec. 1, 1778 - Apr. Ct. 1780. Wife and
Extx: MILLEY. Wit: HENRY H. BURTON, P. WILLIAMS.

EASON, EUNICE
    P. 170. Feb. 22, 1795 - Aug. Ct. 1806. Sis and
Extx: EDITH EASON. Wit: DAVID PRIDGEN, ABIJAH
PRIDGEN.

EASON, SAMUEL
    P. 90. Mar. 1, 1794 - May Ct. 1794. Wife and
Extx: NANCY. Chil: 1. ELY EVERETT EASON, 2. JOHN
SMITH EASON, 3. ALLIS EASON, 4. MARGARET EASON. Wit:
DAVID PRIDGEN, MARY PRIDGEN, SARAH ALLEN.

EASON, SAMUEL
    P. 139. Dec. 3, 1800 - May Ct. 1801. Wife: EDITH.
Sons: 1. WILLIAM - 5 A. south side Sappony Swamp,
2. ISAIAS - 140 A. whereon I live. Daus: 1. EDITH
STRICKLAND, 2. EUNICE STRICKLAND, 3. MARY STRICKLAND,
4. ELIZABETH KEITH, 5. MILLEY EASON, 6. RUTH EASON.
Ex: Son ISAIAS EASON. Wit: DAVID PRIDGEN, ABIJAH
PRIDGEN.

EASON, WILLIAM, Nash Co., Elizabeth Parish
    P. 246A. Mar. 1, 1783 - no probate date. Wife
unnamed. Sons: 1. SAMUEL - 12 A. on Sappony Crk.,
2. DEMPSEY, 3. JOHN. Gr. sons: WILLIAM EASON -
138 A., THOMAS ALLEN. Daus: 1. ANN, 2. EUNICE,
3. EDITH. Gr. dau: MARY WHEDDON. Ex: Son SAMUEL.
Wit: DAVID PRIDGEN, JOHN SHEPPARD, SR., SAM EASON, JR.

EATMAN, RUFFIN
    P. 339. Sept. 22, 1826 - Nov. Ct. 1826. Wife:

AGGATHY. Sons: 1. HENRY, 2. JOHN. Father: JOHN
EATMAN. Daus: 1. JENSEY, 2. NANCY MARIAH, 3. MARTHA,
4. ELIZABETH JANE. No Ex. Wit: JAMES B. CROWELL,
HILLIARD HORN, GREER EATMAN.

EATMAN, THEOPHILUS
     P. 523. Oct. 4, 1848 - Aug. Ct. 1851. Wife:
BEEDY - 90 A. on Mill Stone Br. Sons: 1. GRIMER
(GRIMMER?), 2. WILLIE - 325 A. where he lives, 3. HAYMAN,
4. NOEL - his heirs, 5. GERMAN, 6. MASHEL - part of
DEAN'S land where he lives. Daus: 1. MILLY WILLIAMS -
73 A. near where DRUERY WILLIAMS lives, 2. SENATH
WILLIAMS - 200 A. where she lives, 3. BASHABY NARRON -
and her 3 sons, 4. NICY EATMON - 200 A. where she lives,
5. PRISCILLA WILLIAMS, 6. CHARITY DALTON - 300 A., the
DICKESON tract, 7. ELISHA EATMAN (this dau. appears
several times, always spelled the same), 8. TEMPY
EATMAN - 200 A. of the JAMES DEANS' land, 9. SALLEY
LEWIS, 10. ROEANY WINBOURN. Ex: A. B. BAINES. Wit:
JOHN DOZIER, M. H. DEANS. On May 25, 1849, THEOPHILUS
EATMAN signed a codicil to the above will reducing the
bequest to dau. CHARITY DALTON from 300 A. to 100 A. of
DICKENSON tract and leaving the remaining 200 A. lying
on the road to his gr. dau., CAROLINA BOYKIN, wife of
WILLIE BOYKIN. Wit: JESSE PEELE, EDWIN FULGHUM.

EATMAN, WILEY
     P. 535. June 25, 1853 - Aug. Ct. 1853. Wife:
GINCY - whole estate. "All my children" unnamed. Son
and Ex: LEONARD EATMAN. Dau: ROENY WILLIAMS. Wit:
H. M. BOYKIN, WILL Mc. EATMAN.

EDENS, ANN
     P. 371. ?1824 - May Ct. 1831. Daus: 1. POLLEY
EDENS, 2. NANCY WESTER (also VESTER), at her death, to
NANCY TUCKER. Legatee or dau.: SELLEY (SALLY?)
UNDERWOOD. Ex and Legatee: JOHN DEANS.

EDENS, MARY
     P. 392. Mar. 7, 1833 - May Ct. 1833. Sis: NANCY
SHERROD. Reversion to chil. of ENOS TUCKER: NANCY
TUCKER, JOHN TUCKER. Ex: JOYNER LANGLEY. Wit:
WILLIAM G. SHERROD.

EDENS, RICHARD

P. 187. Feb. 3, 1808 - Feb. Ct. 1808. Mother: ANN EDENS. Cousin: TEMPERANCE UNDERWOOD. Sis: POLLEY, NANCY, SILEY (CEALEY?), and SALLIE. SALLIE'S part to her children. Ex: Friend RICHARD HOLLAND. Wit: SHERWOOD EVANS, JAMES BATCHELOR.

EDWARDS, GEORGE

P. 269. Sept. 6, 1815 - Nov. Ct. 1815. Sons: 1. ETHELDRED, 2. HENRY. Daus: 1. NANCY BARRETT, 2. MARY EDWARDS, 3. LUCY EDWARDS, 4. BETSEY H. EDWARDS, 5. SALLY EDWARDS. Ex: Son HENRY EDWARDS, PHILANDER TISDALE. Wit: ELIAS BARRETT, GUILFORD WHITFIELD, JOHN BRASWELL.

EDWARDS, HENRY

P. 519. Dec. 20, 1849 - May Ct. 1850. Wife: MILLEY-whole estate for her lifetime. Sis: now living in N. C. - 1. NANCY, 2. LUCY, 3. SALLY - to have reversional interest in wife's land. At wife's death all personal property to be equally divided between the following: Bro. DREAD EDWARDS and Sis. BETSEY who moved to Georgia some years ago, and the three children of my wife, known as the MANNING children. Ex: WM. W. BODDIE, E. B. HILLIARD. Wit: JOSEPH A. DRAKE, WM. L. EDWARDS, JAMES DOZIER.

EDWARDS, MARTHA

P. 356. Aug. 4, 1826 - May Ct. 1828. Son and Ex: EDWIN. Daus: 1. PEGGY - wife of Taylor Thorn, 2. BETSEY, wife of Allen Jones, 3. TEMPY, wife of Jonathan Ricks, 4. POLLY, wife of William Westray. Wit: JESSE H. DRAKE.

EDWARDS, MILLEY

P. 533. Mar. 18, 1853 - May Ct. 1853. Sons: 1. MICHAEL MANNING, 2. BRITTAIN MANNING, 3. ALLEN MANNING. The estate to be divided into three parts - the children of each son receiving one part. Legatee: JOEL PRICE - one ax bought of MRS. ANNA RICKS. "MR. PRICE" appears to be farm manager "to carry on as though I were alive until after crop is housed." Ex: WM. W. BODDIE, E. B. HILLIARD. Wit: JESSE BEAL, THOMAS JONES, ELIZABETH BUNTING.

EDWARDS, SOLOMON
    P. 315. Sept. 16, 1820 - Nov. Ct. 1823. Son and
Ex: EDWIN EDWARDS - 382 A. adjoining LEVI S. UNDERWOOD,
CORDAL HUNTER, and HINES DRAKE. Wit: W. D. DORTCH,
CHARLOTTE EXUM.

EDWARDS, WILLIAM H.
    P. 566. Nov. 17, 1859 - May Ct. 1860. Wife:
ELIZABETH. Daus: 1. ELIZABETH C. THOMAS, wife of
ATHANASUS(?) THOMAS, 2. CORNELIA M. BOON, wife of
ROBERT R. BOON. Unmarried chil. unnamed. Ex:
NICHOLAS W. BODDIE. Wit: MADISON SIKES, N. W. BODDIE.
NICHOLAS BODDIE refused to serve as Ex., and ANTHANASIAS?
THOMAS was named Admin. - entering bond of $25,000 with
N. W. BODDIE and MADISON SIKES sureties.

ETHRIDGE, JEREMIAH - Nunc. will
    P. 242. Nov. 28, 1809 - No probate date. Dau:
COURTNEY. Wit: JESSE ADAMS, JACOB PERRY, MICHAEL
VESTER. Sworn before GEORGE BODDIE, J.P., Dec. 4, 1809.

ETHRIDGE, MARTHA
    P. 519. Aug. 6, 1849 - Nov. Ct. 1849. Sis: LIDY
ROSE. Niece: EADY ROSE. Ex: Friend NICHOLAS W.
BODDIE. Wit: W. N. BODDIE, JAS. H. EDWARDS.

EVINS (EVANS), JOHN
    P. 164. Nov. 5, 1805 - Nov. Ct. 1806. Wife: ANN.
Sons: 1. SHERROD, 2. GEORGE, 3. ABRAHAM - land adjoin-
ing BURWELL JOINER, 4. ISAAC - land lying above road.
Dau: ANN EVANS. Gr. chil.: TEMPY WINSTEAD, CALEB
DAVIS, ELIZABETH WARREN EVANS. No relationship - DOLLY
EVANS (gr. dau?) Ex: Son SHERROD EVANS, friends
RICHARD HOLLAND, JESSE JOYNER. Wit: ARCH'D GRIFFIN,
SAM SMITH.

EVANS, SALLY
    P. 598. Jan. 26, 1859 - Nov. Ct. 1866. Sons:
1. ISAAC B., 2. WILLIAM. Hus: ISAAC EVANS dec'd.
Dau: CHARITY BATCHELOR. Gr. chil: ISAAC, GEORGE and
SUSAN, chil. of son ISAAC B., JOEL BATCHELOR, SALLY
WELLS. Grt. gr. dau: LAURA, child of SALLY WELLS -

106 A. adjoining GEORGE W. COOPER - it being the lots
of land drawn by my sons ISAAC B. EVANS and WM. EVANS
in division of lands of their father ISAAC EVANS dec'd
which I purchased of them. Ex: Son ISAAC, B. H.
SORSBY. Wit: T. H. SCOTT, JOHN T. BRASWELL.

FERRELL, ELIZABETH
     P. 581. Oct. 4, 1855 - May Ct. 1862. Sons:
1. BRY FERRELL, 2. BIRTON (BURTON?). Daus: 1. MILLEY,
wife of WILLIAM PRICE, 2. MARTHA, wife of JIMERSON
MORGAN, 3. ELIZABETH, wife of SION SANDERS, 4. LACY,
wife of HENDERSON MORGAN, 5. MASON, wife of WARREN
STRICKLAND. Gr. dau: MARY ANN STRICKLAND, dau. of
WARREN STRICKLAND and wife, MASON. Ex: BARTLEY C.
STRICKLAND. Wit: A. H. SMITH, WESLEY PRIVETTE.

FERRELL, JAMES
     P. 521. Feb. 9, 1850 - May Ct. 1850. Wife:
ELIZABETH. Sons: 1. BENJAMIN, 2. BURTON, 3. ROLLEN
(ROLAND), 4. HENRY. Daus: 1. MILLEY, wid. of DAVID
HOPKINS, 2. MAZIE, late wife of RUFFIN SANDERS,
3. ELIZABETH, wife of SION SANDERS, 4. MARTHA, wife of
JIMERSON MORGAN, 5. MASON, wid. of WARREN STRICKLAND,
6. DELACAY, wife of HENDERSON MORGAN. Gr. chil:
BENJ. FERRELL, son of my youngest son HENRY - 274 A.,
OSCAR K. MASSEY, son of MATTHEW and MILLEY MASSEY -
100 A. Ex: Wife ELIZABETH. Wit: CLABORN PERRY,
A. I. TAYLOR.

FERRELL, WILLIAM of Thomas Co., Georgia
     P. 475. Aug. 25, 1842 - Sept. Ct. 1842. Wife and
children unnamed. He mentions old plantation, LEE
tract, and "collection of money due me in Georgia and
Florida." Ex's: JOHN M. FERRELL and ALSEY STRICKLAND
of Georgia, and DAVID M. DEEN and IESLEY FERRELL of
Nash Co., N. C. This will was probated Thomas Co.,
Ga., Sept. Ct. 1842. Ordered recorded in Nash Co.,
N. C., Feb. Ct. 1845.

FLOWERS, BENJAMIN
     P. 549. Sept. 13, 1852 - Sept. Ct. 1853. Wife:

NANCY - 612 A. Sons: 1. BENNET, 2. GUY - reversion
of mother's land. Daus: 1. WEIGHTY BOYKIN,
2. BLESSING BOYKIN, 3. ZILLA EATMAN, 4. WILLIE BOYKIN,
5. SELOMY WOODARD, 6. GILLY WILLIAMSON. Gr. son:
ADAM FLOWERS. Ex: Son GUY FLOWERS. Wit: WILLIE
DEANS, BARTLEY DEANS, SR. In a certain case in Nov.
term, 1854 Court of Pleas and Quarter Sessions, where
GUY FLOWERS executor was plaintiff and HARDY W. BOYKIN
and wife WRIGHT, HILLIARD BOYKIN and wife WILLIE,
COUNSEL BOYKIN and wife BLESSING were defendants, the
verdict was in favor of GUY FLOWERS. Plaintiffs
appealed to Superior Court, which was held in Wilson
Co., N. C. at which time the verdict of the Court of
Pleas and Quarter Sessions was sustained and the will
of BENJAMIN FLOWERS was ordered probated.

FLOWERS, BENJAMIN SR.
     P. 31. May 12, 1782 - no probate date. Wife:
MARTHA. Sons: 1. WILLIAM - land whereon I live,
2. JACOB, 3. BENJAMIN, 4. JOHN. Daus: 1. LURANA
NICHOLS, 2. JANE ROW, 3. DYCEA (DICIA), 4. MARY,
5. RACHEL. Ex: Wife MARTHA, MICHAEL HORN. Wit:
JOSEPH PHILLIPS, JETHRO PHILLIPS, CORNELIUS JORDAN,
SR.

F. ELLIN (FLEWELLIN), HOWELL (F. ELLIN was FLEWELLIN)
     P. 161. Oct. 17, 1805 - Nov. Ct. 1805. Wife:
ELIZABETH F. Son and Ex: LODERICK F. ELLIN - land on
east side Beaverdam and the HUNT land, also mill.
Daus: 1. SALLY WILLIAMS, 2. POLLY RICKS, 3. ELIZABETH
F. ELLIN, 4. NANCY F. ELLIN, 5. TEMPERANCE F. ELLIN.
Gr. son: HOWELL F. ELLIN (FLEWELLIN) WILLIAMS. Ex:
JAMES WILLIAMS. Wit: DEMSEY BRASWELL, HINES DRAKE,
ARCHIBALD BRASWELL.

FLOYD, AMOS
     P. 173. Oct. 27, 1807 - Nov. Ct. 1807. Bro. and
Ex: FREDERICK FLOYD. "My two brothers". "All my
brothers and sisters" unnamed. Wit: NATHAN WHITEHEAD,
WM. WHELESS.

FOREMAN, CORNELIUS of Edgecombe Co.
P. 588. Oct. 27, 1863 - May Ct. 1864. Nephew:
LEMUEL F. WHELESS (Ex). Legatee: HILLIARD CARLISLE.
These two to share entire estate. Wit: JAMES C.
KNIGHT, W. H. T. KNIGHT.

FOREHAND, DAVID
P. 430. Mar. 30, 1838 - Aug. Ct. 1838. Heirs of
BETSEY RUFFIN: POLLY RUFFIN, DAVID RUFFIN, MARTHA ANN
RUFFIN, SAMUEL HENRY RUFFIN, ELIZABETH FRANCES RUFFIN,
JOHN RUFFIN. Other Legatees: BETSEY RUFFIN, JOHN
MATHS (MATTHEWS?), LUCY TAYLOR, MORNING MORIS, LETTIE
FOREHAND. Ex: BARNEY PEARSON. Wit: DEMSEY
HARRISON, TEACHEN RICKS.

FOX, JACOB
P. 573. April 29, 1861 - Aug. Ct. 1861. Wife: MARY.
Dau: HELEN KEARNEY - all due me from the estate of her
gr. father, BARTHOLOMEW FULLER, and the note I hold
against K. KEARNEY. My 3 youngest chil: 1. ISHAM,
2. READIN, 3. LUCY. Wish to sell PITT's plantation
except ½ A. around grave-yard. Ex: A. H. ARRINGTON,
E. B. HILLIARD. Wit: THOS. W. AVENT, WM. LEONARD.

FRAZIER, ALEXANDER
P. 283. Oct. 21, 1816 - Nov. Ct. 1816. Wife:
SALLY. Niece: SALLY YOUNG. WILLIAM GATLIN of Gates
Co. - all my land in that county - no relationship.
CHARITY HENRY - no relationship. Ex: WILLIAM
HARRISON. Wit: JAMES HARRIS, SEL(?) B. PIPPIN, JESSE
PEALE.

FRAZIER, SALLY
P. 331. April 28, 1825 - Nov. Ct. 1825. Sons and
Ex's: 1. ANCEL FERRELL, 2. JAMES FERRELL. Dau:EUNICE
EDWARDS. Wit: ARCHIBALD LAMON, PATSY MORGAN.

FREEMAN, JOHN - Nuncupative will
P. 157. Nov. 20, 1804 - May Ct. 1805. Mother:
MASSEY DENSON. Bro: MATHEW FREEMAN. Legatee: MILLS
WHITLEY. Sworn by EDWARD COOPER and JAMES TEWELL before
JOSEPH ARRINGTON, ESQ.

FREEMAN, WILLIAM G.
P. 540. July 3, 1854 - Nov. Ct. 1854. Mother:
HARRIET FREEMAN. Sis: AMANDA G. FREEMAN. Bro:
thought to have been maliciously killed by AMARIAH ?
(apparently wife of his brother), and he does not wish
her child to share in his estate if AMARIAH is alive.
Ex: Mother and sister AMANDA, with help of Attn'y
WILLIAM T. DORTCH. Handwriting proved by oaths of
BENJAMIN A. BLOUNT, JAMES HARRIS, and GEORGE N. LEWIS.

GANDY, EDWARD
P. 291. July 23, 1816 - Aug. Ct. 1817. Sons:
1. GRIFFIN GANDY - 100 A. on Sappony Crk.,2. BRINKLEY-
164 A. on lines of JACOB RICKS, WILLIAM RICKS and
DAVID RICKS, 3. AMOS; Daus: 1. TAMSEY GANDY,
2. ELIZABETH GANDY. Ex: Son GRIFFIN GANDY. Wit:
S. WESTRAY, JOHN MELTON.

GARDENER, GEORGE
P. 302. Mar. 24, 1817 - Feb. Ct. 1819. Wife:
SARAH. Sons: 1. GEORGE - 568 A. called the BLANTON
place on the lines of JOSEPH ARRINGTON and JOHN DAVIS,
2. HOLMAN. Daus: 1. SOPHRONA, 2. POLLY P. DARREN,
and 3. MARTHA AVENT - to share 175 A. purchased of
NATHAN WARD. DRUCILLA CAPBELL (CAMPBELL?) is not desig-
nated as daughter but is a legatee. Ex: JOSEPH
ARRINGTON. Wit: BENJAMIN W. AVENT, ELIZABETH AVENT,
NATHANIEL CRUMP.

GAY, JOHN of Franklin Co., N. C.
P. 196. June 8, 1780(?) - Nov. Ct. 1808. Wife:
MARTHA. Sons: 1. JOSIAH - plantation in Nash Co.,
2. MILLS GAY. Dau: BETHANY GAY. Ex: Wife MARTHA,
ELIAS GAY. Wit: EPHRAIM GILLIAM, WILLIAM STEWART,
DAVID VINSON.

GILBERT, NATHAN
P. 192. July 16, 1808 - Aug. Ct. 1808. Wife:
CHARITY. Son: JOHN - land after mother's death.
Daus: 1. SALLEY, 2. PHEBE, 3. ROWENA. Ex: Friend
REDMUND BUNN. Wit: REDMUND BUNN, JOHN ATKINSON.
Codicil July 16, 1808 wit. by: HENRY RICKS, ELI RICKS.

49

GREEN, JOHN
    P. 323. Jan. 29, 1823 - Aug. Ct. 1824. Wife: SALLY-
all land. Sons: 1. ARTHUR, 2. HARDY, 3. JOSEPH.
Daus: 1. TABITHA POWELL, 2. ANN GREEN. Ex: CARTER
ARRINGTON. Wit: JOSEPH ARRINGTON, JR., JOHN DOZIER,
JR.

GREEN, MARY
    P. 488. Dec. 15, 1843 - Nov. Ct. 1846. Dau:
RHODA HARRISON. Gr. daus: MARY HAWKINS of Halifax
Co., N. C., MARTHA WELDON, Nash Co., RHODA KING, Nash
Co. Ex: Son-in-law EMILLIUS HARRISON. Wit: BENJ.
W. AVENT, N. W. ARRINGTON.

GREEN, SALLY
    P. 392. Feb. 5, 1833 - Feb. Ct. 1833. Daus: 3
living children - 1. ANN DRAKE, 2. ELIZABETH CARLISLE,
3. MASON POWELL. Ex: FRED BATTLE. Wit: EMELUS
HARRISON, MATHEW WELDON.

GRICE, JACOB
    P. 296. Feb. 16, 1818 - May Ct. 1818. Wife: LIDDY.
Sons: 1. JAMES, 2. STEPHEN, 3. SHERROD, 4. JOHN. Daus:
1. ELIZABETH, 2. MILLEY, 3. ZILPHEY, 4. PENNEY. Ex:
DAVID WINBORNE, GARRY GRICE. Wit: ARNOLD STRICKLAND,
SIMON TAYLOR.

GRICE, THEOPHILUS
    P. 316. April 18, 1823 - Nov. Ct. 1823. Wife:
POLLEY - home plantation. Sons: 1. JOHN - BLUMERY
land bought of DRED DEBERRY and wife, and IRVIN RICKS,
also land adjoining THEOPHILUS GRICE, CHRISTIAN ROW,
the RALEY Road, JACOB ROW and NICHOLS; 2. THOMAS - all
land in Johnston Co., except 3 A. at Cobb Mill, also
the BOYKIN land adjoining JESSE SIMPSON in Nash Co.
Daus: 1. SALLEY COOK, 2. RODEY, 3. TEMPEY. Ex: Son
JOHN, BARTLEY DEANS. Wit: JOHN L. LYONS, JAMES DEANS.

GRIFFIN, JACOB
    P. 591. Oct. 15, 1856 - Feb. Ct. 1865. Wife:
TEMPERANCE. Sons: 1. JOHN (Ex), 2. NEWELL (Penuel),

3. DOLPHIN - each to have land. Daus: 1. ELIZA,
2. MARY, 3. TEMPE, 4. MARIAH. Wit: JOHN G. F. DRAKE,
LAWRENCE BATTLE, BENJAMIN F. DRAKE.

GRIFFIN, JAMES
   P. 100. May 9, 1779 - May Ct. 1795. Son: ABSALOM.
Daus: 1. CHRISTIAN, 2. ELISAH (ELIZA?). Remaining
estate to friend MARY DRAKE with reversion to her chil:
1. SION DRAKE, 2. LURANEY DRAKE, 3. JESSE DRAKE,
4. ISAAC DRAKE. Ex: MARTHA DRAKE. Wit: JAMES
BATTLE, JAMES BRYANT, MARY WILLIAMS.

GRIFFIN, JOSEPH
   P. 36. Nov. 30, 1776 - Feb. Ct. 1785. Wife: SARAH.
Sons: 1. JOSEPH - land on the lines of Drake, Hilliard,
Parker's Crk., and Spring Branch; 2. PEARCE - land where
he lives; 3. MICAJAH - reversion of land where I live;
4. WILLIAM, 5. DRURY. Daus: 1. SARAH WALKER, 2. MARY
HOLLADAY, 3. APPY, 4. ZILPHA. Ex: Wife SARAH, son
WILLIAM. Wit: W. S. MEARNS, FRANCIS PARKER, JOHN
PARKER.

GRIZZELL, WILLIAM
   P. 168. Jan. 16, 1806 - Aug. Ct. 1806. Wife:
ISABEL. No relation given - PRISCILLA GRIZZELL. Gr.
chil: BONSTER? GRIZZELL, NANCY GRIZZELL, POLLEY O'NEAL,
HARDY GRIZZELL, son of ARTHUR - all land. Chil:
1. RHODA DRIVER, 2. HERROD GRIZZELL, 3. DANIEL GRIZZELL,
4. MASSEY PUGH, 5. ARTHUR GRIZZELL. Ex: WILLIAM
MOORE. Wit: DRUCY WILLIAMS, WILLIAM NEVIN, BRYANT
WILLIAMS.

HACKNEY, RACHEL
   P. 244. Jan. 23, 1788 - no prob. date. Daus:
1. SARAH POPE, 2. PURITY MIALS, 3. UNITY PARKER, 4. PENNY
ADKINS. Gr. chil: BENJAMIN POPE, NANNEY MIALS, CAIN
PARKER, JENNONS (JENNINGS) HACKNEY, RACHEL ADKINS, BETSEY
HACKNEY, PENNY HACKNEY. Ex: NORSWORTHY MIALS. Wit:
JESSE JOHNSON, CHRISTOPHER ING.

HACKNEY, WILLIAM
   P. 241. Mar. 6, 1787 - no prob. date. Wife: MILLEY.
51

Son: 1. JINNENS (JENNINGS) - plantation. Daus:
1. ELIZABETH, 2. PENELOPE. Ex: BENJAMIN FOREMAN.
Wit: JETHRO DENSON, JOSEPH DENSON. Clerk's probate
notes state will proven by oaths of JETHRO and BENJ.
DENSON.

HAMMONS, JESSE
    P. 308. April 9, 1816 - Nov. Ct. 1822.   Wife:
CHARITY. Sons: 1. WILLIS - 350 A. on east side Turkey
Crk., 2. JAMES - 150 A. west side Turkey Crk.,
3. WILLIAM, Daus: 1. MASON MORGIN, 2. POLLEY CARTER,
3. SUSANNEY STRICKLAND, 4. CHARITY HAMMONS. Ex: Sons
WILLIAM and WILLIS HAMMONS. Wit: A. FERRELL, ISHAMEL
STRICKLAND, SION SANDERS.

HAMMONS, WILLIE
    P. 268. Sept. 24, 1814 - Aug. Ct. 1815. My will
and desire is that my brother, JOHN HAMMONS, shall have
my estate.....if I never return from this tower (tour)
that I am now going to serve for SAM VICK as one of the
militia of Nash Co., to wit: (1) filley now in possession
of my father, BURWELL HAMMONS; (2) note for $13.50 due
from ELIZABETH TURLINGTON; (3) note for $10.00 due from
DUNCAN RICKS and ABRAHAM RICKS; (4) note for $4.50 due
from WHITMILL RICKS and ABRAHAM RICKS. All the above to
be held by BURRELL HAMMONS for my brother, JOHN HAMMONS,
and to put them to interest in best manner he can until
my brother arrives at the age of 21 years, or marries.
Wit: S. WESTRAY. Proven in Court by oath of Sam Westray.

HANEY, THOMAS
    P. 24. June 15, 1782 - Oct. Ct. 1788. Wife:
FRANCES. Daus: 1. MARY, 2. ELIZABETH, 3. FRANCES.
Ex: MASON FLOWERS, JESSE BATTLE. Wit: ALISE (ALICE?)
ROSE, FRANCIS ROSE.

HARDEN, NANCY
    P. 288. Feb. 17, 1816 - Feb. Ct. 1817. Sis: BETSEY
POLLY HOPKINS. HARRIET HOPKINS (relationship?) No relationship given: HARRIET CAPEHART. Bros: JOHN
CAPEHART, WM. CAPEHART. No Ex. or Wit. Proven by oath
of WILLIAM FLEETWOOD.

HARPER, WILLIAMSON
    P. 516. Mar. 29, 1849 - Aug. Ct. 1849. Sons: "two
oldest boys" to have two chests of tools. Ex: JOEL
ROSSER. Wit: A. ARRINGTON, W. P. SLEDGE.

HARRELL, LUCRETIA
    P. 422. Mar. 5, 1838 - May Ct. 1838. Son: WILLIAM
HARRELL. Daus: 1. ELIZABETH CULPEPPER, 2. REBECCA
CULPEPPER, 3. EMILLIA TAYLOR, 4. CHARLOTTE WHITLEY. Ex:
Son-in-law ALLEN TAYLOR. Wit: TIMOTHY FERRELL, WILLIE
(WILLIS?) WHITLEY.

HARRIS, RANDOLPH
    P. 271. May 30, 1815 - Nov. Ct. 1815. Sons:
1. JOEL, 2. CANFIELD - his part in a legacy bequeathed
by his uncle EDWIN SEWARD. Daus: 1. REBECCA MASON -
$500 to her children when they come of age, 2. MARY
ATKINSON. Ex: Son JOEL HARRIS, Friends JESSE THORP
and SAMUEL SMITH. Wit: LEWIS HINES, ALEXANDER SMITH,
JOHN A. ATKINSON.

HARRISON, ANN, wid. of JOHN HARRISON, desc.
    P. 476. June 5, 1843 - Nov. Ct. 1844. Sons:
1. HENRY, 2. NATHANIEL, 3. EMELIUS, 4. JOHN, 5. JAMES.
Daus: 1. MILDRED BLOUNT, 2. MARGARET DERING,
3. TEMPERANCE DRAKE. Ex: Son JAMES. Wit: THOMAS
W. AVENT.

HARRISON, HENRY
    P. 537. July 7, 1853 - Feb. Ct. 1854. Bros: JOHN,
EMILIUS. Sis: TEMPERANCE DRAKE. Nephew: NICHOLAS C.
HARRISON, son of JOHN HARRISON. Friend and neighbor:
MRS. PATSEY COLLINS. Ex: Bro. JOHN. Wit: N. W.
COOPER, JOHN POWELL.

HARRISON, JETHRO
    P. 216. Apr. 20, 1811 - Aug. Ct. 1811. Sons:
1. WILLIAM - 500 A. bought of WILLIAM and JETHRO
PHILIPS, 2. JETHRO - land whereon I live as far as the
south prong of Spring Branch, 3. DEMPSEY - land bought
of JOHN SANDERS and all remaining land. Daus: 1. NANCY
HORN, 2. POLLEY GRICE, 3. TEMPERANCE HOLDEN, 4. ELIZABETH
HARRISON, 5. MILBRAY HARRISON, 6. MORNING RICKS. Gr. sons:

Sons of dau. MORNING RICKS (it does not say she is desc'd)
JAMES and JETHRO RICKS. To divide my land: HENRY ATKINS,
WILLIAM HORN, WILLIAM MOORE. Ex: Son WILLIAM HARRISON,
CHARLES COLEMAN, WILLIAM WHITE. Wit: HARDY HORN, WILLIS
MORRIS, ROSANNA BRANTLEY.

HARRISON, JOHN
    P. 347. No date - probated Nov. Ct. 1827.   Wife:
ANN.   Sons: 1. JAMES, 2. BENJAMIN D. HARRISON's chil.
to have 1 share, 3. EMELIUS, 4. JOHN, 5. JAMES.   Daus:
1. MARTHA MASON'S chil. - 1 share, 2. MILDRED BLOUNT,
3. MARGARET HARRISON.   Ex: Son JAMES.   No. Wit.
Proven by oaths of JOHN DERRING, FRED BATTLE and JAMES
AVENT.   Note: It appears there were 9 chil., as estate
was to be divided into 10 parts for wife and children.
See wills of ANN HARRISON and NANCY HARRISON. M.G.G.

HARRISON, JOHN
    P. 603. April 8, 1869 - Feb. 18, 1870. Wife:
CELESTIA E.   Sons: 1. JOHN F. (dec'd), 2. N. C. HARRISON.
Dau: 1. MARY DRAKE. Gr. chil: BETTY, MARY, the chil.
of dec'd son JOHN F. HARRISON. Also chil. of N. C.
HARRISON (unnamed). Ex: B. L. ARRINGTON. Wit: B. L.
ARRINGTON, JOSEPH A. DRAKE.

HARRISON, NANCY
    P. 478. July 7, 1844 - May Ct. 1845. Note: This
appears to be the same person who made will as ANN
HARRISON June 5, 1843 which was probated Nov. Ct. 1844.
M.G.G.   Son and Ex: JAMES HARRISON. Daus: 1. TEMPERANCE
DRAKE, 2. PEGGY DERING. Gr. dau: TEMPERANCE MASON.
Wit: BENJ. W. AVENT, WM. H. HARRISON.

HARRISON, NATHANIEL
    P. 597. Mar. 10, 1860 - May Ct. 1866.   Wife:
MARGARET - land where I live. Son: 1. JOHN H. Daus:
1. FRANCES A. RICKS, 2. ANN E. WILLIAMS. Ex: BENJAMIN
D. MANN. Wit: WM. H. HILLIARD, H. W. WHITAKER. Clerk's
notes: Ex. BENJ. D. MANN being dead, WM. H. JONES was
made Admin., entering into bond of $25,000 with THOS. W.
AVENT, WM. T. WRIGHT and J. W. MITCHELL, sureties.

HARRISON, RHODY

P. 549. Dec. 27, 1855. Legatees: 1. SWIFTON L. SIMS, 2. NATHANIEL L. HARRISON, son of WILLIAM H. HARRISON, 3. MARY ELIZA HARRISON, 4. JOHN C? HARRISON. Ex: NICHOLAS W. ARRINGTON. Wit: ALLEN G. TAYLOR, N. M. HARRIS.

HART, ELISHA B.

P. 519. June 7, 1849 - Feb. Ct. 1850. Wife: NANCY W. HART. Daus: 1. SUSAN E. HART, eldest dau. - certain articles at JAMES GILBERT'S in Franklin Co., 2. VANDELIA C. HART - articles at same location in Franklin Co. Ex: DANIEL L. CRENSHAW. Wit: J. M. TAYLOR, BENJ. B. SMITH.

HART, THOMAS SR.

P. 90. Feb. 4, 1794 - Nov. Ct. 1794. Son and Ex: THOMAS - 100 A. purchased of ISAAC TOMLINSON. Gr. son: JOSEAL NOLLEBOY. Wit: LEWIS VICK, JAMES EVANS, ANN MELTON.

HASKINS, BENJAMIN L.

P. 564. Jan. 27, 1859 - Feb. Ct. 1860. The farm where I live is to be sold, but the house and lot in Wilmington, N. C. is not to be sold, but is left to my wife (unnamed). I do not wish my pew in St. James Protestant Episcopal Church in Wilmington to be sold. Son: 1. BENJAMIN L. HASKINS. Daus: 1. MARIA C. HASKINS, 2. HARRIET ANN JONES. Trustee: JOHN BEVAN, ESQ., of Halifax Co. Ex: L. H. B. WHITAKER of Halifax Co. No wit. There being no witnesses, the handwriting (the will was all in his handwriting) was proved by the oaths of JOHN F. SPEIGHT, JESSE H. DRAKE, and THOMAS L. MANN. L. H. B. WHITAKER having renounced his right to serve as executor, JOHN H. SPEIGHT was named administrator, with bond of $60,000 - L. H. B. BATTLE and HENRY G. WILLIAMS as sureties.

HEDGEPETH, ABRAM

P. 479. Apr. 28, 1843 - May Ct. 1845. Sons: 1. HENRY, 2. JESSE, 3. ELIAS, 4. TAYLOR, 5. ARCHIBALD. Dau: 1. PENELOPY HEDGEPETH. Apparently gr. chil:

heirs of HARTY HARRIS, MARY WILLIAMS, MATHEW DREWRY.
Ex: Sons TAYLOR and ARCHIBALD HEDGEPETH. Wit: JAMES
HARRISON, JOHN A. HARRISON. Note: Included on a list
of Revolutionary Pensioners appearing in the 1840 Census
of Nash County is: ABRAHAM HEDGEPETH, age 72. M.G.G.

HEDGEPETH, HENRY
    P. 548. Oct. 23, 1855 - Nov. Ct. 1855. Wife:
CEALY - 115 A. where I live, with reversion to son
ELIAS GREEN HEDGEPETH. Sons: 1. HENRY W. - 100 A.,
2. WILLIAM T., 3. M. C. HEDGEPETH. Daus: 1. REBECCA
ANN ELIZABETH WOODARD, wife of JOHN L. B. WOODARD;
2. MALVINA HANES (HARRIS?); 3. ROENA MARY ANN HEDGEPETH.
Ex: Wife CEALY. Wit: W. W. BODDIE, FRANCIS WALKER.

HENDRICK, TEMPERANCE
    P. 539. April 1, 1848 - Aug. Ct. 1854. Sons:
1. HENDERSON W. HENDRICK - 29 A. adjoining WM. B.
BRYANT, 2. GRANBERRY, dec'd (his chil.), 3. WRIGHT B.
(his chil.), 4. REDDING. Dau: 1. NANCY STRICKLAND.
Gr. daus: MARY W. STRICKLAND, ELIZABETH M. STRICKLAND.
Ex: J. J. TAYLOR. Wit: ROBERT D. DEANS, GUILFORD H.
WILLIAMS.

HENDRICK, WILLIAM SR.
    P. 454. July 29, 1841 - Nov. Ct. 1841. Wife:
CLOWEY (CHLOE). Legatees: 1. NANCY THOMAS and her
chil., 2. PATSEY LEWIS, 3. FRANCIS LEWIS, 4. children
of ELIZABETH LEWIS, 5. children of ALEXANDER THOMAS.
No relationship given. Ex: WILLIAM B. BRYANT. Wit:
D. W. DEANS (DAVID), N. C. RICE. Clerk's notes: DAVID
M. DEANS AND N. N. RICE.

HIGGS, SAMUEL
    P. 213. May 23, 1810 - Nov. Ct. 1810. Sons:
1. NATHAN, 2. SAMUEL, 3. PHILIP, 4. JONATHAN, 5. JOHN.
Gr. son: THOMAS J. BRADY. Dau: 1. JANE WHITAKER.
Ex: Sons NATHAN and SAMUEL. Wit: WM. DOZIER,
ELIZABETH LANGLEY, WM. DRUERY. Clerk's notes: name
HENRY DRUERY.

HILLIARD, E.(ELIJAH) B.
    P. 582. June 5, 1859 - Aug. Ct. 1862. Wife unnamed.

Sons: 1. JESSE P. - reversional interest in home plantation, 2. SIDNEY P. - land on south side Swift Crk.
and beyond Parker's Crk., 3. Infant not yet named - land
on north side Swift Crk. Daus: 1. ALICE, 2. REBECCA,
3. BETSEY - her guardian is to be JOHN B. WILLIAMS of
Warren Co. Ex: DR. A. T. PERRY, WILLIAM W. BODDIE.
"Whatever errors I may have been guilty of, please to
bury them with me - let me rest by my dear boy JAMES,
at the feet of my mother." Handwriting proved by HENRY
G. WILLIAMS, JOHN B. WILLIAMS and WM. H. ROWLAND.

HILLIARD, ISAAC
    P. 67. June 14, 1790 - Aug. Ct. 1790. Wife: LEAH.
Sons: 1. JAMES - all my land on the s. side of Wateree
River in S. C.; 2. ISAAC - 750 A. in Overseer Meadows,
Northampton Co.; 3. JOHN - 2 tracts bought of JAMES BELL
and ROBERT PYLAND, also my land adjoining same, adjoining Deep Bottom Branch and WILLIAM WRIGHT, also 350 A.
bought of HENRY STEVENS; 4. ROBERT CARTER HILLIARD - 2
tracts bought of JOSEPH MATHEWS, also 350 A. which is
lower part of land bought of HENRY STEVENS, also 75 A.
bought of THOMAS WILSON; 5. HENRY - 440 A. s. side
Swift Crk., it being the JAMES GRIFFIN place, also 50 A.
bought of BENJ. WHITFIELD, 350 A. on lines of JOHN JONES
and JOHN MELTON, the land where the widow THOMAS lived,
also 270 A. in Northampton Co., adjoining DOCTOR PEETE
(PEELE?), also land purchased of THOMAS HORN; 6. WILLIAM-
all land purchased of JESSE BATTLE and ISAAC TALBOT.
Daus: 1. ELIZABETH DAVIS, 2. ANN HILLIARD, 3. MARTHA
HILLIARD. Natural son: ISAAC DORTCH. Ex: Wife
LEAH, son JAMES, bro-in-law HENRY CRAWFORD and cousin
SIMON JEFFRIES. Wit: WILLIAM S. MEARNS, BENJAMIN
SANDERFORD, MILLICAN (MILLIKEN?) JELKS.

HILLIARD, JAMES
    P. 385. Feb. 19, 1830 - Aug. Ct. 1832. Wife:
MOURNING. Sons: 1. ISAAC - 1400 A. bought at my
brother ISAAC'S sale, called Mill Brook; 2. JAMES C. -
land on south side of JAMES GRIFFIN'S Branch and that
along lines of TISDALE, WHITE, HENRY EDWARDS, ALEXANDER
HINES, WHITLEY, ALLEN JONES, GEO. BODDIE, Swift Crk.
and the mill; 3. ELIJAH B. - reversion of land bought

of HENRY PARKER and WILLIAM DRAKE, the SUMNER land and
plantation where I live. Daus: 1. ELIZABETH J. -
1474½ A. PIG BASKET plantation adjoining WILLIE BUNTING,
W. W. BODDIE and others; 2. MARY T. - 703 A. in
MATTHEWS, KITCHEN and TOMLINSON tracts; 3. LEAH M. -
500 A. called Ready Point, bought at my brother, R. C.
HILLIARD'S, sale. Ex: Son ISAAC, WILLIAM W. BODDIE,
WM. BURT. Wit: HENRY DANCE, HENRY ARRINGTON, LUCY E.
HILLIARD.

HILLIARD, JAMES C.
    P. 566. Feb. 26, 1860 - May Ct. 1860.   Wife:
MARTHA. Wife's 4 chil: 1. JAMES CAREY, 2. GEORGE W.
B., 3. WALTER, 4. MARY ELIZA HILLIARD. My 4 chil:
1. MOURNING B., 2. ELIZABETH M., 3. SAMUEL R., 4. JONAS
J. C. HILLIARD. In making bequests of a group of
Negroes to each group of the above children, he speaks
of the Negroes' increase from Sept. 20, 1854. MARTHA
is evidently his second wife, so is it possible that
Sept. 20, 1854 was the date of their marriage? Later,
he names "all my children", naming the above 8 chil.
Very large estate and involved will. Ex: WILLIAM W.
BODDIE, A. H. ARRINGTON. Wit: W. T. ARRINGTON,
BYTHEL BRYAN.

HILLIARD, JOHN T.
    P. 416. Sept. 8, 1836 - Nov. Ct. 1837. Bro-in-
law: ISAAC HILLIARD. Bro and Ex: ROBERT C. HILLIARD.
Half bros: EDMOND and THOMAS C. ARRINGTON. Half sis:
FELECIA ARRINGTON. Wit: JOHN ARRINGTON, BENJ. A. W.
ARRINGTON.

HILLIARD, MRS. LEAH - Nunc. Will
    P. 318. Nov. Ct. 1823. MRS. HILLIARD died 20 of
Oct., 1823. Before she died, she called upon the under-
signed, two of her sons, and remarked: When I die, I
want ROBERT HILLIARD, CAROLINE HILLIARD and WILLIAM
HILLIARD to have a bed each; and LEAH to have my bureau".
The undersigned understood the LEAH mentioned by MRS.
HILLIARD to be LEAH, the dau. of CARTER HILLIARD. - JAMES
HILLIARD, ROBERT C. HILLIARD.

HILLIARD, ROBERT C.
    P. 350. Jan. 7, 1828 - Feb. Ct. 1828.   Wife:
AMMERYLIS. Sons: 1. WILLIAM H., 2. ROBERT C. T.
These, WILLIAM and ROBERT, to have reversional interest
in land lent wife, viz: mansion plantation with all the
land bought of WILLIAM WHITEHEAD, except 100 A. on n.w.
corner of tract, adjoining JACOB ING and DEMPSEY TAYLOR,
also remainder of TALBERT tract on s. side Lane Swamp,
3. JOHN H. - the WILLIAM WRIGHT land, also 100 A. bought
of WILLIAM WHITEHEAD. Daus: 1. MARY S. M. A. E. J.
HILLIARD, 2. LEAH C. HILLIARD, 3. AMMERYLIS W. HILLIARD,
4. REBECCA E. HILLIARD - 140 A. of TALBERT tract on n.
side of Lane Swamp. Ex: Son WILLIAM HILLIARD and
bro. JAMES HILLIARD. Wit: W. L. HUNT, WILLIAM KEA,
LUCY S. LEWIS.

HILLIARD, MOURNING
    P. 503. Feb. 13, 1847 - May Ct. 1847. Sons:
1. JAMES, 2. ELIJAH B. Daus: 1. TEMPE WILLIAMS,
2. LEAH PERRY. "All my children." Gr. chil: ELIAS
CARR, ELLA HILLIARD, MARY B. HILLIARD, MOURNING HILLIARD,
BETSEY M. HILLIARD, SAMUEL HILLIARD, JONAS HILLIARD,
Bond held against JOHN B. WILLIAMS. Ex and Guardian
for the 4 last named gr. chil: Son ELIJAH B. HILLIARD.
Wit: MARTHA SARGENT, ELIZABETH WILLIFORD.

HINES, ELIZABETH
    P. 589. Dec. 21, 1863 - Nov. 1864. Sons: 1. JOHN
C., 2. ALEXANDER W., dec'd. Daus: 1. REBECCA E.
ARRINGTON - my interest in land where I live, 2. MARTHA
DRAKE. Chil. of ALEXANDER W. HINES, dec'd: FRANCIS,
ELIZABETH A. Ex: Dau. REBECCA E. ARRINGTON. Wit:
JOHN E. JONES, JOHN E. LINDSEY.

HINES, HARTWELL SR.
    P. 329. May 20, 1825 - Aug. Ct. 1825.   Dau:
1. ELIZABETH VICK. Gr. chil: LUCY B., dau. of ALEX
HINES, desc., JOSEPH, NANCY, ELIZA (ELIZABETH), PATSEY,
TEMPERANCE and MARY, chil. of FREDERICK HINES, desc.,
chil. of L. V. HINES, desc., ELIZABETH HUNTER, BOLDIN
WALKER, MARTHA VICK and JAMES WALKER, chil. of REBECCA

WALKER, desc. Ex: JAMES HUNTER. Wit: JOHN ARRINGTON, TIMOTHY FERRELL.

HOPKINS, DAVID
    P. 504. Mar. 6, 1847 - May Ct. 1847. Wife: MILLY.
Son: 1. ALSEY - 284 A. where ENOCH HALES lives called
STRICKLAND land. Dau: 1. SUSAN - reversion of 240 A.
whereon I live. ALSEY will come of age in 1863 and
SUSAN will come of age in 1857. Ex and Guardian: A.
I. TAYLOR. Wit: JAMES PIERCE, HILLIARD N. HOPKINS.

HOPKINS, PETER
    P. 183. Nov. 9, 1807 - Feb. Ct. 1808. Wife:
WILMOTH. Sons: 1. JOHN - 250 A. on Little R. in Wake
County, adjoining MATHEW STRICKLAND, Griffin's Br. and
JOSEPH HOPKINS, 2. JOSEPH - 250 A. in Wake Co., adjoin-
ing MATHEW STRICKLAND, WILLIAM HOPKINS, 3. WILEY -
560 A. in Wake Co., adjoining MATHEW STRICKLAND, JESSE
BURNS, ISRAEL PRIVITT and JOHN HOPKINS, 4. WILLIAM -
300 A. on Little R. in Wake Co., adjoining MATHEW
STRICKLAND, JOSEPH HOPKINS, GEORGE BELL, also 300 A.
in Nash Co., adjoining JOHN RICE and Pumping Br.,
5. PETER - 200 A. on Little R. in Wake Co., each side
Moccasin Cr., adjoining BURRELL FOWLER and GEORGE
CRUDUP, 6. DAVID - 400 A. on Little R. in Nash and
Johnston Counties each side of Moccasin Cr., adjoining
HARDY PRIDGEN and BURRELL STRICKLAND, 7. ALSEY,
8. CROFFORD - 300 A. whereon I live. Daus:
1. ELIZABETH RICE, 2. MARY HOPKINS, 3. SUSANNAH HOPKINS.
Ex: Sons ALSEY and DAVID HOPKINS. Wit: BURWELL
STRICKLAND, RICHARD MASON, JOHN HOPKINS.

HORN, ABISHAI
    P. 260. Oct. 12, 1812 - Nov. Ct. 1814. Cousin:
BENNET BUNN of Pitt Co., N. C. Ex: Uncle REDMUN BUNN
and bro. JOSIAH HORN. Wit: ETHELDRED EDWARDS, SALLY
CURL.

HORNE, HENRY
    P. 555. May 9, 1857 - May Ct. 1857. Gr. dau:
POLLY HILL, wife of RUFFIN EATMAN - whole estate includ-
ing my land. Ex: WILEY DEANS. Wit: PETER EATMAN,
A. T. TAYLOR.

60

HORN, JOEL
     P. 85.   June 16, 1793 - Nov. Ct. 1793. Wife unnamed.
Sons: 1. ETHELDRED, 2. MATHEW, 3. HARRIS. My 5 first
chil. to have all my land: 1. HARRIS, 2. HOWELL, 3. HARDY,
4. MILBRIE, 5. REBECCA. Ex: Friends JEREMIAH HILLIARD,
JACOB HORN, JR., and ANSELMA HARRIS. Wit: HARDY HARRIS,
BENJ. WHITFIELD, ELISHA BATTLE.

HORNE, MARY
     P. 447. Aug. 24, 1831 - Feb. Ct. 1837.   Sis:
PATSEY (no other name given) - whole estate.   Ex:
JOSEPH S. BATTLE. Wit: JAMES D. ROSS, C. A. HINES.
Ordered recorded by Nov. Ct. 1840.

HORN, THOMAS
     P. 226. Dec. 2, 1778 - July Ct. 1782. Wife and
Extx: HANNAH. Sons: 1. JOSHUA, 2. HENRY, 3. RICHARD,
4. WILLIAM, 5. WILSON. Wit: JOHN EATMAN, HEROD CLARK,
WILLIAM HALL.

HORN, THOMAS SR. of Edgecombe Co.
     P. 22. Mar. 11, 1772 - July Ct. 1782.   Wife:
CATHERINE. Sons: 1. THOMAS, 2. WILLIAM, 3. MICHAEL-
land where I live and the adjoining 480 A. Legatees:
THOMAS PRIDGEN, WILLIAM FUTRAL (FUTRELL). Ex: Son
MICHAEL. Wit: DEMPSEY BARNES, DEMPSEY DAWSON.

HOWERTON, HENRIETTA
     P. 602. Sons: 1. GEORGE THOMAS, 2. WILLIAM BAKER,
3. WILEY FRANCIS. Daus: 1. SALLY BETTY. Ex: DR.
JOHN A. DRAKE. Wit: H. G. WILLIAMS, (DR.) J. A. DRAKE.

HUNT, SARAH - Nuncupative will
     P. 81. Jan. 10, 1781 - Apr. Ct. 1792. Statement
made by SARAH HUNT Dec. 20, 1780. Son: 1. JESSE.
Daus: 1. DICEY HUNT, 2. SARAH BRASWELL. Gr. dau:
MORNING HUNT, dau. of DICEY. Sworn by WILLIAM BRASWELL,
SR. and JUDITH HUNT before THOMAS HUNTER.

HUNTER, ARCHIBALD
     P. 171. Dec. 21, 1805 - Feb. Ct. 1807. Wife and
Extx: MARY. Ex: JOHN ARRINGTON. Wit: SAM'L WESTER,
REDMUN BUNN, ALEX'R. HINES.

HUNTER, CORDAL
     P. 414. Jan. 19, 1836 - Feb. Ct. 1836.   Wife:
MARTHA.   Sons: 1. THOMAS, 2. ISAAC BLOUNT HUNTER,
3. WELDON SMITH HUNTER, 4. HENRY DREW HUNTER, 5. JOHN
HODGE HUNTER, 6. CORDAL NORFLEET HUNTER, 7. WELDON S.
HUNTER.   Ex: JESSE H. DRAKE and son ISAAC B. HUNTER.
Wit: LEMON LANE, MARTHA A. LANE.

HUNTER, MARTHA
     P. 559. Jan. 28, 1849 - Feb. Ct. 1859.   Son:
1. ISAAC B. HUNTER and wife MARTHA.   Legatees: (no
relationship given) 1. JOHN E. DEANS (Ex), 2. JOANNA
DEANS, 3. HENRY D. HUNTER, 4. JOHN H. HUNTER, 5. CORDAL
N. HUNTER, 6. WELDON S. HUNTER.   Chil. of THOMAS
HUNTER; SALLY ANN HUNTER, JOANNA HUNTER.   Wit: WM.
T. DORTCH, JAMES T. BARNES.

JACKSON, GEORGE
     P. 97. Dec. 25, 1789 - Feb. Ct. 1795. Wife: MARY.
Son: 1. NEWMAN JACKSON. Gr. sons: LEWIS JACKSON -
404 A. whereon I live, NEWMAN RICHESON.   Legatees:
(no relationship given - gr. chil?) 1. JOSEPH JACKSON,
2. BARBARA POPE, 3. SARAH COOPER, 4. RASME TAYLOR. Ex:
DREWRY TAYLOR, LEWIS JACKSON.   Wit: DAVID PRIDGEN,
DREWERY PRIDGEN.

JELKS, MELLECAN (MILLIKEN?)
     P. 247. Nov. 6, 1804 - no prob. date.   Sister:
FILLITHA (FALITHA? FELICIA?) UNDERWOOD.   Ex: GRANBERRY
BAGGETT.   Wit: ELIZABETH HACKNEY, FRANCES DENSON,
JOHN D. COOPER.

JOHNSON, MATHEW
     P. 256. July 17, 1811 - May Ct. 1812. Wife: MARY.
Sons: 1. STEPHEN, 2. MATHEW, 3. HENRY, 4. WILLIAM,
5. LITTLEBURY.   Ex: THOMAS STOKES, HARDY PRIDGEN.
Wit: ELLEN MACOM(?), POLLY SANDERS.

JOHNSON, MOSES
     P. 509. June 21, 1847 - Feb. Ct. 1848.   Wife:
ELIZABETH.   Sons: unnamed, have been provided for.
Daus: 1. POLLY, 2. EMMY, 3. CATHERINE, 4. SALLY,
5. HARRIET.   Ex: JACOB ING.   Wit: KINCHEN TAYLOR,

K. C. TAYLOR.

JOHNSON, TRECY
P. 412. Dec. 22, 1834 - Aug. Ct. 1835. Son and
Ex: MATHEW JOHNSON. Daus: 1. SALLY WINBORNE, 2. NANCY
HINTON, 3. BETSEY BRYANT, 4. PATTIE JOHNSON, 5. TRECY
O'NEAL. Wit: JAMES LEGON, ELLEN NECOME, BETSEY NECOME.

JOHNSTON, BERRY
P. 542. July 31, 1846 - no prob. date. Wife and
Extx: NANCY. Chil: 1. HENRY, 2. LEMMON, 3. JASPER,
4. EMBERSON, 5. WILBY, 6. MILBY, 7. NANCY, 8. DENNIS.
Wit: A. J. TAYLOR, JAMES BRYANT.

JOLLY, JAMES
P. 127. Nov. 12, 1796 - July Ct. 1799. Wife and
Extx: SARAH. Dau: 1. RACHEL JOLLY - all land at
mother's death. Ex: Son-in-law WILLIE BUNN. Wit:
JOEL BUNN, BURWELL BUNN, LEWIS CURL.

JONES, ALLEN - Nunc. will
P. 229. Dec. 21, 1796 - May Ct. 1797. While ill
at home of JOHN JONES, WILLIE JONES, JR. wrote at
request of ALLEN JONES: Legatee - BEN HARRELL. Remaining estate to ALLEN JONES' brother, TAMMERLAIN JONES,
and WILLIE JONES, JR. Wit: WILLIE JONES, JR., NANNY
JONES.

JONES, ALLEN
P. 599. Aug. 26, 1861 - May Ct. 1867. Wife:
ELIZABETH - all estate. Son: 1. JOHN E. Daus:
1. MARTHA THORN, 2. NANCY WHITLEY, dec'd - her heirs.
No relationship: 1. MARTHA ODUM, 2. MARY WRIGHT,
3. AMANDA POPE - their property to remain in the hands
of MARTIN POPE. Ex: Son JOHN E. JONES, JESSE H.
DRAKE. Wit: HENRY A. TODD, CORDAL N. F. ELLIN
(FLEWELLIN).

JONES, ANDES
P. 306. June 4, 1822 - Aug. Ct. 1822. Niece:
EMELINE HIGBY - 160 A. in the ELLINVISE, also 106 A.
conveyed to me by FREDERICK ROGERS and JAMES COURTS.

Bro: ATLESS JONES (ATLAS?)   Ex: REV. WILLIS RIVES.
Wit: OLIVER CUSHING, ASEL J. KNOWLTON, N. B. MASSENBURG.

JONES, COOPER
     P. 251. Aug. 29, 1799 - Feb. Ct. 1800.   Wife:
VIOLET.   Sons: 1. MATHEW, 2. EDMUND - 150 A. purchased
of PENNEL (PENUEL) FLOYD, 3. FRANCIS, 4. ARCHIBALD,
5. BENNET - the three last named to share 217 A. plantation whereon I live. Daus: 1. PENNY, 2. TEMPERANCE,
3. ELIZABETH.   Mother: JULAN JONES.   Ex: Wife VIOLET,
Friends MATHEW DRAKE and THOMAS GRIFFIN.   Wit: SION
BECKWITH, THOMAS WHITE, ISAAC TOMLINSON.

JONES, FRANCIS ALBRIGTON
     P. 45. Jan. 31, 1781 - Nov. Ct. 1788.   Wife and
Extx: JULIAN.   Sons: 1. NEWSOME - reversion of land
whereon I live, 2. JOHN, 3. COOPER.   Daus: 1. MARTHA
GRIFFIN, 2. ELIZABETH MELTON, 3. ANN BASS.   Gr. son:
THOMAS GRIFFIN.   Ex: Son NEWSOME JONES.   Wit:
MATTHEW DRAKE, W. S. MEARNS, ANN SHORES.

JONES, JOHN
     P. 567. Dec. 9, 1846 - May Ct. 1860.   Wife:
MARTHA D.   Son: 1. THOMAS D.   Dau: 1. MARTHA L.
BOON.   Ex: E. W. HILLIARD.   Wit: WM. L. EDWARDS,
JAMES C. HILLIARD.

JONES, JULIAN
     P. 131. Nov. 10, 1799 - May Ct. 1800.   Son and
Ex: COOPER JONES.   Gr. dau: MARGARET JONES.   Wit:
MATHEW JONES, EDMUND JONES.

JONES, LAZARUS
     P. 204. Apr. 3, 1804 - Feb. Ct. 1810.   Wife:
HANNAH.   "All my children" unnamed.   Ex: HARTWELL
HINES, SR.   Wit: LITTLEBERRY HINES, JOHN JONES.

JONES,MARY
     P. 526. Sept. 29, 1850 - Nov. Ct. 1851.   Sis:
MARGARET HARRISON, wife of NATHANIEL HARRISON. Nephew:
JOHN H. HARRISON.   Niece: 1. FRANCES ANN RICKS, wife

of D. A. T. RICKS, 2. ANN ELIZA HARRISON. Ex: Bro-
in-law NATHANIEL HARRISON. Wit: JACOB ING, WILLIAM B.
THORN.

JONES, NEWSOM
P. 115. Mar. 5, 1797 - Aug. Ct. 1797. Wife: CATEY.
Chil: 1. MARY, 2. MARGARET, 3. WINNEY, 4. JAMES,
5. HENRY, 6. CATEY. Ex: WILLIAM DOZIER. Wit: ANN
GRIFFIN, BERSHEBA GRIFFIN, JAMES HILLIARD.

JONES, THOMAS
P. 192. Apr. 4, 1810 - May Ct. 1810. Wife:
TEMPERANCE B. JONES - to her and her heirs (unnamed).
Ex: Father-in-law WILLIAM WILLIAMS. Wit: JAMES
HILLIARD, LITTLE BRAY (BERRY) HINES, WM. OWEN.

JORDAN, SALLY
P. 370. May 1, 1830 - Aug. Ct. 1830. Sons: 1. DAVID,
2. JESSE. Dau: 1. ELIZABETH. Ex: ISAAC F. WOOD.
Wit: ELI MERCER, JOSHUA JORDAN.

JOINER (JOYNER), DREWRY
P. 357. April 17, 1826 - May Ct. 1828. Wife
unnamed - 280 A. Sons: 1. GUILFORD - 240 A. (WILLIAMS
and MILLFIELD tracts), 2. WILLIAM - 180 A. (the WILLIAM
and JOSEPH ARRINGTON land), 3. ALFORD - mother's land
at her death. Daus: 1. OLIFF, 2. PIETY, 3. SELAH.
Ex: WILLIAM JOINER, MOSES JOINER. Wit: AMOS JOINER,
WILLIAM JOINER, JAMES TURNER.

JOINER, ELIZABETH
P. 489. Oct. 30, 1846 - Nov. Ct. 1846. Sons and
Ex: 1. THOMPSON, 2. EXUM L. Dau: 1. UNA TURNER.
Dau-in-law: CHARITY JOINER. Chil. of EXUM L. JOINER:
MARTHA ANN MATILDA, DAVID, ROBERT, RICHARD. Wit: R.
H. RICKS, JOHN H. VICK.

JOYNER, HONOUR (HANOUR in copy. HANNAH?)
P. 293. Mar. 7, 1817 - Nov. Ct. 1817. Son and
Ex: 1. SHADY (SHADRACK?) JOYNER - land bequeathed me by
my father. Dau: 1. FEREBY MENDENDOL (MENDENHALL?)
"All my children" unnamed. Wit: DREWRY JOINER, SARAH
WILLIAMS.

JOINER (JOYNER), JOHN
P. 214. Mar. 7, 1810 - May Ct. 1811. Wife:
ELIZABETH. Sons: 1. JESSE, 2. JOHN, 3. CURTIS. Daus:
1. ELIZABETH LANGLEY, 2. ELIZABETH JACKSON. Note: the
list of children appears twice, and in each instance
both daus. named ELIZABETH. Could one be a step-dau?
M.G.G. Ex: Sons JESSE and CURTIS. Wit: WILLIAM
LANGLEY, ELIZABETH LANGLEY.

JOYNER, JONAS
P. 588. Oct. 8, 1862 - May Ct. 1864. Sons:
1. WILLIAM B. - his chil. - all land north of Great
Branch, 2. GILS (GILES?), 3. NATHAN. Daus: 1. ELIZABETH-
remaining land. Gr. son: WM. N. JOYNER, son of WM.
B. JOYNER. Nephew: WM. N. JOYNER, son of WM. B.
JOYNER. Note: This must be an error. M.G.G. Ex:
Relative B. H. JOYNER. Wit: CALVIN COOPER, IRA E.
JOYNER.

JOYNER (JOINER), JORDAN
P. 507. Mar. 31, 1838 - Nov. Ct. 1847. Wife:
ELIZABETH. Sons: 1. WILLIAM A. - reversion of all
land on e. side road with house and mill, also river
land and piney woods land, 2. CALVIN - 189½ A.,
3. WRIGHT W., 4. MERRITT, 5. DREWRY, 6. JORDAN. Daus:
1. RHODY JOYNER, 2. TAZZY WINSTEAD, 3. TEMPERANCE
JOYNER. Gr. son: ORREN JOYNER. Ex: Sons WRIGHT
W. and DREWRY JOYNER. Wit: SAMUEL W. W. VICK, EXUM
L. CURL.

JOYNER, LEWIS
P. 326. Feb. 11, 1825 - May Ct. 1825. Sons:
1. STEPHEN - 200 A. where I live, 2. MOSES. Daus:
1. MARGARET, 2. RACHEL, 3. SHANNY, 4. GINNEY. My four
daughters to share 74 A. on north side Tar River called
the LEWIS tract, also 100 A. adjoining DREWRY JOYNER.
Gr. son: LEWIS DAUGHTRIDGE. Ex: Son MOSES. Wit:
BENJAMIN BARNES, DREWRY JOINER, WILLIAM JOINER.

JOINER (JOYNER), MOSES
P. 618. Dec. 2, 1853 - Mar. 8, 1873. Sons:

1. DREWERY (dec'd?), 2. GUILFORD L. - all remaining estate so that he may support my wife and my two chil. ELIZABETH and WILLIAM D. JOYNER, 3. WILLIAM D. JOYNER. Dau: 1. ELIZABETH. Ex: Son GUILFORD L. JOYNER. Wit: W. T. DORTCH, JOHN J. BUNN.

JOYNER, NANCY
P. 268. July 20, 1815 - Aug. Ct. 1815. Only dau: MOURNING JOYNER. Ex: WILLIAM LINDSEY. Wit: BENNETT JOYNER, MARY PITTMAN.

JOYNER, NANCY
P. 577. Oct. 27, 1860 - Nov. Ct. 1861. Bros: HENRY DIXON, RANDOLPH DIXON. Sis: POLLY HORN, wid. of GUILFORD HORN, KEZIAH DIXON, SALLY JOYNER, BETSEY WINSTEAD. Nephew: THOMAS G. DIXON, son of bro. HENRY. Relation by marriage: GUILFORD JOYNER, son of ALFORD JOYNER. Relations: Chil. of THOMAS G. DIXON by his first wife, MARTHA. Ex: JACOB H. BARNES of Wilson Co., N. C. Wit: JAMES WIGGINS, ALFRED JOYNER.

JOINER, NATHAN
P. 332. Mar. 14, 1825 - Nov. Ct. 1825. Son and Ex: JONAS. Dau: MARY. Wit: AMOS JOINER, HENRY JOINER, DUNKING (DUCAN) PITTMAN.

JOINER, NATHAN
P. 449. Aug. 4, 1836 - Nov. Ct. 1836. Ordered prob. Nov. Ct. 1840. Wife: ANNIE. Sons: 1. THOMAS, 2. DAVID. Dau: 1. JUDA - all land at death of her mother. If she die without lawful heirs, land to revert to son DAVID. Ex: BRo. MATTHEW JOINER. Wit: POLLY JOINER, DAVID M. DEANS.

JOYNER, NATHAN
P. 611. Aug. 26, 1871 - Oct. 30, 1871. Wife: ORFA(?) - all land. Son: 1. NELSON V. JOYNER. Dau: 1. NANCY JOYNER. Ex: JAMES E. R. WINSTEAD. Wit: JOHN BONE, JAMES W. WINSTEAD.

JOINER, WILLIAM
    P. 37. Jan. 11, 1783 - Feb. Ct. 1785. Wife: SEALEY.
Sons: 1. NATHAN, 2. JACOB, 3. WILLIAM, 4. HARD(Y?) -
150 A. adjoining NATHAN JOINER and WILLIAM JOINER,
5. BURWELL, 6. JORDAN, 7. LEWIS, 8. NEALUS (CORNELIUS?),
9. DRURY. Daus: 1. ANN RICKS, 2. MARY BARNES,
3. ELIZABETH JOINER. Ex: Sons NATHAN and WILLIAM.
Wit: PHILANDER WILLIAMS, WILLIAM SKINNER, HARDY JOINER.

JOINER, WILLIAM SR.
    P. 418. Aug. 22, 1835 - Nov. Ct. 1837. Wife:
PATIENCE. Daus: 1. BASHEBA BARNES, 2. SELAH EVINS,
3. CHARITY DAVIS, 4. UNITY VICK, 5. MORNING JOINER,
6. MILBREY JOINER, 7. MARGARET GRIFFIN. Gr. son:
WILLIAM THOMAS GRIFFIN - 60 A. adjoining WILLIAM GRIFFIN.
Ex: AMOS JOINER. Wit: AMOS RICKS, BARSHABA SMITH,
ABRAHAM SMITH.

KENT, MOURNING
    P. 525. April 14, 1851 - Aug. Ct. 1851. Dau: MILLY
BOTTOMS. Gr. sons: WILLIAM H. BOTTOMS - 114 A. adjoin-
ing JOHN MATHEWS and SAM WILLIAMS, 2. JOHN H. BOTTOMS.
Ex: Friend BRITTAIN H. BOTTOMS. Wit: A. B. BAINES,
JR., JOHN MATHES (MATTHEWS).

KETH (KEITH), JAMES
    P. 168. Mar. 8, 1806 - May Ct. 1806. Wife:
ELIZABETH. Sons: 1. WILLIAM, 2. BENNET, 3. JAMES.
Ex: JACOB HORN, DAVID DANIEL, HENRY THORP. Wit: M.
MASON, COFFIELD HARRIS.

KING, SALLY
    P. 452. Oct. 8, 1834 - May Ct. 1841. Dau: MARY
GRIFFIN - 160 A. I bought of JOHN H. HAWKS - reversion
to her chil. Gr. chil: chil. of MARY GRIFFIN: ROBURTY
(ROBERTA) GRIFFIN, BENJAMIN GRIFFIN, ANDREW I. GRIFFIN.
Ex: JOHN RICKS. Wit: GUILFORD S. WHITFIELD, HARDY
TISDALE.

KNIGHT, GEORGE
    P. 35. Mar. 1, 1784 - May Ct. 1785. Wife and
Extx: SARAH. Son: GEORGE. Wit: WILLIAM WHITEHEAD.

KNIGHT, JOHN
    P. 26. Sept. 14, 1783 - Oct. Ct. 1783. Wife: ANN.
Sons: 1. KINSMERE - reversion of 150 A. tract where I
live at the death of my wife, 2. ELISHA - residue of
lands. Daus: 1. SARAH HARTE, 2. APPY WHITE, 3.KIDDEY
KNIGHT. Gr. son: JOHN KNIGHT. Ex: HARDY GRIFFIN,
ELISHA KNIGHT. Wit: WILLIAM WILLIAMS, JESSE POWELL.

LAMB, EVERETT
    P. 580. April 29, 1858 - May Ct. 1862. Wife:
NANNEY. Sons: 1. JAC KSON, 2. THOMAS. Sons to
have all land. Daus: 1. ELIZA, wife of JONAS PERRY,
2. SYTHONEY, wife of LINDSEY PERRY, 3. ALLEY, wife of
PERRY WHITLEY, 4. PENELOPE LAMB. Gr. dau: MARY
WHITLEY. Ex: ELIJAH H. MORGAN. Wit: A. W. BRIDGERS,
JACOB DANIEL. Codicil, Feb. 13, 1862, wit. by C. M. J.
STRICKLAND, W. C. WILLIAMS. JACOB DANIELS was dead on
date of probate.

LASSITER, WM.
    P. 1. Nov. 1, 1776 - Apr. Ct. 1778. Wife unnamed.
Sis: MARTHA SNIPES. Legatee: BURRELL WHITEHEAD. Ex:
WILLIS POWELL. Wit: NICHOLAS SKINNER, SARAH BARNES.

LAWRENCE, ELIZABETH
    P. 370. July 12, 1819 - Aug. Ct. 1830. JESSE
LAWRENCE and chil. Ex: EDWIN EDWARDS, DAVID SILLS.
Wit: LARK BATTLE, ALEXANDER SILLS.

LAWRENCE, THOMAS
    P. 257. Mar. 19, 1813 - Feb. Ct. 1814. Wife: NICEY.
NANCY WALKER, wife of LEMUEL WALKER, to have her mother's
share of my mother's estate. (She is evidently a niece.)
"All my children" not named. Ex: Friends DAVID SILLS,
WILLIAM WHELESS, SR., JOHN RICHARDSON. Wit: EDWARD
T. BROGDEN, E. EDWIN EDWARDS.

LAWRENCE, WILLIAM
    P. 272. Jan. 8, 1816 - Feb. Ct. 1816. MASSENGALE
land and that onnorth side Swift Creek to be sold. Wife:
VICEY - whole estate - at her death to be sold and
divided between the children of my first wife. Ex:

GEORGE BODDIE, CADER BASS. Wit: JOHN RICHARDSON, ISAAC LAWRENCE, HENRY BRIDGERS. N.B. I, LEVICY LAWRENCE, wife of WILLIAM LAWRENCE, doth agree before witnesses willingly and freely for the land to be sold that I bought of JAMES MASSENGILL under said WILLIAM LAWRENCE'S will and testament this 8 Jan. 1816.

LEE, JAMES
    P. 212. Feb. 23, 1811 - May Ct. 1811. Wife:
BERSHEBA. Sons: 1. JAMES, 2. MOORE LEE - 124 A. on
Tom's Creek, 3. CLAYTON - land whereon he lives,
4. LARRY - land whereon I live and 412 A. in Johnston
Co., N. C. Daus: 1. AMY HORN'S heirs, 2. ELIZABETH
WILLIAM'S heirs, 3. FRACY(?) TUCKER'S heirs, 4. POLLY
WINBOURN, 5. LUCY KING - 231 A. whereon she lives,
6. GILLY MITCHELL - 50 A. on Tomb's (Tom's?) Creek
whereon she lives, and land in Wake Co., N. C. Ex:
HARDY PRIDGEN, MOORE LEE, DAVID WINBOURN. Wit:
WILLIAM HINTON, JOHN DRIVER, JONATHAN DRIVER.

LEIGH, MOORE
    P. 421. Nov. 6, 1837 - Feb. Ct. 1838. Wife:
NANCY. Sons: 1. JAMES, 2. LINDON, 3. LINFORD,
4. LINDSEY, 5. LOAMMA - these four to have reversional
interest in 400 A. in Johnston Co. left their mother,
6. JACKSON - 220 A. plantation whereon I live and 12 A.
in Johnston Co. and mill. Daus: 1. DIDOMY LEIGH,
2. ELIZABETH FULGUM. Ex: GRANBERRY VICK. Wit:
JAMES BRYANT, BERY JOHNSON.

LEWIS, HENRY
    Oct. 8, 1802. This will found among loose papers
in basement of office of Clerk of Court - is not
recorded and bears no probate date. Wife and Extx:
MARY. Ex: WILLIAM DOZIER. Wit: RICHMOND DOZIER,
WINNEY LEWIS.

LEWIS, THOMAS
    P. 57. Jan. 6, 1789 - May Ct. 1789. Wife: LYDA
(LYDIA?) Sons: 1. GEORGE, 2. ABNER, 3. NICHOLSON,
4. JOHN, 5. THOMAS. Daus: 1. MARY BRYANT, 2. MARTHA
LEWIS, 3. NANCY LEWIS. Ex: EDWARD NICHOLSON. Wit:

THOMAS CARTER, BENJAMIN BRYANT, MATHEW WHITFIELD.

LEWIS, THOMAS
     P. 592. Sept. 5, 1863 - Aug. Ct. 1865. Wife:POLLY.
If MATHEW WALKER gives my dau. EMERIAH his estate, she
is not to share in mine. Daus: 1. EMERIAH,
2. CATHERINE. Wit: E. C. LEWIS, WHITMEL HOPKINS.
Codicil June 25, 1864 stipulates that BERRY ALFORD who
married my dau. EMERIAH shall have nothing to do with
my property. Wit: WM. T. BRYANT, ELIZABETH M. or C.
BRYANT.

LINDSEY, WILLIAM
     P. 289. Feb. 16, 1817 - May Ct. 1817. Wife: POLLY.
Sons: 1. JOHN WESLEY LINDSEY - 180 A., part of which I
bought of NATHAN LINDSEY, the remainder I bought of
JEPTHA LINDSEY, on lines of Sappony Crk., JORDAN SHERROD
and JEPTHA LINDSEY, 2. ASBURY LINDSEY - land bought of
EDWARD BALLARD, 3. WILLIAM RAY LINDSEY - 200 A.,
4. EDWARD BUXTON LINDSEY - 200 A. land whereon I live,
on lines of Sappony Crk., PRIDGEN MANNING, NATHAN
JOYNER, CHRISTOPHER TAYLOR and JOHN BISSETT. Daus:
1. JERUSHA LINDSEY, 2. POLLY MINTZ LINDSEY, 3. BETSEY
MARY FLETCHER LINDSEY. Ex: Son JOHN WESLEY LINDSEY,
RICHARD HOLLAND. Wit: BARNA TUCKER, NELSON BONE.

LIPFORD, WILLIAM A.
     P. 303. Mar. 9, 1814 - May Ct. 1819. "Being a
soldier in U. S. Army". Legatees: PHILIP ANDREW
TISDEL, WILLIAM DORTCH of N. C., JOHN IRWIN TISDAL, son
of PHILIP ANDREW TISDALL. Ex: PHILIP ANDREW TISDELL,
BURWELL WOODARD. Wit: ARMISTEAD WORTHINGTON, BENNETT
JONES, JOHN COLLINS. Proven by oath of SAMUEL S. HILL,
who was present at execution of will.

MANN, JAMES N.
     P. 536. Jan. 20, 1851 - Nov. Ct. 1853. Half bros:
SAMUEL L. ARRINGTON - all my land on north side Swift
Crk., adj. JOHN HARRISON; ARCHIBALD H. ARRINGTON.
Nieces: ELIZABETH WILLIAMS, LUCY M. COOPER. Nephews:
HENRY G. WILLIAMS, SOLOMON WILLIAMS, SAMUEL WILLIAMS,

71

WILLIAM T. WILLIAMS, JOHN WILLIAMS, ARCHIBALD WILLIAMS,
THOMAS WILLIAMS. All nephews and nieces are chil. of
my half-sister ELIZABETH A. WILLIAMS. Ex: SAMUEL L.
ARRINGTON, ARCHIBALD H. ARRINGTON. Wit: T. M.
WRIGHT, WILLIAM H. ARRINGTON.

MANN, JOHN
     P. 16. Jan. 11, 1781 - Apr. Ct. 1781. Father:
THOMAS MANN. Bro. and Ex: WILLIAM MANN. Wit: WM.
WHEELESS, AMOS WHEELES, MILDRED WHEELESS.

MANN, THOMAS
     P. 83. June 6, 1792 - Nov. Ct. 1792. Wife:
ELIZABETH. Sons and Exrs: 1. DENTON - 590 A. lying
on no. side Fishing Creek, purchased of PHILIP SHELLEY,
2. ALLEN - reversion of mother's land whereon I dwell
on n. side Swift Crk. and Short Swamp. Dau: ELIZABETH
NICHOLSON. Gr. chil: HENRY DRAKE, CASWELL DRAKE, MARY
DRAKE, PENELOPE DRAKE, SARAH DRAKE, PENELOPE NICHOLSON,
LETTITIA NICHOLSON, MATILDA NICHOLSON, TIMOTHY MANN
NICHOLSON, ELIZABETH NICHOLSON, JAMES MANN NICHOLSON,
GILFORD NICHOLSON, THOMAS NICHOLSON, JOHN MANN. Wit:
WM. AVENT, BENJAMIN DRAKE, W. J. MEARS.

MANN, THOMAS N.
     P. 321. June 18, 1824 - Aug. Ct. 1824. Bro. and
Ex: JAMES N. MANN. Half Bros: SAMUEL L. ARRINGTON,
ARCHIBALD ARRINGTON. Half sis: ELIZABETH N. ARRINGTON.
Handwriting proved by oaths of; JAMES HILLIARD, WELDON
N. EDWARDS, WILLIAM PLUMMER. Will had been given to
JAMES HILLIARD for safe keeping.

MANNING, LEVY
     P. 95. Nov. 30, 1794 - Feb. Ct. 1795. Sons:
1. MATTHEW, 2. JOHN, 3. JOSEPH. Daus: 1. MARY
LANGLEY, 2. DINAH RACKLEY, 3. CATEY MANING, 4. PHOEBE
MANING, 5. MOURNING MANING. Ex: ROBERT CREEKMORE.
Wit: ARTHUR O'NEAL, JOSEPH BATCHELOR.

MANNING,MATHIAS
     P. 59. May 2, 1789 - Aug. Ct. 1789. Wife:MARGARET.
Daus: 1. SARAH RICHERSON - 300 A. whereon she lives,

2. MARY PRIDGEN - 312 A. on Bare Branch. Gr. sons:
MATHIAS MANNING - 640 A. after death of my wife, PRIDGEN
MANNING - 940 A., ELI MANNING, DAVID MANNING. Ex:
DAVID PRIDGEN. Wit: WILLIAM BUNTEN, THOMAS DEANS,
ROBERT CREEKMORE.

MANING, RICHARD
     P. 93. Oct. 19, 1794 - Nov. Ct. 1794. Mother:
SARAH HATFIELD - 300 A. whereon I live. Sons:
1. SAMUEL, 2. THOMAS, 3. MICHAL, 4. JAMES. Daus:
1. PHEREBY POOPE (POPE?), 2. NANCY MANING. Ex:
SAMUEL MANING, THOMAS MANING. Wit: ALEX SORSBY,
LEWIS DORTCH.

MANNING, WILLIAM
     P. 248. April 4, 1791 - no prob. date. Wife and
Extx: MOURNING. Legatee: ELI MANNING. Ex: Bro.
JOHN MANNING. No wit.

MANNING, WILLIBOUGH (WILLOUGHBY?)
     P. 167. Mar. 9, 1805 - May Ct. 1806. Wife:
DRUCILLA. Sons: 1. JOHN WRIGHT MANNING - all land,
2. WILLIBOUGH LANE MANNING, 3. BENJAMIN. Daus:
1. POLLY, 2. ARGEN, 3. RAHAB, 4. ELIZABETH, 5. ABY
(ABBY). Ex: CHARLES HAMMON, GEORGE BODDIE. Wit:
JOHN PARKER, TIMOTHY CREEKMORE.

MARRIOTT, ROBERT H.
     P. 619. July 19, 1873 - Oct. 23, 1873. Wife:
TEMPIE A. "All my children" to be properly educated
and cared for". Children all seem to be minors. I am
under bond to convey my HILLIARD plantation, adjoining
W. H. ROWLAND to HARRY TAYLOR and GEORGE ARRINGTON.
Ex: Wife TEMPIE A. MARRIOTT, bro-in-law JOSEPH J.
BATTLE. Wit: B. H. BUNN, H. S. BUNN.

MASON, ELIZABETH
     P. 244A. Mar. 8, 1811 - Nov. Ct. 1812. Sons:
1. MARK, 2. FOSTER, 3. WILLIAM, 4. ABNER. Ex: Sons
FOSTER, WILLIAM and ABNER. Wit: PETER ARRINGTON.

73

MASON, MARK SR.
P. 86. Mar. 15, 1790 - Nov. Ct. 1793. Wife:
ELIZABETH. Sons: 1. FOSTER, 2. WILLIAM, 3. ABNER -
land on Ralph's Prong, 4. HENRY, 5. MARK - 50 A. adjoining SAMUEL NICHOLSON, ABNER MASON, and Ralph's Prong,
6. BENJAMIN - land whereon I dwell. Daus: 1. MARY
NORRIS, 2. PATTY SMEDLEY, 3. ELIZABETH COOPER,
4. CATHARINE MASON, 5. ALLA MALLARD (appears to be a
dau). Ex: Wife ELIZABETH, son BENJAMIN. Wit: MASON
THOMAS, TISEY THOMAS, FOSTER MASON.

MASSINGALE, JAMES SR.
P. 38. Jan. 22, 1784 - Feb. Ct. 1785. Wife:
ELIZABETH. Sons: 1. JAMES, 2. GEORGE, 3. WALKER,
4. MATTHEW. Daus: 1. MARY HOWELL, 2. HANNAH HARRISON,
3. ELIZABETH CARRILL, 4. ANN ARRABELLA MASSINGALE -
plantation where I live, at her mother's death. Ex:
WILLOUGHBY MANNING, THOMAS MORRIS. Wit: THOMAS MORRIS,
PATIENCE POWELL.

MASSENGAIL, KESSIAH
P. 535. Feb. 6, 1851 - Aug. Ct. 1853. Daus:
1. JUDAH K. WALKER, wife of RICHMOND WALKER - 70 A.
tract purchased of SHERIFF N. W. COOPER, adjoining HENRY
HEDGEPETH, JAMES T. WILLIAMS, and others, with reversion
to her chil: WORREL P. WALKER, SALATHIEL R. D. WALKER,
2. DILLY P. WHITFIELD, wife of ARCHIBALD G. WHITFIELD -
personal property with reversion to her chil: FRANKLIN,
PATRICK L., DILLY ANN WHITFIELD. Ex: WM. W. BODDIE.
Wit: COLEMAN W. W. WOODARD, WM. W. WOODARD.

MASSENGALE, MASSY
P. 265. Feb. 6, 1814 - May Ct. 1815. Sis:
ELIZABETH PASSMORE, MARY MASSENGALE. Heirs of KIZA
MASSENGALE: WARREN MASSENGALE and REDDICK MASSENGALE.
No Ex. Wit: WILLIAM FLETMORE, WILLIAM LAWRENCE.

MASSENGILL, WALKER
P. 281. Sept. 30, 1794 - May Ct. 1816. Wife:
ELIZABETH. Sons and Ex: 1. JAMES, 2. WALKER - land
whereon I live. Daus: 1. HONOUR RICHARDSON, 2. MILLY
TURNER, 3. ANNIS MASSENGILL, 4. SEALAH LAWRENCE. Wit:

74

JOHN GAY, ANNIS MASSENGILL, E. EDWARDS. Handwriting proved in Court by oath of DAVID SILLS.

MATHES (MATTHEWS?), JOSIAH
P. 574. Aug. 12, 1861 - Nov. Ct. 1861. Wife: PENELOPE. Son: FRANCIS - to have all land. Daus: 1. ARMINDA, 2. ELIZABETH, 3. ISLEY, 4. LECY. Ex: BENJAMIN BILBRO. Wit: W. E. MANNING, URIAH CREEKMORE.

MATHEWS, WILLIAM H.
P. 590. April 19, 1864 - Feb. Ct. 1865. Wife:LUCY R. Niece: LUCY H. MATHEWS, dau. of bro. and Ex: JOHN G. MATHEWS. Wit: J. D. MATHEWS, GEO. COLLINS. Clerk's notes: GEO. COLLINS was out of the state - will proved by J. D. MATHEWS.

McDADE, JOHN
P. 360. No date - Aug. Ct. 1828. Wife: DREWSILLA. Sons: 1. JOHN J., 2. WILLIAM. Daus: 1. MARY, 2. SALONY, 3. DREWSILLA, 4. NANCY. Ex: BENNETT BARNES. Wit: EXUM S. CURL, JOHN BARNES.

MECOM, ELLEN
P. 599. Sept. 17, 1866 - Nov. Ct. 1866. Dau: BETSEY P. MECOM - entire estate, including land. If no heirs, to my two gr. chil: CHARLES C. JOHNSON, unnamed infant, the children of LUCY JOHNSON. Ex: B. C. STRICKLAND, HENDERSON HOCUT. Wit: JOHN M. MORRIS, CALVIN ALLEN.

MELTON, ANDREW
P. 321. April 8, 1824 - Aug. Ct. 1824. Wife: CHRISTIAN - 412½ A. Ex: WILLIAM COOPER. Wit: WILLIAM BOWERS, JOEL MATHEWS.

MELTON,BOLEN
P. 610. May 24, 1871 - Sept. 28, 1871. Wife: ZILPHA D. - land on lines of Cocoa Crk., GOOCHE, W. B. WILLIAMS, ALERSON STRICKLAND and Halifax Rd. Friend: ALERSON STRICKLAND - all land on west side Halifax Rd., also a tract on lines of JENKINS, Turkey Crk., Thos. Carter's Spring on east side Halifax Rd. Sons of ALERSON STRICKLAND: JASPER G., ROBERT N. - to have land on lines of Thos. Carter's Spring, B. WOOD and J. T. WEBB. Ex: BENNET GAY. Wit: WILLIAM POWELL, WILLIAM S. GAY, BENNET GAY.

MELTON, JOHN
    P. 133. April 29, 1797 - Aug. Ct. 1800. Wife:
ELIZABETH. Sons: 1. COOPER - 150 A. purchased of
BRIANT O'NEAL, 2. THOMAS - 146 A. purchased of ARTHUR
O'NEAL whereon I live, 3. DAVID, 4. MATHEW, 5. JOSEPH.
Daus: 1. MARY HART, 2. ANN MELTON, 3. FEREBY MELTON,
4. MARTHA MELTON. Ex: Sons DAVID and JOSEPH. Wit:
LEWIS VICK, JACOB VICK, ACHRIH VICK.

MELTON, NATHAN
    P. 152. May 20, 1804 - Aug. Ct. 1804. Father
unnamed. Ex: Father and ARCHIBALD GRIFFIN. Wit:
DAVID RICKS, JOEL VICK.

MELTON, ROBERT
    P. 578. Oct. 26, 1860 - Nov. Ct. 1861. Wife:
SARAH - 156 A. with reversion to my two youngest chil:
Sons: 1. ROBERT BOLDEN TIMOTHY MELTON, 2. JOSEPH DRAKE
MELTON. Second dau: REBECCA BOON - land where she
lives. Gr. chil: REBECCA BURNETT, MARTHA, wife of
HARDY GRIFFIN, 3. CALVIN BURNETT. Ex: WILLIAM W.
BODDIE. Wit: J. B. H. BODDIE, WILLIAM WESTER.

MELTON, ZACHARIAH
    P. 77. Oct. 23, 1786 - May Ct. 1792. Wife: SARAH.
Sons: 1. JOHN - one half all my land, 2. JOSIAH - one
half all land. Daus: 1. ELIZABETH SELAH, 2. PHARABY
TUCKER, 3. MARY MELTON, 4. PRISCILLA MELTON, 4. BATHSEBA
WHITLEY. Ex: WILSON VICK. Wit: WM. MATHEWS, THOS.
BARROT (BARRETT?).

MERCER, ELI
    P. 389. June 1, 1832 - Aug. Ct. 1832. Wife:
MARGARET. Sons: 1. JAMES - north half my land at
death of his mother, 2. THOMAS - south half my land,
including plantation, at death of his mother, 3. JOHN.
Daus: 1. NANCEY MERCER, 2. ABBA MERCER, 3. MARY GARDNER,
4. SALLY WILLIAMSON. Ex: Friends ISAAC WILLIAMSON,
JOHN MERCER. Wit: BARTLEY DEANS, STEPHEN BOYKIN.

MERCER, MARGARET
    P. 510. Oct. 30, 1847 - Feb. Ct. 1848. Son and

Ex: THOMAS MERCER. Dau-in-law: RHODA, wife of THOMAS
MERCER. Gr. daus, chil. of THOMAS MERCER: JANE and
TEMPE ANN MERCER. Wit: JAMES F. MERCER, LAZARUS COOK.

MERRITT, BENJAMIN
     P. 3. No date - Jan. Ct. 1779. Wife: SARAH. Sons:
1. WILLIAM - 140 A. on south side Swift Crk. and Garles
Br., 2. HENRY - 200 A. adjoining WILLIAM MERRITT,
3. BENJAMIN. 2 daus. unnamed. Ex: Wife SARAH, son
WILLIAM. Wit: ISAAC NEWSOME, LEWIS DORTCH, SARAH
CAMMEL (CAMPBELL?).

MITCHELL, HENRY
     P. 529. Jan. 9, 1851 - Aug. Ct. 1852. Wife:
PENELOPE - 248 A. where I live. Sons and Exs: 1. JOHN
W. - reversion of mother's land, 2. HENRY C. D. Daus:
1. MARY, wife of JEREMIAH JOHNSTON, 2. ELIZABETH, wife
of WILLIAM S. DOZIER, 3. MARTHA, wife of WILLIAM PITTS.
Wit: JOHN G. F. DRAKE, JOHN J. DRAKE.

MOONEHAN, THOMAS
     P. 145. Nov., 1801 - Feb. Ct. 1804. Wife: MARY.
Sons: 1. JOHN, 2. THOMAS, 3. SHADRICK, 4. ENOCH. Daus:
1. ANN, 2. AMY, 3. JUDEY. At wife's death all land to
go to REDDICK ELLIS, son of SUSANNA ELLIS. If he die
without lawful heir, property left him must "fall back
into my family". Ex: OWEN SILLANT(?), WILLIAM MOORE.
Wit: JOEL TAYLOR, JAMES PERKINS.

MOORE, EDWARD
     P. 24. May 23, 1783 - Oct. Ct. 1783. Wife:
ELIZABETH. Sons: 1. JAMES - all land on Peach Tree
Crk., 2. WILLIAM - 275 A. on Contentney Crk., adjoin-
ing WILLIAM PUGH, 3. EDWARD - all land on Tar R. Daus:
1. JUDAH FLOWERS, 2. MARY, 3. ELIZABETH, 4. SUSANNA.
Ex: Wife ELIZABETH and son JAMES. Wit: EDWARD MOORE,
THOMAS CARTER, HARDY STRICKLAND.

MORGAIN (MORGAN), ELIZABETH SELAH
     P. 70. May 4, 1790 - Nov. Ct. 1790. Sons:
1. JAMES (eldest), 2. WILLIAM. Ex: Bro. WILLIAM
MORGAIN, ELIAS OWENS. Wit: JAMES TALER (TAYLOR),ROBERT
VICK.

MORGAN, HARDY
    P. 218. Mar. 21, 1811 - Aug. Ct. 1811. Wife:
ELIZABETH. Sons: 1. HENRY, 2. WILLIAM - my land.
"All my children" unnamed. Ex: Son HENRY MORGAN,
JOHN MORGAN, SR. Wit: JESSE HAMMOND, ANSEL ALFORD.

MORGAN, JAMES of Elizabeth Parish, Edgecombe Co.
    P. 19. Nov. 24, 1774 - no prob. date. Wife and
Ex: ELIZABETH. Sons: 1. JOHN - land on lines of
BENJ. TANN and Norfleet's Branch, 2. JAMES - land on
lines of JOHN TAYLOR and Bogg Branch, 3. HARDY -
reversional interest in his mother's land, 4. STONE.
Dau: BETTE CEALLE MORGAN. Wit: C. W. MOORE, JOHN
FINCH, MARY KEFF?

MORGAN, JOHN
    P. 440. Apr. 4, 1836 - Aug. Ct. 1837. Wife:
RUTHA. Sons: 1. JAMES, 2. JOHN. Daus: 1. SELA-
wife of HUTCHENS FERRELL, 2. ANNA - wife of BENNETT
SMITH, 3. SUSANNA - wife of IRVIN FINCH, 4. NANCY
MORGAN - reversion of all land. Ex: IRVIN FINCH.
Wit: H. FINCH, CLABORN FINCH. Ordered recorded
Nov. Ct. 1840.

MORRIS, THOMAS
    P. 178. Feb. 13, 1806 - Nov. Ct. 1807. Wife:
PRESTON - 500 A. adjoining JAMES HILLIARD, BRASWELL,
DEMSEY MORRIS and HARDY MORRIS. Sons: 1. DEMCY,
2. HARDY, 3. JESSE, 4. ALLEN, 5. ASEY HILL MORRIS.
Daus: 1. CLOAH (CHLOE), 2. SILVAH (SYLVIA),
3. BATHSEBA, 4. BETSEY. Ex: JOHN H. DRAKE, son
JESSE MORRIS. Wit: RHODA VAUGHAN, GEORGE BODDIE,
DAVID MELTON. Note: THOMAS MORRIS stipulates that at
the death of his wife, PRESTON, her property should be
divided between JESSE, ALLEN and ASEY HILL MORRIS,
which may indicate that she is mother of only the
younger children. M.G.G.

MURRAY, JOHN SR.
    P. 474. Jan. 8, 1845 - Feb. Ct. 1845. Sons:
1. JOHN, JR., 2. BURNEL, 3. VINCENT, 4. ABSALOM. Daus:
1. POLLY EARP, 2. ELIZABETH HOLLAND. No Ex. Wit:
A. B. B. BAINES, SR., BURKLEY CONE.

MURRAY, WILLIAM
    P. 494. Mar. 23, 1839 - Nov. Ct. 1846. Wife:
MORNIN - all land. Son: ELIJAH. Dau: NANCY MORGAN.
Wife's oldest son: JOEL WHITFIELD, "balance of her
heirs" unnamed. No ex. Wit: WILLIAM JOHNSON, ISAAC
WHITFIELD.

NICHOLS, JEREMIAH
    P. 401. Dec. 18, 1827 - Feb. Ct. 1834. Daus:
1. SARAH NICHOLS, 2. PATSEY DAVIS. Gr. sons: 1. JOHN
NICHOLS, 2. ARNOL (ARNOLD) NICHOLS - land adjoining
JOSIAH DAVIS, JR., BARTLEY DEANS and BENJAMIN FLOWERS.
Gr. dau: ELIZABETH NICHOLS. Ex: BARTLEY DEANS. Wit:
JOHN PEELE, JAMES DEANS.

NICHOLSON, EDWARD
    P. 129. Dec. 26, 1799 - Feb. Ct. 1800. Wife:
WINNEFORD. Dau: BEARSHEBA ELY. Gr. daus:
LUCREASIA BONDS (BARNES?), PATSEY DUE (DEW). Ex:
DUNCAN DUE (DEW). Wit: THOMAS CARTER, TIMOTHY TUCKER,
LYDDA SELLERS.

NICHOLSON, GEORGE of Edgecombe County
    P. 12. Feb. 3, 1773 - Apr. Ct. 1780. Wife unnamed.
Sons: 1. WRIGHT, 2. DAVID - land he lives on, 3. GEORGE,
4. EDWARD, 5. MALACHI, 6. JOSIAH. Daus: 1. TRESSA
LEWIS, 2. LYDIA LEWIS, 3. CLOE PETMOND (PITMAN?),
4. ELIZABETH WALKER. Gr. dau: LYDIA NICHOLSON. Ex:
Wife and son WRIGHT. Wit: WINFIELD WRIGHT, JOSEPH
NICHOLSON, ABBAGIL NICHOLSON.

NICHOLSON, JAMES M.
    P. 201. Feb. 7, 1809 - Nov. Ct. 1809. Wife: MARY.
Dau: ELIZA ANN. Unborn child. The land left wife and
two chil. is as follows: manor plantation whereon I
live, also plantation on n. side Fishing Crk. in Halifax
Co., known as the BATTS and ETHERIDGE places and adjoining land. Ex'rs. ordered to sell land in Halifax Co.,
known as THROWER place. If children die without heirs,
estate to go to brothers: GUILFORD and THOMAS NICHOLSON.
Ex: Father-in-law WILLIAM ARRINGTON, Bro. THOMAS
NICHOLSON. Wit: W(ILLIA)M H. (M?) GREGOR, MILLS WHITLEY.

NICHOLSON, LYDIA
    P. 58. Oct. 24, 1782 - Feb. Ct. 1789. Son and
Ex: JOSIAH NICHOLSON. Wit: BENJ. JOYNER, LAZARUS
WHITEHEAD, MARY WHITFIELD.

NICHOLSON, TIMOTHY M.
    P. 188. Mar. 15, 1808 - May Ct. 1808. Mother:
PENELOPE NICHOLSON. Dau: SALLY NICHOLSON - all land
which fell to me from my father's will, also the adjoin-
ing LANDINGHAM place, also the land whereon I live,
which I bought of JOSEPH MARES (MEARS), also land in
Edgecombe Co. on Fishing Crk., which was part of the
lands of ABSALOM BENTON, desc'd. Sis: LATITIA
CROWELL, SALLY M. PHILIPS, MARTHA NICHOLSON, PENELOPE
WHITFIELD, POLLEY JELKS, FEREBY SHELTON, ELIZABETH
NICHOLSON, NANCY NICHOLSON. Ex: Bro-in-law: EXUM
PHILIPS, cousin THOMAS NICHOLSON. Wit: ALEX SORSBY,
MAJOR GLANDEN.

ODUM, JACOB
    P. 455. Sept. 2, 1841 - Nov. Ct. 1841. Wife:
CHRISTIAN. Sons: 1. JAMES, 2. WILLIAM - upper part
of mill place, 3. JACOB RICHARD - the ATKINSON place,
4. JOHN - middle part of mill place, 5. EXUM - lower
part of mill place, 6. DAVID M. - land whereon I live.
Daus: 1. NANCY, wife of VINCENT COOPER, 2. ELIZABETH,
wife of DANIEL BRAKE, 3. MILDRED, wife of JESSE BRASWELL.
Ex: Son JAMES 'ODUM and HENRY BLOUNT. Wit: B.
BATCHELOR, WILLIS WARD.

O'NEAL, CONDARY
    P. 391. Oct. 12, 1832 - Nov. Ct. 1832. Wife: LUCY-
482 A. whereon I live, and also the entry I hold on land
in Johnston Co., N. C., now in possession of RICHARD
MASON - executor to obtain grant for same. All this to
wife LUCY and her heirs (unnamed). Ex: Friend STEPHEN
O'NEAL. Wit: HILLIARD HINTON, ROBERT LUIS (LEWIS).

O'NEAL, MICAJAH
    P. 579. Wife: AMY. Sons: 1. AXUM (EXUM) oldest,
2. CALVIN WATON (WATSON?), 3. JOSEPHUS. Dau?: WITHY
ANN. Ex: PETER EATMAN. Wit: ALEX EATMAN, C. H.
FINCH.

OWENS, DANIEL
P. 138. Aug. 11, 1800 - May Ct. 1801. Wife:
ELIZABETH. Sons: 1. JOHN - 40A., 2. ELIAS - 150 A.,
3. WILLIAM - 310 A., 4. ENOCH. Daus: 1. ANN BUTLER,
2. MARY OWENS. Ex: Son ELIAS OWENS, JOHN RICE, ESQ.
Wit: JOSEPH HEARP (EARP?), HARDY MORGAN.

PARKER, ANN - Nunc. will
P. 233. Sept. 25, 1795 - no probate date. Nieces:
ELIZABETH WHITFIELD, dau. of ELIZABETH WHITFIELD, desc.,
LUCY DREWRY, dau. of FRANCIS PARKER. Nephew: WILLIAM
PARKER, son of FRANCIS PARKER. Wit: ANN GRIFFIN,
BARBARY KEARNEY, LEAH PITT. Sworn before B. BOON
Sept. 28, 1795.

PARKER, FRANCIS
P. 111. Jan. 9, 1797 - Feb. Ct. 1797. Wife: MARY.
Sons: 1. WILLIAM - land where he lives, also 100 A.,
2. JOHN - 440 A. where I live. Dau: 1. LUCY DREWRY.
Gr. son: SAMUEL DREWRY. Ex: Sons WILLIAM and JOHN
and son-in-law JAMES DREWRY. Wit: CASWELL DRAKE,
LEWIS WELLS.

PARKER, SOLOMON
P. 448. Feb. 9, 1837 - Nov. Ct. 1837. Sons:
1. CALVIN - 100 A. adjoining his land and the HAMMON
tract on the swamp, 2. OFFE - 350 A. adjoining JESSE
BARNES, 3. WEEKS - 239 A. known as the EARSENCEY place
and the BALDEY place, 4. SOLOMON - 200 A. known as the
VINUSE(?) place. Daus: 1. POLLY UERS (EURE?),
2. KIZZEY UERS (EURE?). Gr. chil: BECKY, JOE and
DEMPSEY? Ex: Son CALVIN, son-in-law ALFORD URES
(EURE?). Wit: D. WINSTEAD, D. Y. HARRISON.

PARKER, WILLIAM
P. 292. June 15, 1805 - Feb. Ct. 1807. Wife:
MARTHA NAILER PARKER. Nephews: JOHN DREWRY, JAMES
DREWRY, SAMUEL DREWRY. Nieces: NANCY DRAKE, POLLEY
DRAKE. Bros-in-law MATHEW DRAKE and FRANCES DRAKE
and their heirs. Ex: Wife MARTHA NAILER PARKER and
bro-in-law MATHEW DRAKE. Wit: ALLEN DRAKE, DELILAH
DRAKE, NATHANIEL DRAKE.

PARROTT, JOSEPH
     P. 477. Oct. 13, 1844 - May Ct. 1845. Bro:
WILLIAM'S heirs. AUSTIN (bro?). Sis: MARY, ANNA.
No Ex. Wit: BENJAMIN BILBRO, WILLIAM SAVAGE, THOMAS
SAVAGE.

PEELE, JOHN
     P. 502. Jan. 26, 1847 - May Ct. 1847. Wife:
EDITH. Sons: 1. NATHAN - 448 A. whereon I live,
2. DAVID - 670 A. in Johnston Co. called the HOLLAND,
RICHARD PIERCE and CLARKEY PIERCE tracts. Daus:
1. PATIENCE, 2. MARTHA, 3. REBECCA BELL, 4. SARAH,
5. ANNE P. WILLIAMS in Ohio. Ex: Sons-in-law: JOHN
PEELE, JOHN BELL. Codicil - same date provides that
son DAVID have tract bought of ZADOC PEACOCK on Turkey
and Moccasin Crks. in lieu of the Johnston Co. land,
which exs. shall sell. Wit: JAMES FULGHUM, HARDY
WILLIAMSON, NATHAN STOTT, HENRY STOTT.

PENDER, ELIZABETH H.
     P. 614. Sept. 11, 1863 - May 9, 1872. Nephews:
LEWIS H. HINES (ex), DAVID D. HINES. All estate,
including that due me from the estate of my brother,
KINCHEN HINES. Wit: JOHN THORP, ROB'T H. MARRIOTT.

PIERCE, JOSHUA
     P. 60. May 6, 1789 - Aug. Ct. 1789. Wife:
ELIZABETH. Son: 1. JOSHUA - all land after death of
wife. No relationship given: CELIA BRASWELL, DINAH
BRASWELL, PEGGY BUNTIN, JEREMIAH BUNTIN. Ex: WILLIAM
BUNTIN. Wit: THOS. CARTER, THOMAS DEANS, JOHN
SELLERS.

PITMAN, MARY WHITE
     P. 435. Nov. 7, 1838 - Aug. Ct. 1839. Son:
1. BRINKLEY GANDY PITMAN - 60 A. on north side Polecat
Branch, and all my real estate. Legatee: ELIZABETH
SMITH. If son dies without heirs, to JOHN FRANCIS
MERRILON SMITH. Ex: AMOS JOINER. Wit: WILLIAM
GRIFFIN, BATHSHEBA SMITH.

PITTMAN, JOHN
     P. 545. May 28, 1848 - no probate date. Wife:

RHODA - the BURRELL tract. Sons: 1. WILLIAM - the
ATKINSON tract, also the STRICKLAND and WILLIAMS tracts,
2. ROBBIN R. - MARY PITTMAN tract, also the BAKER and
MOSELY tracts. Dau: 1. SALUDA PITTMAN. Gr. sons:
JESSE, JOHN, sons of WILLIAM PITTMAN. Ex: WILLIAM
JOYNER, NELSON BONE. Wit: EXUM CURL, FRANCIS M. B.
CURL.

PITTMAN, WILLIAM
    P. 355. Nov. 27, 1827 - Feb. Ct. 1828. Wife:
SUSAN - land adjoining FOSTER GANDY. Son: 1. WILLIAM
B. Dau: 1. MARYAN - her 2 chil. to share remaining
land. Ex: JAMES JOYNER. Wit: BENNETT ATKINSON,
FOSTER GANDY, DUNCAN PITMAN.

POPE, DEMPSEY
    P. 411. June 6, 1835 - Aug. Ct. 1835. Wife:
BEDAH (BEADY?). Sons: 1. WILLIAM, 2. LITTLEBERRY.
Daus: 1. ELIZABETH, wife of RICHARD ROSE, 2. PENELOPE,
wife of WILLIAM H. FOUNTAIN, 3. MARY POPE. Ex: Son
LITTLEBERRY POPE. Wit: JACOB ING, NATHAN MANNING.

POPE, HARDYMAN
    P. 231. Nov. 11, 1789 - No probate date. Wife:
SARA. Sons: 1. ELISHA - land whereon he lives,
bought of ROGERS JENKINS, 2. DEMSEY - land bought of
JESSE JENKINS, 3. JESSE, 4. JOSEPH, 5. HARDYMAN,
6. ARCHIBALD, 7. WILLIAM - these 4 youngest sons to
have land whereon I live at my wife's death. Daus:
1. MARY POPE, 2. ANN POPE, 3. SUSANNA NEWTON. Ex:
Son ELISHA, REUBEN TAYLOR. Wit: JESSE JOHNSON,
JOSIAH POPE.

POPE, LAZARUS
    P. 61. Oct. 16, 1789 - Nov. Ct. 1789. Wife and
Extx: BARBARA - 190 A. adjoining PHILANDER WILLIAMS,
JOHN DEW, and DRURY TAYLOR. Bro: ARTHUR POPE. No
relationship given: RICHARD POPE, ARTHUR POPE, JR.,
WINEY (WINNIE?) JACKSON RICHARDSON. Wit: PHILANDER
WILLIAMS, DRURY TAYLOR, ABSALOM WILLS.

POPE, WILLIAM
    P. 458. Mar. 21, 1838 - Feb. Ct. 1842. Daus:

1. SALLEY EDWARDS - land whereon I live with reversion
to her 4 sons, 2. CHRISSEY BENNETT - the JOSEPH POPE
tract, with reversion to the sons of SALLEY EDWARDS.
Gr. chil: WILLIAM EDWARDS, HENDERSON BATTLE EDWARDS,
EDWIN FRANCIS EDWARDS, JAMES R. CLINTON EDWARDS, SARAH
ANN ELIZABETH EDWARDS, chil. of CULLEN EDWARDS. Ex:
JACOB ING. Wit: JOHN D. CAUTHON, EDWIN EDWARDS.

POPE, WILLIAM A. of Edgecombe Co.
    P. 513. Jan. 5, 1848 - Aug. Ct. 1848. Wife:
MARY ANN. Ex: WILLIAM T. DORTCH. Wit: THOMAS
NEWLY (NEWBY?), KINDRED POPE.

PORTIS, GEORGE
    P. 97. Dec. 17, 1794 - Feb. Ct. 1795. Wife:
MARY. Son: WILLIAM. 3 daus. unnamed. Money coming
in from my father's estate to pay debts. No Ex. Wit:
DEVX. BALLARD, IRA PORTIS.

POULAN, JOHN
    P. 26. Dec. 9, 1783 - Jan. Ct. 1784. Son:
WILLIAM. Daus: 1. JEAN WILLIAMS, 2. MARY TAYLOR,
3. ELIZABETH POULAND. Ex: Son-in-law JONAS WILLIAMS.
Wit: EDWARD MOORE, WILSON TAYLOR, ROWLAND WILLIAMS.

POULAN, JOHN
    P. 361. Mar. 16, 1826 - Feb. Ct. 1829. Wife:
SALLEY. Sons: 1. JOSEPH - 109 A. bought of WILLIAM
HARRISON, north side Tar R., 2. GUILFORD - land whereon
I live at death of his mother, 3. WILLIAMSON, 4. JOHN.
Daus: 1. CHARITY RICKS, 2. SUSAN PITTMAN, 3. ZELPHIA
BAKER, 4. BETSEY JOINER. Ex: Son WILLIAMSON POULAN.
Wit: JOSIAH VICKS, LITTLE G. B. VICK.

POWELL, WILLIAM
    P. 269. Nov. 22, 1814 - Aug. Ct. 1815. Daus:
1. ELIZABETH POWELL, 2. MARY ANN POWELL. Ex: Friend
JAMES WILLIAMS, wife POLLY POWELL. Wit: ETHELDRED
EDWARDS, RATCHFORD VALLENTINE.

POWELL, WILLIE
    P. 570. Mar. 28, 1860 - Nov. Ct. 1860. Wife: MARY.

Son: 1. WILLIE POWELL'S heirs, among whom is SARAH
ELIZ. POWELL. Daus: 1. MARTHA, 2. MARGARET. Gr.
dau: MARTHA BURNETT. Gr. son: J. B. BOWERS (Ex).
Wit: B. D.MANN, L. F. WHELESS. Note: Probably other
heirs, but these only ones named.

PRIDGEN, ABIJAH
    P. 459. Dec. 12, 1841 - Feb. Ct. 1842. Wife:
SARAH. Son: ABIJAH THOMAS PRIDGEN. Dau: ZELBYANN
BATCHELOR. Ex: WILLIAM COOPER. Wit: JOSIAH VICK,
MARTHA CRICKMAN.

PRIDGEN, DAVID
    P. 275. May 26, 1814 - Aug. Ct. 1816. Wife:
PINKEY L. PRIDGEN - 150 A. whereon I live, it being the
land my father bought of BENJAMIN FLOWERS, also 140 A.,
it being the land bought of JOSEPH HARRWOOD and wife
SARAH, also 25 A. bought of SOLOMON WELLS; reversion to
my sons. Sons: 1. HARDY - 330 A. on Sappony Swamp,
bought of JOHN ATKINSON, 2. ABIJAH - 175 A. on north
side Tar R., bought of HARDY PRIDGEN. Daus: 1. PIETY
TISDALE, 2. CLOAH ATKINSON - 158½ A. on north side Tar
R., bought of JAMES PRIM and wife MARY, also 141 A. on
north side Tar R., bought of JAMES PRIM and wife MARY,
3. ATESHIA HARPER, 4. PRIMMY LAMKIN,5. POLLY HARRIET
PRIDGEN (minor) - 150 A. adjoining DREWRY PRIDGEN,
bought of RHODA ALLEN, also 150 A. bought of ELIZABETH
ALLEN and 320 A. bought of JOSEPH SELAH, JR. Gr. son:
WILLIAM HUTSON TISDALE, PHILANDER TISDALE, ALEXANDER
HENRY TISDALE, sons of WILLIAM TISDALE and wife PIETY.
Gr. dau: MOURNING TISDALE. Ex: Son ABIJAH PRIDGEN,
BENJAMIN ATKINSON. Wit: JOHN VICK, JACOB BARNES,
NANCY B. BOTTOMS.

PRIDGEN, DREWERY
    P. 409. Jan. 29, 1835 - May Ct. 1835. Wife:
SARAH. Son: WILLIAM A. PRIDGEN. Daus: 1. PIETY
COCKRELL - the ALLEN tract, 2. MOURNING BONE - 100 A.
near TOM ALLEN, 3. DANA PRIDGEN - 88½ A. bought of
SAMUEL LAMPKIN and wife, 4. SARAH COCKRELL, 5. ELIZABETH
COCKRELL, 6. NANCY LINDSEY - 100 A. west of the ALLEN

tract, 7. MARY CARTER - 100 A. northeast of the ALLEN
tract. Gr. son: JOHN C. TAYLOR - 100 A. Ex: SAM.
W. W. VICK, son WILLIAM A. PRIDGEN. Wit: O. D. BARNES,
W. T. BARNES.

PRIDGEN, JESSE
P. 312. Feb. 1, 1816 - Aug. Ct. 1823. Wife: MARY.
Sons: 1. PATRICK - 125 A. lower end of old plantation,
2. COLEN (CULLEN?) E. - 125 A. at upper end of old plantation, 3. JESSE - 250 A. whereon he lives. Reversion
of 250 A. whereon I live to be divided between sons at
death of mother. "All my children" - names no daus.
Ex: DREWRY PRIDGEN, HARDY PRIDGEN. Wit: SAM W. W.
VICK, DAVID WINSTEAD, JOHN WELLS.

PULLEN, WILLIE
P. 565. Nov. 25, 1851 - Feb. Ct. 1860. Wife:
ELIZABETH. 5 chil: 1. CLARISSA, 2. MARY, 3. ETHELINDA,
4. JOHN C., 5. ELIZABETH. Ex: WILLIAM D. HARRISON.
Wit: JOHN F. HARPER, JAMES HARPER. WILLIAM D. HARRISON
renounced his executorship and EMILUS PULLEN was made
Admin. Sureties: A. MATHEWS, JOHN E. MATHEWS.

PURCELL, EDWARD
P. 63. Feb. 18, 1785 - Feb. Ct. 1790. Wife and
Extx: ELIZABETH. Son: 1. JEREMIAH - 500 A., 2. HARDY-
300 A. both sides Turkey Crk., 3. JAMES - 300 A. both
sides Little Crk. Daus: 1. SARA PURCELL, 2. JANE
PURCELL. Ex: JEREMIAH ETHRIDGE. Wit: DANIEL
TAYLOR, JAMES CULPEPPER.

RACKLEY, CHERRY
P. 558. April 6, 1855 - Aug. Ct. 1858. Sons:
1. JOHN H., 2. LEMON D., 3. FRANCIS R. Daus:
1. MARGARET CHERRY RACKLEY, 2. ROENA W. WHITLEY,
3. SELETER R. MATTHEWS. Ex: Son JOHN H. RACKLEY.
Wit: WILLIAM H. JOYNER, DAVID JOYNER.

RACKLEY, FRANCIS SR.
P. 416. June 3, 1837 - Nov. Ct. 1837. Wife:
CHERRY. Sons: 1. FRANCIS RACKLEY, JR. - 400 A. on
lines of THOMAS JOINER, 2. LAMON DEW RACKLEY - my two

youngest sons. Daus: 1. SELETER PANSY RACKLEY,
2. ROEANNA WARD RACKLEY, 3. MARGARET CHERRY RACKLEY.
Ex: Son FRANCIS RACKLEY. Wit: DAVID W. DEANS, JOHN
DEANS.

RACKLEY, PERSON
    P. 261. Oct. 18, 1814 - Nov. Ct. 1814. Sons:
1. JOSEPH (his heirs), 2. FREDERICK, 3. FRANCIS,
4. MATHEW, 5. SILAS, 6. PERSONS. Daus: 1. CITYVIAS?
RACKLEY, 2. SARAH ETHERIDGE, 3. MOLLEY RACKLEY,
4. ELIZABETH BATCHELOR. Gr. sons: FREDERICK, son of
FREDERICK, WILLIAM, PERSONS, son of PERSONS, PERSONS,
son of SILAS, JOHN BATCHELOR, son of JOHN BATCHELOR.
Gr. daus: LUCY, dau. of MATHEW RACKLEY, MARGARETT, dau.
of PERSONS RACKLEY. Ex: Son FRANCIS, friend DAVID
RICKS. Wit: DAVID MELTON, PATSEY TUCKER.

RAWLS, DAVID
    P. 523. July 2, 1850 - Nov. Ct. 1850. All my
land in Martin Co. to my bro. and sisters: HARDY
RAWLS, MILLEY BAILEY, MARTHA WOODARD, NANCY RAWLS.
Bro-in-law: DANIEL BAILEY. Legatee: MARY T. FOSTER
and her chil: SALLY ANN, KELLY RAWLS. Ex: BENJ. F.
FOSTER. Wit: T. W. WRIGHT, T. C. WHITEHEAD. Note:
MARY T. FOSTER may have been a sister. M.G.G.

RAWLS, KELLY of Hilliardston, Nash Co.
    P. 512. Nov. 26, 1847 - Feb. Ct. 1848. Father:
DAVID RAWLS - DOZIER place. Mother: SALLY RAWLS.
Wife: MARY. Son: CORNELIUS. Dau: SALLY ANN.
Ex: JOSHUA WATSON, DOC (DR.?) JOHN ARRINGTON. Wit:
THOMAS C. ARRINGTON, JOHN T. WATSON.

REVEL, ELIJAH
    P. 173. Nov. 3, 1806 - Nov. Ct. 1807. Wife: DOLLY.
Sons: 1. JONNATHAN (JONATHAN), 2. PAUL - land joining
BENJ. WHITFIELD and DANIELS, 3. BARNABAS - land north
side Lassiter's Branch, 4. MATHEW - lands west side
Lassiter's Branch, 5. HUMPHREY - residue of land. Daus:
1. EDITH REVEL - lands adjoining DANIELS, 2. CELAH
MALONE - land adjoining EDITH REVEL, DANIELS and THORP,
3. FAITHFUL MALONE - land adjoining DREW HUNTER. Ex:

Friends REDMUN BUNN, NATHAN GILBERT, JOSEPH STRICKLAND.
Wit: MARMADUKE MASON, MATHEW REVEL, JOSEPH STRICKLAND.
Codicil witnessed Oct. 24, 1807 by JOSEPH STRICKLAND,
MATHEW REVEL.

REVEL, HUMPHREY
    P. 379. Nov. 28, 1831 - Feb. Ct. 1832. Wife:
DELILAH. Sons: 1. WILLIAM N. (minor) - land whereon
I live, 2. ELIJAH H. (minor) - land bought of WILLIAM
DOZIER. Ex: WILLIAM N. (to take possession of his
property whether he be of age or not), TIMOTHY FERRELL.
Negroes to be divided between heirs by: BENNETT BUNN,
BENNETT BARNES, JAMES T. BARNES, JAMES HUNTER, WILLIE
RICKS.

RICE, JOHN
    P. 443. April 29, 1836 - Aug. Ct. 1837. Wife:
ELIZABETH. Son: WILLIAM - reversion of 800 A. where-
on I live. Dau: NANCY CARPENTER. The following (no
relationship given) have received their property:
WILLIAM RICHARDSON, HOPKINS RICE, REDEN RICHARDSON,
WILLIAM EARPPE, BENJAMIN RICE. Gr. son: RICHARDSON,
son of WILLIAM RICE. Chil. of BENJAMIN RICE (and their
representatives): JOHN RICE, NICHOLSON RICE, BOYKIN
RICE, heirs of JINCY STRICKLAND. Legatee: JOHN
LEONARD. Ex: BENJAMIN MERRITT, JOHN RICE. Wit:
WILLIAM M. B. ANNDELL, BOYKIN DENTON, HOPNE (Clerk:
HOPIN) PUCKETT.

RICE, JOHN SR.
    P. 480. Mar. 28, 1845 - Nov. Ct. 1845. Wife:
MARTHA - land whereon I live - on Tar R. and Red Oak
Spring, lines of WM. WINSTEAD and BRYANT RICE. Sons:
1. JAMES M., 2. HENDERSON - land south side Tar R.,
3. BRYANT - land on Tar R., Dickinson Br., and lines
of WILLIAM WINSTEAD. Daus: 1. SUSAN WINSTEAD,
2. MORNING WILLIAMSON, 3. MARY RICE. Ex: A. B.
BAINES, JR., MARTHA RICE. Wit: KINCHEN TAYLOR,
ROBERT D. DEANS.

RICE, JOHN B.
    P. 591. Nov. 20, 1863 - Feb. Ct. 1865. Son:

NATHANIEL - to have "english education". All chil. and property to be held together until chil. come of age or marry. Ex: A. B. BAINES. Wit: J. T. WEBB, W. E. MANNING. Clerk's notes: Will proved by W. E. MANNING, also the signature of J. T. WEBB, who is out of the state.

RICE, MARTHA
    P. 572. Jan. 13, 1855 - Aug. Ct. 1861. Sons: 1. BRYANT D. RICE, 2. HENDERSON RICE (Ex). Dau: 1. MOURNING WILLIAMSON. Gr. chil: the chil. of HENDERSON RICE and MOURNING WILLIAMSON. Wit: KINCHEN TAYLOR, A. B. BAINES, JR.

RICHARDSON, WILLIAM
    P. 254. Aug. 19, 1812 - Feb. Ct. 1813. Sons: 1. NUMAN (NEWMAN), 2. GEORGE, 3. JOHN, 4. ALSEY. Dau: TEMPY. Ex: Son JOHN, friend AUGUSTIN BASS. Wit: GIDEON BASS, JESSE BASS, JONES WALKER.

RICKS, ABRAHAM
    P. 394. April 12, 1833 - May Ct. 1833. Wife: RACHEL. Sons: 1. EXUM, 2. ISAAC - sons to share reversional interest in all land, 3. WILLIE. Daus: 1. ISABELLA RICKS, 2. DRUSILLA RICKS, 3. NANCY VICK, desc. Gr. chil: TEMPERANCE JACKSON, JOHN RICKS, WILLIAM RICKS. Ex: Son WILLIE RICKS. Wit: BERRYMAN BATCHELOR, DAVID RICKS.

RICKS, ACKSEY
    P. 604. May 2, 1863 - no prob. date. Sons: 1. WILLIAM J. B. HARPER (Ex. and guardian to my gr. chil., the chil. of ALFORD JOYNER To Wit: WILLIAM D. JOYNER, GUILFORD JOYNER, JAMES JOYNER, MARY E. JOYNER, MALVINA JOYNER, ASHLEY JOYNER, HENRY JOYNER. Also GEORGE HARPER, son of my gr. son, JOHN H. B. HARPER. Wit: W. W. BODDIE, JAMES BUNTING. Handwriting of JAMES BUNTING, dec'd, proven by C. W. WARD.

RICKS, D. A. T.
    P. 608. June 8, 1871 - no prob. date. Only son: AUGUSTUS H. RICKS - all residue of land, provided he

care for his mother.   Wife: FRANCES A. RICKS - the
ING tract, also land willed to her by her father,
NATHANIEL HARRISON.   Daus: 1. LAURA F., wife of W. C.
TAYLOR - ½ the BYNUM tract, 2. ANN ROSELL RICKS - ½ the
BYNUM tract.   Ex: Son A. H. RICKS, bro. GEORGE RICKS.
Wit: (DR.) J. A. DRAKE, PINKIE PARKER, (DR.) R. H.
MARRIOTT.

RICKS, ISBELL (ISABEL?)
    P. 453. Dau: MARTHA RICKS.   Ex: AMOS JOINER.
Wit: BERRYMAN BATCHELOR, EXUM L. CURL.

RICKS, JOHN
    P. 245. Feb. 15, 1790.   Wife and Extx: MARY.
Sons: 1. ISAAC - 280 A. on Tyancoky Swamp whereon he
lives, 2. JOHN and 3. RICHARD to share 401 A. land
whereon I live, 4. JESSE, 5. GIDEON, 6. REDMUN, 7. CARY
or LARY? - 150 A. at mother's death, 8. JACOB.   Daus:
1. ANN WATKINS, 2. SARAH DENSON, 3. JOHANNA, 4. DELILAH.
Ex: Son ISAAC RICKS.   Wit: R. BUNN, WILLIAM SKINNER,
JAMES RICKS.   Codicil dated Feb. 16, 1790 was wit. by
R. BUNN, JAMES RICKS, DAVID BUNN.

RICKS, JOHN
    P. 504. Jan. 6, 1845 - Nov. Ct. 1847. Wife: ANNA-
land bought of DAVID RICKS, where I live, also tracts
bought of ELIZABETH BARRETT, with reversion to sons
NERO RICKS and JOHN A. RICKS.   Sons: 1. DAVID A. T.
RICKS of Alabama, 2. JEROME RICKS of Alabama, 3. GEORGE
RICKS - 640 A. where he lives on Back Swamp - with
regard to the will of GEORGE BODDIE, SR., and deeds
proven in Nash Co. Court in 1844, also deeds of trust
from NICHOLAS C. HARRISON and JOHN G. F. DRAKE,
4. WILLIAM RICKS - 440 A. of SION BECKWITH land,
5. BUCKANAN RICKS - 306 A. of THOS. BECKWITH land,
6. NERO RICKS, 7. JOHN A. RICKS.   Daus: 1. FRANCES
RICKS - 220 A. bought of HOWELL F. ELLEN (FLEWELLEN)
and THOS. F. ELLEN, also ½ the land bought of HARRIET
and SERINA SNEED, 2. SIDNEY S. B. HARPER, wife of
WILLIAM J. B. HARPER - land bought for her from ALFORD
JOYNER and wife PRIMMY and from BENNET ATKINSON and wife
MARY.   She is also to have 98 A. of PHILANDER TISDALE

land I bought of SAMUEL W. W. VICK, also 97½ A. I drew
in the division of lands of the late DAVID RICKS, and
land where JAMES BUNTING lives, which is my interest in
the dower land of ALSEY RICKS, 3. INDIANA RICKS.   I
have already contracted away my land on south side Tar
R. to GEORGE H. WHITLEY and LAMON R. WHITLEY.   I wish
$50 set aside for a tombstone, to bear the following
engraving: "John Ricks, born 1786. Died _____.   An
honest man in all his dealings, but badly slandered
and much belyed."   Ex: Son GEORGE RICKS, son-in-law
WILLIAM J. B. HARPER, with the aid of BENJAMIN BLOUNT.
Sis: SALLY MANNING of Lawrence Co., Georgia.   Debt
due me by GEORGE BODDIE of Jackson, Miss.   Guardian
for chil., FRANCES, WILLIAM and BUCKANAN RICKS: son-
in-law WILLIAM J. B. HARPER.   Guardian for chil.,
INDIANA, NERO and JOHN A. RICKS: my son GEORGE RICKS.
Wit: JESSE BEAL, ELIAS BARRETT, HENRY EDWARDS, JAMES
F. ELLIN (FLEWELLEN).   Codicil Aug. 20, 1845 giving
additional Negroes to dau. SIDNEY S. B. HARPER.   Codicil #2 Jan. 31, 1846 dismissing guardians named in will
and appointing son DAVID A. T. RICKS, who is to give
bond and is ordered to spend not to exceed $1500 for
dau. Indiana Ricks.

RICKS, LYDIA
    P. 411. June 15, 1835 - Aug. Ct. 1835.   Son:
DICKERSON RICKS.   Dau: ELIZABETH RICKS.   Ex: RUFFIN
H. RICKS.   Wit: JOHN H. HANKS, EMELDRED WHITFIELD.

RICKS, MICAJAH
    P. 513. Oct. 1, 1841 - May Ct. 1848.   Son:
MICAJAH - land on Sapponey Crk., formerly the land of
RUFFIN H. RICKS.   Daus: 1. APPY ANN RICKS - land
between Little Swamp and Toisnot Swamp, including that
whereon I live, 2. AQUILLA ANN VICK - land on north
side Little Swamp and Toisnot Swamp.   Gr. son: IREDELL
VICK.   No Ex.   Wit: ROBERT D. DEANS, G. W. WARD.

RICKS, RHODA
    P. 403. June 12, 1834.   Father: WILLIAM RICKS.
Mother: LYDIA RICKS.   Bro: DAVID RICKS, dec'd. Sis:
MOURNING JOINER.   Others mentioned: JOHN RICKS, RUFFIN

RICKS, and LUCY BASS. Nieces: ANNALIZAR BUNTING,
FRANCES BUNTING, HARRIETT, dau. of MOURNING JOINER.
Ex: Bro-in-law JAMES BUNTING. Wit: ROBERT MELTON,
WILLIAM B. HARPER.

RICKS, THOMAS - Nunc. will
   P. 247. Sept. 13, 1789. Wife: PRISCILLA. Son:
ELLEXANDER (ALEXANDER) URBAN(?). Dau: MILBERRY. Ex:
Father-in-law ROLAND WILLIAMS, bro. ABRAHAM RICKS. Wit:
BENJ. RICKS, JOEL RICKS, ABRAHAM RICKS. Sworn within
15 hours after his death. Wit: R. BUNN, EDWARD
NICHOLSON.

RICKS, WILLIAM
   P. 388. May 7, 1832 - Aug. Ct. 1832. Wife: LYDIA.
Sons: 1. JOHN, 2. DICKESON. Daus: 1. RHODA RICKS,
2. MILLANEY BUNTING, 3. ELIZABETH RICKS, 4. MOURNING
JOINER (JOYNER), 5. SALLY MANNING. "At death of wife,
estate to be divided among all my children, with following exception: SALLY MANNING'S part, say one eighth
part, is to be held by my executor, and paid her according to his judgment of her need." Note: Did he have 8
children? Son-in-law: ALEXANDER MANNING. Ex: Son
JOHN RICKS. Wit: MOSES R. MOORE, WILLIAM J. B. HARPER.

RICKS, WILLIE
   P. 545.
   A paper purporting to be the will of WILLIE RICKS is
offered for probate on the testimony of JESSE H. DRAKE,
RUFFIN H. RICKS and JAMES T. BARNES; the said JESSE H.
DRAKE proves that the paper was deposited with him for
safe keeping.....whereupon the paper was admitted for
probate. There being no executor named in the will,
BENTON A. RICKS was appointed administrator, who enters
into bond of $20,000 with WILLIAM S. BATTLE, JAMES P.
BATTLE and JOHN E. LINDSEY sureties. The will follows.
   P. 545. Sept. 7, 1846 - no prob. date. Wife:
CHARLOTTE - land north of the Creek to Halifax Rd.
Legatees: PININAH SARY, formerly PENINAH RICKS (and her
chil.), ARTIMESIA LANDMAN, formerly ARTIMESIA RICKS (and
her chil.), MILLICENT WALKER, formerly MILLICENT RICKS
(and her chil.), NANCY H. RICKS. Note: He does not

call them daughters, but states they are to have their lawful share of his estate, so they probably were daughters. M.G.G.   Sons: 1. WILLIE B. RICKS, 2. ISAAC W. RICKS, 3. JAMES W. RICKS, 4. BURTON A. RICKS, 5. ADDISON E. RICKS.   Written in his own hand.

ROGERS, ROBERT
     P. 227. June 3, 1791 - Aug. Ct. 1791. Wife: ANN. Sons: 1. JACOB - 160 A. whereon he lives, 2. JESSE, 3. ROBERT - these two sons all remaining land.   Daus: 1. BETEY (BEEDIE or BETSEY?) BASS, 2. NANNY ROGERS, 3. CHARITY ROGERS, 4. MOURNING ROGERS, 5. ZANY ROGERS. Ex: Sons JACOB and JESSE.   Wit: HILL JONES, WILLIAM RICHARDSON.

ROGERS, THOMAS
     P. 42. Nov. 14, 1785 - Feb. Ct. 1786. Wife: MARY. Sons: 1. JOHN - land, 2. JAMES - 250 A. whereon I live, 3. THOMAS - 400 A., 4. PELEG (PEALICK).   Daus: 1. MARY THOMAS, 2. ONEDIANCE BARRON, 3. ANN CHAPMAN, 4. ELIZABETH DUNN, 5. UNY ROGERS, 6. MOORE ROGERS, 7. MOURNING ROGERS, 8. PATIENCE ROGERS.   Ex: Son JAMES ROGERS, WILLIAM DUNN.   Wit: EDWARD NICHOLSON, THEOPHILUS HICKMAN, WINIFRED NICHOLSON.

ROPER, JOEL
     P. 522. April 10, 1842 - Aug. Ct. 1850. Wife: MARY-all the Negroes and their increase that came by her at our marriage. No Ex. No Wit. Proved in Court by oath of T. W. WRIGHT.

ROSE, ANN
     P. 326. May 6, 1824 - May Ct. 1825.   Daus: 1. ANN MOORE, 2. MOURNING SIKES, 3. CHARITY ODOM, 4. ZANY LINDSEY.   Gr. dau: INDES ? MOORE   Ex: COLLUM (CULLEN?) MOORE, JOHN W. LINDSEY.   Wit: WILLIAM M. HAMMONDS, WILLIAM WALKER.

ROSE, ELIZABETH of Edgecombe County
     P. 1. May 25, 1774 - July Ct. 1778.   Sons and Ex: 1. EDWARD CLINCH - 350 A. south side Swift Crk. on lines of COL. WM. WHITEHEAD and JEREMIAH WILLIAMS, 2. JOSEPH

JOHN CLINCH - 450 A. where I live, purchased of WM. BELLAMY. Dau: 1. MARY BELLAMY, wife of WM. BELLAMY. Gr. dau: ELIZABETH CLINCH. Wit: JAS. W. NEELE, LENOR MACK, NATHAN ATKINSON, RICH'D MANNING, BENJ. MERRITT.

ROSE, FRANCIS
    P. 111. May 7, 1795 - Nov. Ct. 1796. Wife: PATTY. Sons: 1. WILLIAM, 2. BENJAMIN, 3. TOMKINS. Daus: 1. MARY WRIGHT, 2. MARTHA ROSE, 3. ANN ROSE. Ex: Wife and JOHN ARRINGTON. Wit: JAMES SANDERFORD, JETHRO DENSON (?), WILLIAM SANDERFORD, JR.

ROW, WILLIAM
    P. 123. Jan. 6, 1797 - Nov. Ct. 1798. Wife: JEAN. Children unnamed. Ex: THOMAS HORN of Wayne Co., JETHRO HARRISON. Wit: THOMAS HORN, CHARLES HOWELL, JESSE PARKER.

SANDEFORD, HENRY - Nuncupative will
    P. 235. HENRY SANDEFORD died May 16, 1800. POLLEY HUNTER. NATHAN? Chil. of BENJ. WILLIAMS - no relationship shown for any of above. Wit: JOSEPH ARRINGTON, JR. Sworn before JOSEPH ARRINGTON, J.P. May 21, 1800.

SANDERFORD, TOMPKINS
    P. 31. Dec. 2, 1782 - Apr. Ct. 1783. Wife: MARY. Sons: 1. HENRY, 2. TOMPKINS, 3. NATHAN. Ex: Wife MARY, bro-in-law ARTHUR ARRINGTON. Wit: WILLIAM ARRINGTON, MARTHA ROSE, MARTHA ARRINGTON.

SANDERS, PRIMMY
    P. 609. June 20, 1869 - no probate date. Sis: CALLY SANDERS - 150 A. known as SION SANDERS place, and all remaining estate. Ex: BARTLY C. STRICKLAND. Wit: H. H. MEDLIN, SARAH BENTON.

SANDERS, ROBERT
    Page 29. Jan. 3, 1783 - no prob. date. Wife: MARY. Sons: 1. PHILANDER and 2. RICHARD - to have 190 A. on Burn Coate Swamp. Reversion to their sons and daughters

unnamed. Ex: JAMES CAIN, PHILANDER SANDERS. Wit:
JAMES CAIN, PHILANDER SANDERS.

SANDERS, SION
    P. 586. June 19, 1861 - Nov. Ct. 1863. Wife:
ELIZABETH - 300 A. where I live. Sons: 1. RUFFIN H.-
land where he lives, 2. STARLING E., 3. LINDY M. Gr.
chil: WILLIAM B. SANDERS - 110 A. of FAISON tract,
SALLY ROUNTREE, JINCY ROUNTREE, FRANKY ROUNTREE, ELLEN
JANE FINCH. Daus: 1. TEMPERANCE, wife of KINCHEN
FINCH, 2. NANCY, wife of JOHN BAILEY, 3. RAHAB, wife of
IRWIN FINCH, 4. ELIZA, wife of JOHN H. HENDRICKS - 250
A. north side Tar River, 5. CALLY - 110 A. of FAISON
tract, 6. PRIMMY, 7. LAUTORY SUSAN FRANCES. Ex: A. H.
DENTON. Wit: WESLEY PRIVETT, JAS. S. DENTON. Clerk's
notes: WESLEY PRIVETT proved handwriting of JAMES S.
DENTON who is in the army out of the state. Ex.
renounced - EVAN H. MORGAN and RUFFIN H. SANDERS named
Admin. - who entered bond of $75,000 with D. W. WINSTEAD,
JOHN B. RICE, WILLIS WARREN, MADISON SIKES and W. D.
STRICKLAND as sureties.

SCREWS, HENRY
    P. 87. Oct. 14, 1793 - Nov. Ct. 1793. Sons:
1. JOHN, eldest son, 2. JAMES, 3. WILLIAM and
4. LITTLETON - these two to have all the land. Daus:
1. SARAH, 2. POLLY. Gr. dau: ANNA ROBERTSON. Ex:
JOSIAH NICHOLSON, JOHN POWELL. Wit: JOHN WIGGINS,
SUSANNA POWELL.

SCREWS, SALLEY
    P. 197. Dec. 14, 1808 - Feb. Ct. 1809. Legatee
and Ex: ALEX W. HINES. Niece: ANNE ROBERTSON.
Legatees: Children of my bro. JAMES SCREWS. Wit:
L. LEWIS, HARTWELL HINES, SR.

SELAH, JOSEPH JR.
    P. 99. Aug. 16, 1792 - May Ct. 1795. Wife:
ELIZABETH. Sons: 1. BENJAMIN - 100 A. on north side
Sappony Crk., 2. RICHARD - 100 A. lower part of same
plantation. 4 youngest chil: RICHARD, RODAH, ELIZABETH
and MOURNING. Ex: Wife ELIZABETH SELAH, friend SAM
WESTRAY. Wit: EDWARD GANDY, ELIJAH ATKINSON.

SELAH, JOSEPH
    P. 200. Feb. 16, 1807 - Aug. Ct. 1809. Gr. Son:
CORDY SELAH. Dau: SILLEAR SEGRAVES (PRISCILLA?) Ex:
CORDY SELAH, JESSE JOINER. Wit: BENNETT JOINER.

SELAH, REBECCA
    P. 143. July 14, 1803 - Nov. Ct. 1803. Son:
BILLEY BAKER SELAH. Daus: 1. BARSHEBA, 2. MOURNING.
Ex: JESSE JOINER, JORDAN SHERROD. Wit: EDWARD SELAH,
PARTHENA JOINER.

SHERROD, JOHN J.
    P. 512. April 11, 1848 - May Ct. 1848. Wife:
ANSELINA - whole estate. Ex: PRIDGEN MANNING. Wit:
JOS. B. MANN, WILLIAM H. MATHES, EVERT (EVERETT?)
MATHES (MATTHEWS).

SHERROD, JORDAN
    P. 462. Oct. 8, 1841 - Feb. Ct. 1843. Wife: NANCY.
Wife's sis: MARY EDENS, desc. Sons and Ex: 1. SILAS-
100 A. called JOINER land and part of my land in fork
of ODUM Branch and JACOB Swamp, 2. REDMUND - residue of
land north side JACOB Swamp. Daus: 1. CATHERINE
WILLIAMS, 2. SALVA JOINER, 3. MARY TAYLOR, 4. ELIZABETH
ROBINSON, 5. CHRISCHANEY LINDSEY's chil., 6. JANE
POULAND. Gr. daus: CHRISCHANEY PENELOPE ELIZABETH
ANN STRICKLIN, 2. LEVINEY SHERROD - the ODUM field,
south of the field and east of JACOB Swamp. Ex:
ABSALOM B. BAINES, JR., ISAAC STRICKLAND. Wit: JOINER
LANGLEY, CORDAL SELEY.

SHORT, RICHARD
    P. 594. April 22, 1863 - Aug. Ct. 1864. Wife:
MATHEW? - the FULLER tract. Sons: 1. GEORGE C.,
trustee, 2. RICHARD. Daus: 1. MARY, 2. LOUISIANNA,
3. MASORA?, 4. HARRIET BRYANT, 5. ELISA TAYLOR (ANN
ELIZA). Ex: JESSE F. TAYLOR, JESSE H. DRAKE. Wit:
D. W. WINSTEAD, B. D. RICE.

SIKES, JOHN
    P. 117. July 3, 1797 - Nov. Ct. 1797. Gr. sons:
JOHN SIKES, son of MOURNING SIKES, JOSEPH SIKES, son of
JACOB. Ex: NATHAN BODDIE. Wit: GEORGE BODDIE,
MOURNING SIKES.

SIKES, MOURNING
P. 529. July 4, 1852 - Nov. Ct. 1852. Sons:
1. EDMOND, Ex., 2. MADISON. Dau: 1. JULIAN, wife of
AUGUSTIN BASS. Gr. son: WILLIAM JOURDING SIKES. Gr.
daus: JULIAN SIKES, MARYAN SIKES, SARA SIKES, MARGARET
SIKES. Wit: W. H. EDWARDS, HARRIET WHITE. On
July 18, 1852, MOURNING SIKES added a codicil to the
above will, bequeathing a loom to HARRIET WHITE, the
wife of JOSEPH H. WHITE - no relationship expressed.
Wit: W. H. EDWARDS.

SILLS, DAVID
P. 395. Mar. 27, 1832 - Aug. Ct. 1833. Wife:
ELIZABETH. Wife's father: WILLIAM WILHITE. Wife's
sis: SALLY PEARCE (formerly WILHITE). Sons: 1. GRAY-
land where I live, containing tract purchased of DR.
MALONE on the Raleigh-Halifax Rd. on lines of WILLIS
WEBB, Nashville Rd., ABRAM HEDGEPETH, WELDON BRASWELL,
Redbud Crk., the Meeting House, EBEN NELMS and ARCHIBALD
PEARCE. Daus: 1. SUSAN MARY DAVIS - the RODGERS
tract, adjoining BENJAMIN WHELESS, HEDGEPETH, Gay's Old
Mill and the swamp, 2. LUCY, 3. VIRGINIA REBECCA SILLS-
all other land adjoining above land - the JOSIAH
JOHNSTON tract, KING and DICKINSON tracts, JAMES
HARRISON tract, that I own on Cypress Crk. in Franklin
Co., called MICAJAH BRIDGE'S tract adjoining ALLEN
HINES, also the land of HENRY MITCHELL called the DAVID
TURNER tract, 4. ISADORE SILLS - the MALONE tract, both
sides Raleigh-Halifax Rd., the UNDERWOOD tract adjoin-
ing JAMES HARRISON, the CYNTHIA BASS tract in Franklin
Co., adjoining MRS. JOSIAH THOMAS, 5. SALLY J. THOMAS -
plantation where she lives, called the JACOB BASS tract,
with reversion to her 3 chil: SUSAN BATTLE, DAVID
BATTLE and ANGELINA BATTLE. Ex: W. W. BODDIE. Wit:
JAMES HARRISON, JOHN Q. A. DRAKE. Attached is reference
to a Marriage Contract made Jan. 20, 1820 between DAVID
SILLS and his wife ELIZABETH and WILLIAM WHELESS, executor of WILLIAM WHELESS, dec'd. Preface to will of
WILLIAM WHELESS is found on P. 365 of W. Bk. 1, and
precedes the will of WILLIAM WHELESS in this volume.

SMITH, BENJAMIN
P. 125. Jan. 19, 1799 - Aug. Ct. 1799. Sons:

1. BRITTAIN, 2. SIMON, 3. SAMUEL - 38 A. s. side Sapony
Crk., also 600 A. adjoining, bought of DUNCAN LAMON,
4. JORDAN - 287 A. lying on Limestone Crk. in Washington
Co., Ga., bought of WILLIAM WHITEHEAD, also 300 A.
adjoining same, bought of SION SMITH, 5. BENNETT - 500 A.
whereon I live, 6. SION'S heirs (apparently he is
deceased). Daus: 1. ELIZABETH WHITEHEAD, 2. MOURNING
SMITH, 3. CHARITY GRIFFIN, 4. MARY VICK. Ex: Son-in-
law ARCHIBALD GRIFFIN, son SAMUEL SMITH, friend JESSE
JOINER. Wit: JESSE JOINER, BENJAMIN WHITLEY.

SMITH, BENNETT
     P. 527. May 7, 1852 - Aug. Ct. 1852. Wife: AMEY-
150 A. where I live. Sons: 1. JOHN (eldest) - land
where he lives, 2. A. W. SMITH (youngest) - 813 A. where
I live, except life estate of wife AMEY. Daus:
1. ZILPHA (eldest), wife of CLABORNE PERRY, 2. MARTHA
(youngest), wife of JOSHUA BRANTLEY. Residue to be
divided between wife and children. Ex: Son A. W.
SMITH. Wit: A. B. BAINES, JR., A. T. TAYLOR.

SMITH, MOURNING
     P. 8. May 12, 1778 - July Ct. 1781. Sons:
1. JOSIAH, 2. MICAJAH. Daus: CHLOE. Gr. son: JAMES
RICKS. Gr. daus: MOURNING and RHODA RICKS. Ex:
NATHAN BODDIE, JOSIAH CRUDUP. Wit: STEPHEN YOUNG,
JOHN BIGGS, SR., JAMES SMITH.

SMITH, WILLIAM H.
     P. 528. June 24, 1852 - Aug. Ct. 1852. Friends:
DR. JOHN H. DRAKE, DR. JOHN C. DRAKE, DR. JOHN G. F.
DRAKE, and JOHN WILLIAM WALLACE DRAKE to have whole
estate. Ex: DR. JOHN H. DRAKE. Wit: JOHN J. DRAKE,
GEORGE EVANS.

SIMS, HENRY
     P. 560. Dec. 28, 1854 - Feb. Ct. 1859. Son:
L. S. SIMS. Daus: 1. HARRIET W. B. SIMS, wife of
DR. RICHARD S. SIMS, of Brunswick Co., Va., 2. SARAH
E. A. BUNN, wife of WILLIAM B. BUNN. Friends: DR.
RICHARD S. SIMS, DR. JOHN G. RIVES (Ex), JAMES P.
BATTLE (Ex). Wit: FREDERICK PHILIPS, JAMES P. PHILIPS.

SOREY, ROBERT

P. 555. Oct. 29, 1855 - Aug. Ct. 1857. Wife:
GRACY. Sons: 1. JESSE SOREY, 2. WILLIAM. Daus:
1. NANCY MOORE dec'd, her chil: MARY ELIZABETH MOORE,
DENNIS MOORE, 2. ELIZABETH TREVATHAN dec'd, her chil.,
3. MARY GOOD. Gr. chil: WHITMAEL SOREY, MARY ELIZA
SOREY. Ex: Bro. DENNIS MOORE, son WILLIAM SOREY,
JOHN THORP. Wit: ROB'T H. MARRIOTT, GEO. A. WEEKS,
JOEL WELLS.

SORSBY, ALEX

P. 299. Feb. 2, 1818 - Nov. Ct. 1818. "All my
children" unnamed. Ex and Guardians: GEORGE BODDIE
and JAMES HILLIARD. Wit: EXUM RICKS.

SORSBY, BENJAMIN

P. 221. Sept. 10, 1811 - Nov. Ct. 1811. Wife
unnamed. Sis: LIDDA, ANN, JEREMAH (?) SORSBY -
plantation in Sussex Co., Va. Sons: 1. SAMUEL,
2. HENRY, 3. BENJAMIN. Daus: 1. ELIZABETH WRIGHT,
2. POLLEY SORSBY, 3. SUSAN SORSBY. Ex: JOSEPH
ARRINGTON. Wit: B. DRAKE, WOOD TUCKER, MITCHELL LONG.

SORSBY, B. H. SR. (BENJ. H.)

P. 605. Jan. 19, 1869 - July 18, 1870. Sons:
1. BENJA. H. (Ex), 2. SAML S., 3. CHARLIE B. No wit.
Handwriting proven by R. B. GRIFFIN, WM. T. GRIFFIN
and G. M. BLOUNT. FRANCES M. E. SORSBY, wid. of late
BENJAMIN H. SORSBY entered her dissent to the above
will.

SORSBY, ELIZABETH

P. 131. June 4, 1799 - Feb. Ct. 1800. Sons:
1. WILLIAM, 2. ALEX. Daus: 1. ELIZABETH BURGE,
2. FRANCES DEW. Ex: LEWIS DORTCH, ALEX W. HINES,
FREDERICK B. HINES. Wit: JAS. WILLIAMS, POLLEY
WALKER.

SORSBY, SAMUEL

P. 73. Oct. 14, 1790 - Aug. Ct. 1791. Wife:
ELIZABETH. Sons: 1. WILLIAM - all land south side of
Wateree R. in S. C., 2. ALEXANDER - land whereon I live.

99

Son-in-law: ARCHIBALD DAVIS and his sons: ALEXANDER
DAVIS and BALDY SORSBY DAVIS. Daus: 1. ELIZABETH
B. BURGE, 2. FRANCES SORSBY - lot #6 in Tarborough,
N. C. Ex: Wife ELIZABETH, son ALEXANDER. Wit:
ETHELDRED JELKS, SAMUEL MANNING, N. DAVIS.

SORSBY, SAMUEL D.
    P. 312. Dec. 19, 1822 - May Ct. 1823. Bro:
HENRY SORSBY - land in Illinois, also my share of land
inherited from our bro. BENJAMIN SORSBY, also my share
of our mother's dowry and my expected legacy in Virginia
at the decease of our aunt. Ex: BENJAMIN BLOUNT.
Wit: JAMES DOZIER, MARY BLOUNT.

STEVENS, JEREMIAH
    P. 159. Mar. 25, 1805 - Aug. Ct. 1805. Sons:
1. JOHN - land bought of JOHN BONDS, 2. JOSEPH. Daus:
1. REBECCA AVENT, 2. SARAH JONES, 3. ELIZABETH STEVENS.
Gr. daus: NANCY CARTER, NANCY HARRIS, ELIZABETH
STEVENS, dau of JOSEPH STEVENS. Ex: PILGRIM L.
WILLIAMS, ROBERT WILLIAMS. Wit: OSBORN STRICKLAND,
WILLIE TAHLOR (TAYLOR).

STONE, McCULLAR
    P. 583. Dec. 18, 1860 - Nov. Ct. 1862. Wife:
MARY E. - lands in Wilson Co., adj. PETER EATMAN, also
the legacy willed to me by my dec'd mother, HAPPY STONE.
She is also to have property left her by her dec'd
mother TEMPERANCE FINCH. Ex: MADISON SIKES, Nash Co.,
EDMON SIKES, Franklin Co. Wit: G. R. MARSBURN, GOODMAN
MASSENGALE.

STRICKLAND, ARNOLD
    P. 585. Jan. 8, 1859 - no prob. date. Wife: LUCY -
100 A. where I live. Sons: 1. B. T. STRICKLAND, B.
C. STRICKLAND. Daus: 1. ELIZABETH DENTON, 2. GILLY
HILL, 3. LINDAMARY DANIEL, 4. LUCY MARRIOTT MEDLIN. Gr.
son: GEORGE A. G. MEDLIN - a cow, at HILSMAN H. MEDLIN'S.
Ex: B. T. STRICKLAND. Wit: WM. BALLENTINE, SAMUEL
BRYANT. Clerk's notes: "Paper proven by McBRANTLEY and
CATHERINE KEMP, who testify to handwriting of witnesses
one of whom is dead, the other in the army".

STRICKLAND, DINAH

P. 408. Dec. 12, 1834 - May Ct. 1835. Friend:
WARREN STRICKLAND - all estate. Ex: A. B. B. BAINES,
SR. Wit: HARRY FERRELL, A. B. B. BAINES.

STRICKLAND, JACOB

P. 66. Aug. 18, 1788 - May Ct. 1790. Sons:
1. ELISHA, 2. JACOB, 3. MATTHEW, 4. MARKE, 5. HARDY -
362 A., 6. HENRY, 7. SOLOMON. Dau: CREESY HICKMAN.
Gr. chil: ISAAC, son of ELISHA STRICKLAND, JACOB, son
of JACOB STRICKLAND, MARY, dau. of MATTHEW STRICKLAND,
ISMEL, son of MARKE STRICKLAND, THEOPHILUS STRICKLAND,
CARROLUS, son of HENRY STRICKLAND, CREESY HICKMAN, SARAH
HICKMAN. Ex: Son MARKE STRICKLAND. Wit: EDWARD
NICHOLSON, CHRISTOPHER TAYLOR, WILLIAM BYRD (or BURDEN).

STRICKLAND, JACOB

P. 559. May 14, 1858 - Aug. Ct. 1858. Wife:
ELIZABETH. Sons: 1. C. M. J., 2. F. K. W., 3. WILLIAM,
4. WAYMORE, 5. WALTER R., 6. NALBY M. Daus:
1. MAHALY, 2. MARGARET. Ex: Son F. K. W. STRICKLAND.
Wit: JNO. B. RICE, J. T. WEBB.

STRICKLAND, JOSEPH

P. 17. Mar. 4, 1779 - Apr. Ct. 1781. Sons:
1. JESSE, 2. DAVID. Daus: 1. PATIENCE, 2. MARY,
3. ELIZABETH. Gr. sons: MARMADUKE MASON - 100 A.
whereon I live, BURWELL STRICKLAND. Ex: Sons DAVID
STRICKLAND and RALPH MASON (son-in-law?). Wit: DUN.
LAMON, ARCH. LAMON, MARY LAMON.

STRICKLAND, MARKE

P. 218. Aug. 6, 1811 - Nov. Ct. 1811. Wife:
MARTHA. Sons: 1. GIDEON - 500 A. south side Toisnot
Swamp, 2. ISHMEAL, 3. OSBORN - land whereon he lives
except 250 A., 4. ELIE - land and mill whereon he lives,
also 250 A. reserved, where OSBORN lives, 5. MARK - land
whereon I live, also the other half of mill and 300 A.
on Turkey Crk. Gr. sons: MARK, son of ISHMEAL - 300 A.
on Turkey Crk., JACOB, son of GIDEON - 300 A. on Turkey
Crk. Daus: 1. ELLENDER SAUNDERS, 2. JINNY STRICKLAND,

3. REBECCA STRICKLAND.   Gr. dau: NANCY SANDERS (?).
Ex: Son OSBORN, friend NOAH STRICKLAND.   Wit: THOMAS
HAMILTON, DAVID CREEKMORE, WM. TAYLOR, SR. (Clerk's
notes say WILSON TAYLOR, SR.)

STRICKLAND, NANCY
    P. 407. Dec. 12, 1834 - May Ct. 1835.   Friend:
WARREN STRICKLAND - all estate.   Ex: A. B. B. BAINS,
SR.   Wit: HARRY FERRELL, A. B. B. BAINS.

STRICKLAND, NOAH
    P. 277. Oct. 21, 1809.   Wife: ELIZABETH - lend
part of plantation whereon I live adjoining my son
BOLLIN STRICKLAND, ADKINS and THOMAS CARTER - with
reversion to my son WILLIAM DEW STRICKLAND.   Sons:
1. BOLLIN - land whereon EDWARD CLINCH lived adjoining
s. side Tar R., Horse Pen Branch and Tarboro Rd.,
2. EDWARD - land north side Tar River, 3. NOAH - land
adjoining THOMAS CARTER, WILLIAM DEW STRICKLAND, and
Tar R., also 80 A. adjoining THOMAS CARTER and ROLAN
WILLIAMS, also 300 A. on both sides Turkey Creek adjoining HARDY STRICKLAND and BENJAMIN RICE, 4. WILLIAM DEW
STRICKLAND - land on Board (?) Tree Branch and THOMAS
CARTER'S line, also 150 A. on both sides Turkey Crk.,
adjoining HARDY STRICKLAND and ROBERT VICK.   Dau:
1. MARY ADKINSON - 218 A. whereon she lives, also
100 A. joining ROLAND WILLIAMS and HARDY STRICKLAND.
Ex: WILLIAM BUNTIN, HENRY ADKINS, JR.   Wit: MATHEW
CARTER, ROBERT CREEKMORE, THOMAS CARTER.

STRICKLAND, OSBON (OSBORNE)
    P. 534. June 5, 1850 - no probate date.   Sons:
1. ISAAC - land where he lives, 2. HARDY - money to buy
land, 3. WILLIAM D. - 80 A. where he lives, 4. OSBON -
all land on north side ARTHUR WILLIAM'S Branch, also
my grist mill and 100 A. on north side Cooper's Crk.
and part of land around the mill.   Dau: 1. ELIZABETH
TISDAL, my son ISAAC to be guardian for her children.
Gr. sons: HENDERSON MORGAN, WILLIAM MORGAN, WILLEY
(WILEY?) MORGAN - the three of them to have land. Ex:
JOHN W. BRYANT, JACOB STRICKLAND.   Wit: EVAN H.
MORGAN, WM. B. MORGAN.

STRICKLAND, ZADOCK
    P. 578. Aug. 30, 1860 - Nov. Ct. 1861. Wife:
REBECCA. Sons: 1. ALLISON - 100 A. on Bidatoe (?)
Br. adj. SION SANDERS and F. K. W. STRICKLAND,
2. MADISON, 3. REDDING, 4. C. O. STRICKLAND'S heirs.
Daus: 1. RENNY, wife of RUFFIN TAYLOR, 2. ROENNY,
wife of HILLIARD PERRY, 3. NANCY, wife of EVAN H.
MORGAN, 4. SUSAN, wife of PRESLEY ROOKER, 5. CHARITY,
wife of ELIAS BERGERON. Ex: Son ALLISON. Wit:
JOHN W. PERRY, WM. STONE.

SULLIVANT, JAMES
    P. 525. Feb. 1850 - Nov. Ct. 1851. All estate
left in trust for the use and care of MARGARETT HAMMOND
(now aged about 14 yrs.) and for her mother CHARITY
HAMMOND. The trust to be administered by my Ex: JACOB
STRICKLAND. Wit: DANIEL S. CRENSHAW, J. M. TAYLOR.

SULLIVANT, OWEN
    P. 433. Jan. 29, 1838 - May Ct. 1839. Wife:
MARTHA. Sons: 1. CORNELIUS, 2. TIM. Daus:
1. BETSEY BOYKIN, 2. POLLY ANDERSON, 3. LUCY SULLIVANT.
No Ex. Wit: LEVI BAILY, EXUM EATMAN.

SUMNER, EDWIN
    P. 446. Dec. 24, 1836 - May Ct. 1837. Wife:
SALLY. Son and Ex: JOHN LEWIS SUMNER. "Children"
unnamed. Wit: JO BELL, CHARLES HARRISON. Ordered
recorded Nov. Ct. 1840.

SUTTON, THOMAS
    P. 179. Dec. 2, ? - Nov. Ct. 1807. Wife: CATHERINE.
Sons: 1. LEMWELL, 2. JOHN, 3. VINSON. Daus:
1. CHARLOTTE LANDMAN, 2. MARGET, 3. CATHERINE - legacy
from her uncle GEORGE SUTTON. Gr. sons: NELSON LANDMAN,
OWEN LANDMAN. Ex: Wife CATHERINE, son VINSON. Wit:
EDWARD YORK, THOMAS BRYANT.

TANN, BENJAMIN
    P. 170. Sept. 11, 1806 - Nov. Ct. 1806. Wife:
PRECILER (PRISCILLA). Son and Ex: BENJAMIN - 190 A.
Dau: OMEY LOUIS (LEWIS). "All my children" unnamed.
Ex: JOHN RICE, ESQ. Wit: J. TAYLOR, EDW. YORK.

TAYLOR, ARTHUR

   P. 319. Sept. 9, 1823 - Nov. Ct. 1823. Wife and
Extx: ALSEE. Sons: 1. ARTHUR DEW TAYLOR - all land
on n. side of road except 3 A. adjoining the new house,
2. DREWRY TAYLOR - 3 A. adjoining the new house and
land on south side of the road adjoining FORD TAYLOR,
3. HENRY HINES TAYLOR - the other half of land lying on
south side of the road, adjoining JOHN RICE. Daus:
1. SALLY WIET TAYLOR, 2. NANNEY (NANCY) TAYLOR,
3. LITHA HORN TAYLOR. Wit: D. WINSTEAD, JOHN RICE,
JR., DREWRY JOINER, JR.

TAYLOR, CHRISTOPHER

   P. 310. May 31, 1808 - Nov. Ct. 1822. Wife: MARY.
Sons: 1. MILES - 250 A. adjoining HENRY ATKINSON,
2. WILLIAM - 350 A. adjoining MILES, 3. MERRY - 400 A.
whereon I live, at death of his mother. Daus:
1. ZILPHA BRANTLEY, 2. TEMPY TAYLOR. Ex: Wife MARY,
WILSON TAYLOR. Wit: WM. TAYLOR, JOHN POULAN, HENRY
W. H. POULAN, DREWRY TAYLOR.

TAYLOR, DEMPSEY

   P. 477. Apr. 6, 1837 - May Ct. 1845. Sons:
1. TALTON SCREWS, 2. LABON SCREWS, 3. DEMPSEY CALVIN
TAYLOR. "I hereby authorize my executors.....to
legitimate and alter the names of my two sons, TALTON
SCREWS and LABON SCREWS, agreeable to an act of the
General Assembly, to TALTON TAYLOR and LABON TAYLOR".
Daus: 1. LUCINDA TAYLOR, 2. POLLY TAYLOR. Friend:
JOHN FLETCHER. Ex: JACOB ING, KINCHEN TAYLOR, SAMUEL
L. ARRINGTON. Wit: JOSHUA LONG, GUILFORD COLEY, FED
BATTLE.

TAYLOR, DRURY

   P. 198. Feb. 13, 1808 - Feb. Ct. 1809. Wife:
ROSAMOND. Sons and Ex: 1. ARTHUR - 60 A. land south
side Tar River on lines of DINAH POULAN and WILSON
TAYLOR, SR., 2. SIMON - 150 A. on south side Tar River
on lines of Dickenson Br. and DAVID WINSTEAD, 3. DRURY-
remaining land. Gr. son: JOHN C. TAYLOR. Wit:
URIAH HATCHER, EDWARD TAYLOR, HENRY W. POULAN.

TAYLOR, HARDY

P. 203. Sept. 15, 1809 - Nov. Ct. 1809. Mother:
SARAH WREN. Bros: BOYKIN, SAMUEL. Sis: SELAH
DRAKE. Ex: Bro. SAMUEL TAYLOR. Wit: MICAJAH
BRIDGERS, MONFORD WILHEIGHT.

TAYLOR, HARRY

P. 46. May 31, 1788 - Nov. Ct. 1788. Wife:
SARAH. Sons: 1. ETHELDRED - 3 tracts of land lying
in Franklin County, lying on Turkey Creek - one tract
purchased of JAMES BRADLEY, one from THOMAS GLOVER,
the third from ARTHUR BOWDEN - altogether 802 A.,
2. SAMUEL, 3. HARRY, 4. HARDY, 5. JOHN, 6. BOYKIN -
HARDY, JOHN, and BOYKIN to have plantation whereon I
live, at mother's death. Daus: 1. ELIZABETH BODDIE,
2. CELIA TAYLOR. Gr. son: ELIJAH BODDIE. Ex:
Son ETHELDRED TAYLOR, friend WILLIAM LANCASTER of
Franklin Co. Wit: WILLIAM LANCASTER, THEOPHILUS
ODOM, ROBERT ROGERS.

TAYLOR, JAMES - Nuncupative will

P. 110. May 4, 1796 - Aug. Ct. 1796. Son: JOHN.
Daus: 1. FERELIZE (?), 2. PATSEY. Gr. dau: SILFE
(SYLVIA or ZILPHA?). Proved by oath of HARDY MORGAN
before WILLIAM HAMMONDS.

TAYLOR, JOHN

P. 106. Sept. 28, 1794 - May Ct. 1796. Wife:
RUTH. Sons: 1. DEMPSEY - land where he lives,
2. WILLIAM - land where he lives, 3. JOHN - part of
land I purchased of ROBERT VICK on Bogg Branch,
4. WILEY - 279 A. where I live, including mill, part
of land on Toisnot Swamp, purchased of ROBERT VICK,
also 200 A. on south side the Swamp adjoining
STRICKLAND STALLINGS. Daus: 1. DELILAH, 2. ELIZABETH,
3. JUDAH. Ex: Sons DEMPSEY, WILLIAM and JOHN TAYLOR.
Wit: WILSON TAYLOR, JACOB WHEELER, RICHARD DEAN.

TAYLOR, JOSIAH

P. 497. Dec. 8, 1846 - Feb. Ct. 1847. Sis: MARY
MANN, WINNIFRED TAYLOR. Bro: KINCHEN TAYLOR. Ex:
BENJAMIN MANN. Wit: WILLIAM E. BELLAMY, WILLIAM
DOZIER.

TAYLOR, KINCHEN

P. 544. Feb. 3, 1851 - No probate date. Wife: MARY-
the NICHOLSON land where I live, also the adjoining land
purchased of REBECCAH HILLIARD. Sons: 1. NICHOLSON
TAYLOR, 2. KINCHEN TAYLOR - the DUNCAN CAIN land and the
HINES land adjoining it, 3. HENRY A. TAYLOR and
4. BENJAMIN B. TAYLOR - to share the BALDY CAIN tract,
the POWELL tract and the CROWELL tract, 5. JOHN A.
TAYLOR and 6. THOMAS H. TAYLOR - to share the C. POWELL
tract, N. POWELL tract and mill tract, 7. WILLIAM C.
TAYLOR - reversion of mother's land. Daus: 1. ELIZA
BRADDY, 2. WINEFORD ROSSER, wife of WM. ROSSER,
3. CAROLINE KNIGHT, wife of WM. H. KNIGHT - the GARRET
land and WM. DOZIER land, 4. LUCY H. TAYLOR - the
WHELESS tract, 5. ELIZABETH TAYLOR - the NINES tract.
Gr. dau: MARY MANN. Ex: Son KINCHEN, and JACOB ING.
Wit: WILLIAM D. BRYAN. TARTTON (TARLETON?) TAYLOR.

TAYLOR, MARINDA

P. 543. Mar. 28, 1850 - Nov. Ct. 1854. Sons:
1. RUFFIN, 2. BENNETT, 3. DENNIS, 4. DEMPSEY. Dau:
1. LUCY WILLIAMS. Gr. chil: JOSEPH TAYLOR, JANE
TAYLOR, MARY TAYLOR, CALVIN TAYLOR, BOLIN TAYLOR, JAMES
TAYLOR, DANIEL TAYLOR, ZADOCK TAYLOR. Ex: MATHEW
WILDER. Wit: BRYANT BILBRO, MATHEW WILDER. When
offered for probate, the court declared the paper, not
having been executed according to law, is not the last
will and testament of MARINDA TAYLOR, and refused to
admit it to probate.

TAYLOR, REUBEN

P. 307. Dec. 6, 1821 - Nov. Ct. 1822. Wife:
WINEFORD. Sons: 1. WILLIAM - ½ all my Nash Co. land,
joining JOHN F. BELLAMY, 2. ALLEN - other ½ of Nash Co.
land, 3. REUBEN - land in Edgecombe Co., 4. DEMPSEY,
5. KINCHEN, 6. JESSE. Daus: 1. PENELOPE POPE,
2. ELIZABETH WHITEHEAD, 3. POLLY HOUSE. Ex: Sons
DEMPSEY and WILLIAM TAYLOR. Wit: JACOB ING, LITTLEBERRY
POPE.

TAYLOR, WILSON

P. 346. Jan. 21, 1827 - May Ct. 1827. Wife:

ELIZABETH. Sons: 1. ASA, 2. CALVIN - land whereon I
live at his mother's death. Dau: 1. POLLY. Ex:
DUNCAN YORK. Will signed in city of Raleigh. Wit:
JAMES M. HENDERSON, J. D. BARR, G. BOBBITT.

TERRELL, JOEL
    P. 305. Jan. 29, 1820 - Feb. Ct. 1820. Wife:
POLLY. Ex: Father-in-law WILLIE BUNN. Wit: WM.
TAYLOR, MATT CARTER, WILSON WILLIAMS.

THOMAS, JESSE
    P. 147. Jan. 6, 1804 - Feb. Ct. 1804. Wife: MARY.
Sons: 1. JESSE - land on lines of Peachtree Crk., JOHN
ALSTON, JOSEPH THOMAS, Spring Branch, REUBEN WHITFIELD,
Marsh Branch and JACOB THOMAS at mother's death,
2. JOSEPH, 3. JACOB (is intimated - but not clear).
Daus: 1. MARY, 2. ELIZABETH, 3. CHLOE, 4. MOURNING.
Ex: Friends ARCHIBALD GRIFFIN, JOHN LEWIS. Wit:
JOHN MELTON, JAMES UZELL.

THOMAS, JETHRO
    P. 144. June 20, 1803 - Nov. Ct. 1803. Wife and
Extx: SUSANNA. Sons: 1. RICHARD, 2. ETHELDRED,
3. HENRY B. - sons to have all land. Daus: 1. SALLY
VICK, 2. MILDRED THOMAS, 3. SOPHIER THOMAS, 4. SUSANNA
THOMAS. Ex: Son-in-law JOEL VICK. Wit: ARCH.
GRIFFIN, CHARITY GRIFFIN.

THOMAS, MICAJAH
    P. 49. May 17, 1778 - Nov. Ct. 1788. Half-bro:
JOSIAH CRUDUP. Father-in-law: PHILEMON HAWKINS.
Nephews: GEORGE BODDIE - 5000 A. lying on the waters
of the Tennessee R., entered in JOHN ARMSTRONG'S office
in my own name; BENNETT BODDIE; Nieces: MOURNING
ARRINGTON, RHODA RICKS, TEMPERANCE PERRY, MARY PERRY.
Legatee: ANN JACKSON, mother of my 3 daus., MOURNING
THOMAS JACKSON, MARGARET THOMAS JACKSON, and TEMPERANCE
THOMAS JACKSON. Natural daus: 1. MARY CRAWFORD,
child of the late ELIZABETH CRAWFORD of Surry Co., Va.-
all my land on north side Roanoke R. in Northampton
Co., N. C. purchased of SAMUEL COTTEN and the estate
of FREDERICK RUFFIN - 1500 A., 2. MOURNING THOMAS
JACKSON - 2500 A. on lines of NATHAN BODDIE, WILLIAM

BODDIE, JAMES WOODARD, RICHARD HOLLAND, DAVID EVANS, GEORGE WIMBERLEY, JULIAN KING, and JESSE THOMAS on Peachtree Crk., Pig Basket Crk., and Tar R., also 420 A. on north side Tar R., and also 640 A. on western waters of N. C., it being a soldier's warrant, 3. MARGARET THOMAS JACKSON - 3000 A. between Peachtree Crk. and Sappony Swamp, including the Court House, the WHEDDEN and REUBEN WHITFIELD places, also 600 A. on Pig Basket Crk., and also 640 A. on western waters of N. C., it being a soldier's warrant, 4. TEMPERANCE THOMAS JACKSON - 2000 A., all my lands on both sides Tar R., lying within the following lines: SAMUEL BRYANT, MALPHUSSES OWENS, JULIAN KING, REUBEN WILLIAMS, WILLIAM BRASWELL, JOSHUA STEVENS, EDWARD PURCELL and JOHN WARREN, also 2000 A. on lines of HENRY TAYLOR, ROBERT ROGERS, DRURY ALFORD, JESSE BASS, MATTHEW DRAKE, WILLIAM LINDSEY, and JOHN JONES, also 800 A. on Back Swamp on lines of THOMAS HILL (Franklin Co.), JOHN WEBB, JOSIAH JOHNSON, MASSINGALE, and ROBERT ROGERS, also 640 A. on western waters of N. C., it being a soldier's warrant. If these 3 last named natural daus. die without heirs, their property is to be equally divided between BENNETT BODDIE, GEO. BODDIE, JOHN CRUDUP, and GEORGE CRUDUP. Legatees: JULIAN KING - 200 A. on lines of ROBERT BRASWELL, DAVID EVANS, GEORGE WIMBERLEY, and Pig Basket Crk., SOLOMON COTTEN - 5000 A. on western waters of N. C., entered in the name of WILLIAM McDONALD, also 2 yrs. boarding, clothing, and schooling, JACOB BUTTS- 1 yrs. board and schooling. Ex: NATHAN BODDIE, WILLIAM BODDIE, BENJAMIN HAWKINS, SHADRACK RUTLAND. Wit: WILSON VICK, SAMUEL WESTRAY, THADDEUS BARNES, HARDY BROWN.

THOMAS, REBECCA
    P. 132. Mar. 24, 1797 - May Ct. 1800. Son: JETHRO THOMAS. Dau: MARY STRICKLAND, wife of JOSEPH STRICKLAND. Gr. dau: CHARITY STRICKLAND, dau. of MARY. Ex: Son-in-law JOSEPH STRICKLAND. Wit: WILLIAM ARRINGTON, ARCHIBALD HUNTER.

THOMAS, RICHARD
    P. 28. Oct. 15, 1784 - No prob. date. Wife: REBECCA.

Son: JETHRO - 400 A. on north side Maple Crk. Daus:
1. MOURNING, 2. MARY. Ex: Son JETHRO, DUNCAN LAMON,
MICAJAH THOMAS, WILSON VICK. Wit: DUN. LAMON, WILSON
VICK, HENRY BUNN.

THORN, TAYLOR
P. 536. Nov. 25, 1853 - Feb. Ct. 1854. Sons:
1. RED, 2. JOHN E., 3. WILLIAM B., 4. JOSEPH,
5. THEOPHILUS T. Daus: 1. MARTHA RICKS, 2. MARY JONES,
3. TEMPERANCE L. THORN. Ex: JOHN E. THORN. Wit:
JAMES W. RICKS, MOURNING DRAKE.

THORP, PRISCILLA
P. 259. Nov. 2, 1814 - Nov. Ct. 1814. Sons:
1. JAMES - land south side of the road, 2. ANSELEM and
3. HENRY - to share all land on north side of the road,
4. JESSE. Daus: 1. FRANCES HORN, 2. PHEBE HARRIS,
3. NANCY BUNN, 4. PRISCILLA THORP, 5. REBECCA THORP.
Ex: Son JESSE, JOSIAH HORN. Wit: SAM SMITH, JOHN
ATKINSON, MARY HARRISON.

TISDAL, ELIZABETH
P. 602. July 12, 1865 - No prob. date. Sons:
1. GEORGE W., 2. JOSEPH - 30 A. adjoining WM. WOODARD
and H. T. BENNETT. Dau: SALLIE ANN. This document
is in the form of a deed of gift. No Ex. Wit: H. G.
BENNETT, W. P. WALKER.

TISDEL (TISDAL), HENRY
P. 193. June 20, 1808 - Aug. Ct. 1808. Father
unnamed. Wife: MOURNING. Sons: 1. RENNISON, 2. JOEL,
3. ELISHA. Daus: 1. NANCY O'NEAL, 2. ANZADA TISDEL.
Son-in-law: THEOPHILUS O'NEAL. Ex: Son RENNISON
TISDEL, friend FREDERICK HOLMAN. Wit: JACOB WHEELER,
JOHN THOMAS, REBECCA WHEELER.

TOMLINSON, ISAAC
P. 147. Sept. 27, 1802 - Feb. Ct. 1804. Legatee:
Friend JAMES HILLIARD - 60 A. lying on lines of JESSE
KITCHEN and JONATHAN WHITEHEAD. Ex: JESSE KITCHEN.
Wit: HENRY MITCHELL, JACOB BARROTT, JAKE HILLIARD,
JESSE KITCHEN.

TOMPKINS, ROSANAH
    P. 518. April, 1845 - Aug. Ct. 1849. Sons: 1. PETER
R. HINES - his present wife being his second wife,
2. JOHN FRANKLIN TOMPKINS. Ex: RICHARD HINES and my
son PETER R. HINES. Wit: BENNETT H. BUNN, MOURNING
DRAKE. Clerk's notes: Proven by the oath of MOURNING
DRAKE; proof of handwriting by BENJAMIN F. KNIGHT.

TREVATHAN, WILLIS
    P. 264. Jan. 5, 1815 - Feb. Ct. 1815. Wife: MARY.
Sons: 1. WILLIAMSON, 2. MATTHEW. Daus: 1. SALLY
TREVATHAN, 2. SELAH (or LILAH) TREVATHAN, 3. NANCY ROSE,
4. PENELOPE PRICE, 5. CHARLOTTE PRICE. Ex: Son
MATTHEW. Wit: JOHN ATKINSON, LEWIS HINES.

TUCKER, BENJAMIN
    P. 367. Oct. 15, 1829 - Feb. Ct. 1830. Wife: AMEY.
Sons: 1. BARNABAS, 2. THOMAS. Daus: 1. MARTHA
MUSAW?, 2. ELIZABETH VESTER, 3. BARSHABA WILLIAMS,
4. ELIZA VESTER. Gr. chil: HIXSEY, KELLY, EDWIN, and
JOHN STYLES. Son of wife: DREWRY SAVAGE. Son-in-
law: GUILFORD GRIFFIN. Ex: SION UPCHURCH. Wit:
R. (RICHMOND) UPCHURCH, ALBERT UPCHURCH.

TUCKER, DINAH
    P. 208. Sept. 11, 1795 - May Ct. 1810. Son and
Ex: JOAB. Daus: 1. DINAH YOUNG, 2. TAMMEN WHITFIELD,
3. ANAS PARROT, 4. PATIENCE TAYLOR, 5. ANN BATCHELOR.
Wit: ROBERT E. CREEKMORE, DANIEL BATCHELOR, BALLENTINE
CREEKMORE.

TUCKER, EASTER
    P. 401. Feb. 10, 1830 - May Ct. 1836. Legatees:
ELIZABETH PRIVETT, LUKE PRIVETT. Wit: WILLIS WARD,
JOHN S. MATHIS.

TUCKER, JAMES
    P. 228. Feb. 11, 1797 - Feb. Ct. 1797. Wife:
FARABEE. "My children" unnamed. Ex: MARCOM COOPER.
Wit: ROBERT CREEKMORE, WILLIAM TISDAL, JOSIAH MELTON.

TUCKER, LEWIS B.
   P. 439. Aug. 21, 1840 - Nov. Ct. 1840. Wife:
ELIZABETH. Bro: JOAB TUCKER of Miss. Mother: FANNEY
TUCKER. Sis: NICY TUCKER, UNA LINDSEY. Legatee:
MARIAH BILBRO - all land (dau?). Ex: LEROY MITCHELL.
Wit: BENJAMIN BILBRO, THOMAS GAY.

TUCKER, THOMAS of Edgecombe Co.
   P. 16. Mar. 5, 1778 - no probate date. Wife:
MARGRET. Sons: 1. THOMAS - 25 A. whereon I live,
2. WILLOBY. Daus: 1. CUZIAH (KIZZIAH), 2. BETTY.
Ex: Wife MARGARET, son THOMAS. Wit: STEPHEN YOUNG,
THOMAS MORRIS.

TUCKER, THOMAS
   P. 620. Feb. 21, 1871 - Aug. 12, 1872. Wife:
MARTHA - 50 A. Sons: 1. TAYLOR - remaining land,
2. WRIGHT (Ex). Daus: 1. FRANCES - to share mother's
land, 2. MARTHA ROWLAND, wife of DR. ROWLAND, 3. REBECCA
KING (is not designated as dau). Gr. sons: GEORGE
K. TUCKER - land, DITSON TUCKER - land. Wit: N. W.
COOPER, JAMES T. AVENT. Codicil, Mar. 18, 1872, will-
ing 15 A. to dau. MARTHA ROWLAND, it to be woodland
taken from that left my gr. sons GEO. K. TUCKER and
DITSON TUCKER, and adjoining THOMAS H. GARNER and
THOMAS W. AVENT. If she leaves no heir, it is to revert
to gr. sons named above. Wit: N. W. COOPER, JAMES T.
AVENT.

TUNNELL, BYRD B.
   P. 587. May 1, 1861 - May Ct. 1864. Wife:
DRUSILLA. Son: 1. MASSILON L. (minor) - 298 A.
Daus: 1. MARY A. E. FORT, wife of JACOB G. FORT -
278 A., 2. VIRGINIA BRADLEY - 288 A. Trustee for care
of MARY A. E. FORT and her chil - and for MASSILON L.
TUNNELL: JOHN E. THORN. Ex: WILLIAM W. PARKER. Wit:
WILLIE WHITLEY, HENRY A. WHITLEY.

TURLINGTON, JOHN
   P. 27. Sept. 22, 1783 - Apr. Ct. 1784. Wife:
ELIZABETH. Sons: 1. TIMOTHY, 2. THOMAS. Dau: MARY.
Ex: JACOB RICKS. Wit: WILSON VICK, PENELOPE CLARK.

TURNER, JAMES

P. 103. April 30, 1788 - Feb. Ct. 1796. Wife: ANN.
Son: JAMES - 313 A. Daus: 1. NANNY TURNER,
2. ELIZABETH TURNER, 3. MARTHA GRIFFIN, 4. MARY
VALENTINE, 5. JULIAN TURNER. Gr. son: LAZARUS TURNER,
JOHN VALENTINE. Ex: Wife ANN, son JAMES. Wit:
ALANSON POWELL, JOHN POWELL.

TURNER, LAZA

P. 532. April 20, 1852 - Feb. Ct. 1853. Wife:
REBECCA. Sons: 1. HENRY and 2. GEORGE - the two young-
est; other sons unnamed. "Each of my daughters" unnamed.
Ex: NATHANIEL H. MURPHY. Wit: WILLIAM WHITLEY, HENRY
WHITLEY.

TURNER, WILLIAM

P. 467. Jan. 30, 1838 - Feb. Ct. 1843. Wife:
MILLY - plantation. Son: SION. "All my children"
unnamed. Ex: W. W. BODDIE. Wit: ELIAS BARRETT,
E. WILLIE GRIFFIN.

UNDERWOOD, JACOB

P. 120. Sept. 11, 1798 - Nov. Ct. 1798. Wife:
HANNAH. Sons: 1. HOWELL, 2. MALECHI, 3. ZACHARIAH,
4. LEVI - land whereon I live and that on north side
Compris (Compass?) Crk. Daus: 1. SALLY HATTIN
(HATTON?), 2. DOLLY UNDERWOOD. Ex: REDMUN BUNN,
ARCHIBALD HUNTER. Wit: JOHN FLETCHER, PHILLIP ALSTON.

VAUGHAN, DEMPSY

P. 70. Oct. 17, 1789 - Aug. Ct. 1790. Wife:
EASTER. Sons: CHRISTOPHER - all land. Ex: BURREL
ROSE. Wit: CHRISTOPHER VAUGHAN, EFRAM VAUGHAN.

VAUGHAN, EPHRAM

P. 128. Feb. 10, 1797 - May Ct. 1797. Wife and
Extx: PATY (PATTY). Son: Vinson - 103 A. whereon I
live. Daus: 1. MOLLEY, 2. PRESTON, 3. PATTY, 4. HULDAY.
Three youngest: PATTY, HULDAY, VINSON. Ex: ROBERT
CREEKMORE. Wit: JOSIAH MELTON, STEPHEN VAUGHAN.

VESTER, BENJAMIN
P. 472. June 22, 1844 - Nov. Ct. 1844. Wife:
CHERRY. Sons: 1. ABISHA, 2. WILEY, 3. NATHAN,
4. SOLOMON, 5. ELIJAH, 6. BENJAMIN H., 7. JORDAN
(youngest) - reversion of land whereon I live. Daus:
1. SEBRINA SUTTON, 2. NANCY VESTER, 3. FRANCES VESTER
(youngest). Ex: JARMAN WARD. Wit: J. W. HOPKINS
(Clerk: J. H.), ALFRED UPCHURCH.

VESTER, WILLIAM
P. 137. Mar. 3, 1801 - May Ct. 1801. Wife:
ELIZABETH. Sons: 1. NATHAN and 2. WILLIAM (two
eldest) - to have 100 A. at mother's death. Other
children: POLLEY VESTER, ELIZABETH VESTER MERRITT,
GREEN VESTER, TEMPERANCE VESTER, SUCKEY VESTER. Ex:
JETHRO BASS. Wit: PETER ETHRIDGE, WILLIAM VESTER,
REBECCA JONES.

VESTER, WILLIAM
P. 145. Jan. 12, 1804 - Feb. Ct. 1804. Sons:
1. JOSEPH, 2. WILLIAM'S heirs (apparently deceased).
Dau: DINAH ETHRIDGE. CORNEALIAS? BRUCE'S heirs.
Ex: GEORGE BODDIE. Wit: ABIJAH PRIDGEN, PETER
ETHRIDGE.

VICK, BENJAMIN
P. 152. June 12, 1804 - Nov. Ct. 1804. Wife:
MARY. Sons: 1. RICHARD - all land east side Mill
Branch, 2. BENJAMIN, 3. ASEL. Dau: CHARITY BECKWITH.
Ex: Bro. JOHN VICK, friend ARCHIBALD GRIFFIN. Wit:
JAS. WILLIAMS, ACHASH VICK.

VICK, BENJAMIN
P. 186. Oct. 11, 1807 - Feb. Ct. 1808. Mother:
MARY VICK. Bro: ASAEL VICK. Ex: Friend ARCHIBALD
GRIFFIN. Wit: DELILAH HUNT, PATIENCE VICK.

VICK, B. S.
P. 585. Jan. 28, 1862 - Nov. Ct. 1862. Wife:
NANCY K. VICK - entire estate. Ex: NEVERSON W. COOPER.
Wit: H. (HENRY) G. WILLIAMS, W. F. ROWLAND.

VICK, ELIZABETH
    P. 368. April 17, 1830 - May Ct. 1830. Sis: LUCY
TUNSTALL. Nephews: BOLDEN WALKER, JAMES WALKER, JOHN
C. HINES. Nieces: NANCY HINES, MARY ANN HINES.
JAMES HARTWELL WALKER, son of BOLDEN WALKER. Ex:
TIMOTHY FERRELL. Wit: ELIZABETH VICK, MARTHA VICK.

VICK, ELIZABETH
    P. 597. Oct. 28, 1863. Gr. dau: ARABELLA C.
WALKER - first choice, and an equal portion of estate.
Should she die without an heir, property to be divided
between legal heirs. Ex: Neph. JOHN THORP. Wit:
E. L. CURL, VIRGINIA L. D. CURL. JOHN THORP refused
to qualify, and DAVID RICKS was named Admin.

VICK, HENRY
    P. 563. June 23, 1859 - Aug. Ct. 1859. Mother:
MARTHA VICK. Bro: JOSIAH VICK (Ex). Sis: LOUISA
ODUM. Aunt: PHERABA WHITEHEAD. Wit: T. P. WESTRAY,
DAVID L. BUNN.

VICK, ISAAC
    P. 380. Jan, 1832 - Feb. Ct. 1832. Wife: CHARITY.
Sons: 1. HENRY, 2. JOHN. Daus: 1. SALLY, 2. POLLY
HARRIET. Ex: Friend GRANBERRY VICK. Wit: JOINER
LANGLEY, SHERROD WILLIAMS.

VICK, JOHN
    P. 282. Feb. 5, 1816 - May Ct. 1816. Wife:
ELIZABETH. Unnamed children appear to be quite young.
Ex: EDMUND BARROW, SAM WESTRAY. Wit: REUBEN HARRELL,
ELIZABETH HINES.

VICK, JOHN
    P. 402. Oct. 25, 1826. Wife: SUSANNAH. Sons and
Ex: 1. JOSIAH, 2. LITTLE GRANDBERRY VICK. Daus:
1. NANCY DEBERRY JOINER, 2. CATHERINE WINSTEAD. No
Wit.

VICK, JOHN "old and infirm"
    P. 374. April 5, 1831 - Nov. Ct. 1831. Wife: MARY.
Sons: 1. JOEL (apparently dec'd) - "his children",
2. ELI (apparently dec'd) - "his children", 3. JOSIAH

(apparently dec'd) - "his children", 4. ELIJAH - land
on lines of Allen's Branch and LODERICK F. ELLEN,
5. JOHN VICK (apparently dec'd) - "his children". Daus:
1. PRISCILLA WHITFIELD, 2. PATIENCE VICK - chil. she now
has or may have. Gr. chil: LOUISA, JOHN and BENJAMIN,
who are chil. of JOSIAH VICK; WILLIAM VICK, son of JOHN-
remaining land; LUDENDA and MARY M. V. VICK, chil. of
ELI VICK - 30 A. each, adjoining ASHAEL VICK; VILETT
GRIFFIN (VIOLET); POLLY JONES; ORPHALINE VICK, dau. of
JOHN VICK; CHARITY BATCHELOR, dau. of JOEL VICK; ISAAC,
JOHN, PENELOPE and ELI WHITFIELD, chil. of PRISCILLA
WHITFIELD. Note: POLLY JONES and VILETT GRIFFIN are
not designated as daus. or gr. daus., but are listed
along with gr. chil. Ex: Son ELIJAH VICK, Nephews
SAMUEL W. W. VICK, ASHAEL VICK. Wit: JOHN RICKS, WM.
H. HALL. Codicil, dated April 9, 1831, provides for:
JACKY C., ELIZABETH W., HARRIET JANE, RAHAB, and EBELINE
(EVELINE?), chil. of son ELIJAH VICK. Wit: JOHN RICKS,
RUFFIN GRIFFIN.

VICK, LEWIS
    P. 230. Mar. 6, 1801 - Aug. Ct. 1806. Son: JACOB-
150 A. whereon I live, purchased from HARTWELL and THOMAS
HART. Daus: 1. ACHRAH (?), 2. ELENDER, 3. MARY -
daus. to share 150 A. purchased of DAVID DANIEL. Ex:
Son JACOB and JAMES WILLIAMS, constable (?). Wit: JOHN
VICK, JOS(H)UA VICK.

VICK, LEWIS
    P. 568. Aug. 25, 1859 - Aug. Ct. 1860. Sons:
1. JOSEPH JOHN - 191 A. adjoining BLUFORD WILLIAMSON,
R. D. WELLS, W. R. CARTER, 2. HOWEL R., 3. B. L. VICK.
Daus: 1. ELIZABETH, wife of JOSEPH POLAND, 2. JINCY
VICK, 3. TEMPY, wife of JOSIAH PARKER. Ex: Son JOSEPH
JOHN VICK, son-in-law JOSIAH PARKER. Wit: BLUFORD
WILLIAMSON, J. J. Q. TAYLOR, DREWRY PRIDGEN.

VICK, MARGARET
    P. 593. Sept. 27, 1853 - Aug. Ct. 1865. Son and
Ex: W. W. PARKER - entire estate. Wit: MARMADUKE
RICKS, SPENCER D. RICKS. SPENCER D. RICKS dead on pro-
bate date.

115

VICK, MARY
    P. 399. Sept. 30, 1821 - May Ct. 1836. Son and
Ex: ASAEL - all my land adjoining ELI VICK, JOHN VICK,
and JOSEPH STRICKLAND. Dau: CHARITY BECKWITH. Wit:
HARDY G. WHITFIELD, WILLIAM DORTCH.

VICK, NATHAN SR.
    P. 408. Oct. 28, 1834 - May Ct. 1835. Wife: MARY.
Sons: 1. NATHAN, JR., 2. MATTHEW, 3. WILLIAM. Daus:
1. CHLOE WATKINS, 2. CHRISTIAN ODOM, 3. POLLY BRASWELL.
Ex: Neph. SAM W. W. VICK. Wit: JOHN H. VICK, PHEREBE
WHITEHEAD.

VICK, ROBERT
    P. 108. June 30, 1796 - Aug. Ct. 1796. Sons:
1. ROBERT, 2. JACOB (Ex). Wit: JOHN TAYLOR, JEREMIAH
CREMER.

VICK, SUSANNAH
    P. 471. Feb. 22, 1842 - May Ct. 1842. Sons:
1. GRANBY, 2. JOSIAH (Ex). Daus: 1. NANCY DLECY ?
JOYNER, 2. CATHERINE WINSTEAD - 85 A. called the SAMUEL
WINSTEAD PINEY WOODS, adj. ELI CRUMPLEY and JOSIAH VICK,
whereon she lives. Wit: A. B. BAINES, JR., DUNCAN
FLOYD.

VINSON, SALLIE
    P. 620. Mar. 19, 1857 - Feb. Ct. 1868. Nephew:
THOMAS WOOD - 132 A. known as the COLLINS place, adjoin-
ing HENRY ROBERTSON, provided he returns to North
Carolina. Nieces: SALLIE COLLINS, IRENE COLLINS,
MARTHA HOPKINS, wife of WHITMEL HOPKINS. Legatees
(apparently nephews and niece): BRITTON WOOD, SALLIE
COLLINS, wife of CLIFTON COLLINS, JOHN WOOD, son of my
dec'd bro. BRITTON WOOD. Ex: DR. THOMAS DAVIS. Wit:
WM. HUNT, W. H. EDWARDS. Clerk's notes: THOMAS DAVIS
being dead, BRITTON WOOD was appointed Admin. entered
into bond of $2000 with JAMES VINSON, J. T. WEBB,
BENNETT GAY and WHITMEL HOPKINS as sureties.

VIVERETT, THOMAS
    P. 78. Oct. 12, 1791 - Nov. Ct. 1792. Wife:
ELIZABETH. Sons: 1. HENRY - land s. side Little Swamp,

2. LAUNCELOT - land both sides a prong of Town Crk.,
3. MICAJAH - land on north side Tar R., 4. JAMES - land
whereon I live.   Ex: LAMON RUFFIN, NATHAN TART, JESSE
PITMAN. Wit: THOMAS WELLS, ROLAND ROBBINS, JESSE
PITMAN.

WALKER, JOEL
    P. 267. July 12, 1813 - Aug. Ct. 1815.   Wife:
SILVIA. Sons: 1. MICAJAH - 100 A. where he lives,
2. JONATHAN, 3. LEMUEL - 25 A.where he lives, also that
already given him, 4. JACOB - 75 A. where he lives on
north side Tumblin Crk. on lines of EDWARDS and WILLIAMS,
also what is in his possession, 5. JESSE - 100 A. where
I live. Daus: 1. JEMIMA HEDGEPETH, 2. POLLY KITTLE,
3. PATSEY WALKER. Ex: Sons JACOB and JESSE. Wit:
JACOB JOHNSTON, ABRAHAM HEDGEPETH.

WALL, JAMES
    P. 10. Feb. 21, 1778 - April Ct. 1780. Daus:
1. SARY (SARAH), 2. BETTY.   If daughters die without
heirs, my estate shall go to NATHAN POWELL, son of
NATHANIEL POWELL. Ex: JOHN POWELL, JAMES CAIN. Wit:
JOHN DAVIS, HENRY SCREWS.

WARD, FRANCIS
    P. 133. Oct. 20, 1800 - Nov. Ct. 1800. Wife: SARAH.
Sons: 1. BENJAMIN - mill, until JOHN WARD comes of age,
2. JOHN WARD, alias MATHEWS, the child my wife had before
wedlock - all my land in Halifax Co., N. C., except 112 A.
purchased of MARK PITTS, 3. FRANCIS - land where I live
at mother's death, also land purchased of MARK PITTS,
ARCHILBALD DAVIS, SAMUEL MILLER, LEWIS MILLER, BENJAMIN
SANDEFORD and SAMUEL MITCHELL, 4. NATHAN - land purchased
of POLLACK, 5. WILLIAM - land purchased of JAMES GOODWIN.
Daus: 1. FANNY WARD - land purched of PRYOR GARDNER,
2. MARY SOUTHALL, 3. SALLEY AVENT - 400 A., part of land
purchased of ARCHIBALD DAVIS, 4. NANCY JONES, 5. PRISYLA
NEWSOM (PRISCILLA).   He does not indicate which are "my
four youngest children by my last wife".   Gr. chil:
BETSEY JONES, BETSEY JARRATT (JARRETT), THOMAS ANDERSON.
Ex: ARCHIBALD DAVIS, BENJAMIN WARD, JOHN HARRISON. Wit:
MARK PITT, BENJAMIN BLUNT, GEORGE GARDNER, JOE WARD.

WARD, NATHAN
   P. 311. Apr. 27, 1821 - May Ct. 1823. Bro: JOHN
WARD (alias MATTHEWS) - 1000 A. Ex: Neighbor JOHN
HARRISON, SR. Wit: BENJ. BLOUNT, JAMES HARRISON, JOHN
N. BURNETT.

WARD, WILLIS
   P. 563. Dec. 19, 1857 - Nov. Ct. 1859. Wife: LUCY.
Sons: 1. CALVIN - part of remaining land, 2. GERMAN -
part of remaining land, 3. JOHN - 50 A. where he lives.
Daus: 1. NANCY DOZIER, 2. CHERRY WINSTEAD, 3. AQUILLA
WINSTEAD, 4. LUCINDA EVANS, 5. DOROTHY HAMILTON,
6. SALLIE ANN BATCHELOR. No Ex. Wit: B. H. SORSBY,
T. I. BODDIE.

WARREN, MARY
   P. 528. May 30, 1852 - Aug. Ct. 1852. Son and
Ex: WILLIS WARREN. Daus: 1. FANNY, 2. NANCY MANNING-
her heirs, 3. SUSAN BOON - her heirs. Son-in-law:
THOMAS CREEKMORE. Wit: BENJAMIN BILBRO, URIAH
CREEKMORE.

WATKINS, HENRY
   P. 150. Mar. 23, 1804 - May Ct. 1804. Wife: MARY.
Sons: 1. THOMAS - 50 A. whereon I live on north side,
Kerbey's Crk., 2. STEPHEN, 3. HENRY, 4. JAMES, 5. JOSEPH.
Daus: 1. AMY DAVENPORT, 2. ANNA AMMONS?, 3. SUSANNA
ROBBINS, 4. SARAH CLIBON, 5. ELIZABETH WEAVER, 6. JINNEY
WATKINS, 7. ? COBB, 8. RHODA SANDERS, 9. MARY REVELL,
10. BEVETON WATKINS, 11. MOURNING WINSTEAD, 12. RACHEL
WATKINS. Ex: JACOB HORN, JOHN ATKINSON. Wit: JOHN
ATKINSON, ELIZABETH PAETRICK.

WATKINS, ISAAC
   P. 308. Sept. 23, 1814 - Nov. Ct. 1822. Mother:
NANCY WATKINS. Bro: JOHN WATKINS. Sis: CHARLOTTE
RICKS, SARRY RICKS, ELIZABETH WATKINS, NANCY SCARBOROUGH,
DELILA WATKINS. Ex: MARMADUKE MASON. There being no
wit - handwriting proven by DREW HUNTER, JOHN RICKS and
SAMUEL VICK. It was further sworn by JAMES W. DANCE
that will was found among papers of ISAAC WATKINS.

WATKINS, JOHN

P. 189. May 2, 1808 - May Ct. 1808. Wife: NANCY-
400 A. on north side Kirbey's Crk., reversion to sons.
Sons: 1. JOHN - land on north side Kirbey's Crk.,
2. ISAAC - land on south side Kirbey's Crk., also ½ my
interest in mill. Daus: 1. CHARLOTTE WATKINS,
2. SALLEY RICKS. Ex: JACOB HORN, son ISAAC WATKINS.
Wit: JOHN WATKINS, SAM SMITH, M.(MARMADUKE) MASON.

WELLS, ABSALOM - Nunc. will

P. 106. Jan., 1795 - May Ct. 1796. Bro: REDMAN
WELLS. Estate to be settled by STEPHEN WELLS. Sworn
statement by STEPHEN WELLS and JOEL BUNN.

WELLS, ELIZABETH

P. 208. Nov. 27, 1809 - Feb. Ct. 1810. Son and
Ex: JEREMIAH. Dau: MARTHA DAUGHTRIDGE. Wit:
SAMUEL L. LAMKIN, THOMAS POPE.

WELLS, FREDERICK

P. 3. Nov. 16, 1778 - Jan. Ct. 1779. Bros:
JOSHUA - land received from my father; SOLOMON WELLS.
Ex: JOS. CROWELL. Wit: JOANNA ROBINS, BARBARA POPE.

WELLS, JOEL

P. 618. Oct. 16, 1869 - July 23, 1873. Friends:
ROBERT H. RICKS - 16 shares capital stock in Wilmington
and Weldon Railroad and $1000, JOHN H. THORP of Rocky
Mount, N. C. - all remaining estate. Ex. Wit: JOHN
E. LINDSEY, DAVID B. RICKS.

WELLS, SOLOMON

P. 64. May 8, 1789 - Feb. Ct. 1790. Legatee:
JOHN WELLS, son of STEPHEN WELLS. Sis: PRISCILLA
POPE. Cousins: LEWIS JACKSON, JOHN WELLS, son of
REDMON WELLS - 350 A. whereon I live, in case he dies
without heirs, land reverts to his brother, STEPHEN
WELLS, STEPHEN WELLS, son of REDMON WELLS. Ex:
Friend WILSON VICK. Wit: SAM WESTRAY, RICH. VICK,
THOMAS HORN.

WELLS, STEPHEN

P. 171. Mar. 18, 1807 - May Ct. 1807. Wife:

ELIZABETH. Sons: 1. JEREMIAH - 150 A. where I live, 2. STEPHEN, JR. - 100 A. adjoining VICK, PRIDGEN, and JOSHUA WELLS, 3. JOHN. Dau: MARTHA DAUGHTRIDGE. Ex: Sons JOHN and JEREMIAH WELLS. Wit: JOHN VICK, JOSEPH COCKRELL, DELILAH POPE.

WELLS, STEPHEN
P. 533. Mar. 6, 1850 - May Ct. 1853. Wife: MARY-all land where I live. Sons: 1. BARTLEY, 2. REDMOND D. - Ex. Ex: Friend J. J. T. TAYLOR. Wit: NELSON BONE, DREWRY PRIDGEN, WILLIAM ASBURY PRIDGEN.

WESTER, ARTHUR
P. 75. Feb. 10, 1792 - Feb. Ct. 1792. Sons: 1. HARDY, 2. WILLIAM, 3. BENJAMIN. Gr. son: ELI WESTER. Daus: 1. MARY WESTER, 2. KISSIAH WESTER, 3. PATIENCE JOYNER. Gr. dau: POLLY WESTER. Ex: Son HARDY, friend LEWIS CURL. Wit: ROGER REESE, JOSIAH WHITLEY.

WESTRAY, SAMUEL
P. 353. April 1, 1827 - Feb. Ct. 1828. Wife: SALLY. Son: TURNER P. WESTRAY - the GANDY place on Great Sapponey Crk., adjoining JACOB BARNES, also the Academy with the 25 A. around it, also the reversion of the land whereon I live, at the death of his mother. Dau: MARTHA, wife of DR. JOHN ARRINGTON - lower part of Fishing Crk. plantation, adjoining DANIEL WALKER, also the ELI B. WHITAKER land. Legatee: JAMES S. BATTLE. No Ex. Wit: H. BLOUNT, ELIZA H. EDWARDS.

WESTRAY, SARAH B.
P. 434. Sept. 8, 1838 - May Ct. 1839. Son and Ex: 1. TURNER P. WESTRAY, 2. WILLIAM SHORT. Daus: 1. SARAH HARRIETT, wife of JAMES S. BATTLE, 2. MARTHA SMITH, wife of DR. JOHN ARRINGTON, 3. MARY ANN, wife of DR. ISAAC SESSUMS. Gr. chil: SARAH B. SHORT, JOURDAN HILL SHORT, THOMAS SHORT, the chil. of my son WILLIAM SHORT; gr. chil: HARRIET ELIZA, wife of DR. JOSEPH DRAKE, SOLOMON and? DAVID SESSUMS, chil. of my dau. MARY ANN SESSUMS. Gt. gr. child: WILLIAM SMITH JOURDAN, child of MARY JANE JOURDAN. Wit: J. W. CLARK.

WESTRY, WILLIAM
     P. 514. Mar. 7, 1847 - Nov. Ct. 1848. Sons:
1. WILLIS, 2. WILLIAM, 3. BENNETT. Daus: 1. CHARLOTTE
BATCHELOR, 2. MARGARET MANNING, 3. TEMPERANCE WESTRY,
4. ELIZABETH BATCHELOR. Gr. chil: NANCY I. WESTRY,
MARY MANNING, MARTHA MANNING, ELIZABETH MANNING,
ELIZABETH WESTRY, WILLIAM S. WESTRY. The last two
gr. children were children of son WILLIAM WESTRY.
JOHN THORN appointed by the will as Guardian for the
two children of WILLIAM WESTRY. Friend BENNETT BARNES
trustee for son BENNETT WESTRY JUNIOR (?). Ex. and
Guardian for dau. TEMPERANCE WESTRY - son-in-law
SAMUEL McBATCHELOR. Wit: CORDAL N. F. ELLIN, JOHN
E. JONES.

WHELESS, AMOS
     P. 130. Jan. 18, 1800 - Feb. Ct. 1800. Wife and
Extx: MILBRY. Chil: 1. SUFFIA (SOPHIA?),2. ARCHIBALD,
3. DOLPHIN, 4. PATSEY, 5. CHARLOTTE. Ex: COOPER
WILLIAMS, ARCHIBALD DAVID (DAVIS?). Wit: BENJAMIN
BRIDGERS, DENTON MANN, WM. WHELESS.

WHELESS, WILLIAM
     P. 186. Nov. 12, 1807 - Feb. Ct. 1808. Sons:
1. HARDY, 2. DREWERY. Daus: 1. EDNEY, 2. POLLY.
"My 8 chil." Ex: WM. B. WHELESS, JOEL WHELESS, HARDY
WHELESS. Wit: CHARLES GANT, WILLIAM GANT.

Preface to will of WILLIAM WHELESS
     P. 365.   .....My will is that all estate, both real
and personal, which was conveyed to me in trust by a
deed or marriage contract executed Jan. 20, 1820 between
DAVID SILLS of the first part, ELIZABETH WILHITE of the
second part, and myself (WILLIAM WHELESS) of the third
part, shall be by my executors, administrators or heirs
at law conveyed and transfered to each and every person
who shall be named in the said DAVID SILLS' will or in
any other instrument of writing, my executors, administrators or heirs shall convey aforesaid estates as the
aforesaid deed or marriage settlement directs.

WHEELESS, WILLIAM
     P. 365. Feb. 6, 1829 - Nov. Ct. 1829. Wife:

ELIZABETH. Sons: 1. BENJAMIN WHEELESS, 2. AMOS
WHEELESS, 3. JOHN WHEELESS, 4. ELIJAH WHEELESS. Daus:
1. PATSEY WHELESS, 2. BATHANY STOKES, 3. ELIZABETH
WHELESS, 4. MILDRED HAMMONDS. Ex: DAVID SILLS,
WILLIAM HAMMONDS, son B ENJAMIN WHELESS. Wit: AZARIAH
KING, THOMAS W. WRIGHT.

WHIDDEN, LOTT SR.
    P. 30. Dec. 28, 1784 - Feb. Ct. 1785. Wife: SARAH.
Chil: 1. MAXWELL, 2. ELIZABETH, 3. JAMES. Ex: Son
WILLIAM WHIDDEN, MARCOM COOPER. Wit: WM. HALL,
BRINKLY GANDY, ISHAM GANDY.

WHITE, ELIZABETH
    P. 404. May 9, 1833 - Nov. Ct. 1836. Son: JOSEPH
WHITE. Dau: PATSEY WHEELESS. Wit: G. BASS, MARY
LANDFORD.

WHITE, GULIELMUS
    P. 151. Feb. ?, 1804 - May Ct. 1804. Gr. dau:
MARY WHITE. Ex: Friend JAMES WILLIAMS. Wit: T. W.
WHITE, SION WHITLEY.

WHITE, JOSEPH SR.
    P. 96. Dec. 4, 1794 - Feb. Ct. 1795. Wife:
GUELMINUS (?). Sons: 1. THOMAS, 2. JOSEPH, 3. ARMEGER.
Daus: 1. ANN HALL, 2. ESTHER SMITH, 3. GULIEMA ?
GRIFFIN. Gr. daus: MARY WHITE, MILICENT WHITE. Ex:
Son JOSEPH WHITE. Wit: JAMES WILLIAMS, HOWELL ELLIN,
BETTY ELLIN.

WHITE, JOSEPH JR.
    P. 240. Jan. 18, 1795 - Feb. Ct. 1795. Wife:
SARAH. Son: THOMAS - 650 A. land. Daus: 1. ELIZABETH,
2. MARTHA, 3. MARGARET. Ex: Friends EDMUND DRAKE,
LEWIS VICK. Wit: PENWELL (PENUEL) FLOYD, JOHN MELTON,
MARGARET BASS.

WHITE, LITTLEBERRY
    P. 469. Sept. 29, 1831 - Nov. Ct. 1842. Wife:
ELIZABETH - 216 A. whereon I live, bought of HENRY

BANDES (BANDY?). Sons: 1. JOSEPH HARTSFIELD WHITE - land bought of WILLIAM BILBRO, tract bought of TITUS LEWIS, 2. JOHN WHITE des'd (his chil.), 3. WILLIAM HEATH WHITE, 4. LITTLEBERRY, 5. CHARLES, 6. EDWARD, 7. ABRAHAM, 8. WORTHAM. Daus: 1. MARY HUNT, 2. ANN FOLKS, 3. PEGGY COOPER, 4. ELIZABETH BUNTING, 5. MARTHA WHELESS. Ex: Son JOSEPH HARTSFIELD WHITE, LEROY MITCHELL, CULLOM MOORE. Wit: THOMAS SAVAGE, W. L. ABERNATHY, WILLIE HINDRIOT (?). Codicil, Dec. 23, 1834 - wife ELIZABETH now deceased, the land left to her shall be divided between my chil. JOSEPH H. WHITE and MARTHA WHELESS. Wit: A. H. DAVIS, W. L. ABERNATHY, THOMAS SAVAGE.

WHITEHEAD, ELIZABETH
    P. 384. Dec. 4, 1828 - May Ct. 1832. Daus:
1. ABIAH CULPEPPER, wife of MATHEW CULPEPPER,
2. MOURNING BALEY, wife of RICHARD BALEY (BAILEY).
Gr. chil: RICHARD THOMAS BALEY, ROBERT WILLIAMSON
BALEY, LAVINA MOURNING BALEY, EVALINA F. BALEY, SALLEY
BALEY (BAILEY). Ex: JOSEPH ARRINGTON. Wit:
BENJAMIN BLUNT (BLOUNT). "Same had been established
in Superior Court in Warren Co., as will of ELIZABETH
WHITEHEAD - ordered recorded."

WHITEHEAD, BENJAMIN
    P. 232. Dec. 6, 1794 - no probate date. Wife:
MARY (and Ex.). Sons: 1. JONATHAN, 2. CHARLES,
3. BENJAMIN, 4. JAMES, 5. WILLIAM, 6. JOSEPH. The last
named 4 to share my land. Daus: 1. MILBURY (MILBRY)
MASON, 2. ISABEL MASON, 3. MARY WHITEHEAD, 4. MARTHA
WHITEHEAD. Ex: Son BENJAMIN, Friend JOSEPH ARRINGTON.
Wit: JAMES SANDERFORD, HENRY WHITEHEAD, JOEL COOPER.

WHITEHEAD, JAMES
    P. 542. April 6, 1847 - Nov. Ct. 1854. Nephew and
Ex: PORTLAND C. WHITEHEAD - whole estate. Wit: JOSHUA
WATSON, GEO. W. POWELL.

WHITEHEAD, MARY
    P. 169. Jan. 17, 1797 - Nov. Ct. 1806. Chil:
1. BENJAMIN, 2. MARY, 3. JAMES, 4. WILLIAM, 5. JOSEPH,

6. MARTHA.   Ex: Bro. JOSEPH ARRINGTON, son BENJAMIN
WHITEHEAD.   Wit: MARTHA ARRINGTON, ELIZABETH C.
ARRINGTON.

WHITEHEAD, NATHAN
   P. 4. Mar. 20, 1778 - Apr. Ct. 1779. Wife:
RACHEL.   Sons: 1. NATHAN - 540 A. where I dwell (2
tracts), also 312 A. on Moccasin Crk., 2. BENJAMIN,
3. THOMAS, 4. HENRY.   Daus: 1. RHODA NICHOLSON,
2. PHERIBY SANDERFORD, 3. CHLOE CULPEPPER, 4. ISABEL
BELL, 5. MARY SANDERFORD.   Gr. son: NATHAN, son of
THOMAS.   Ex: Wife RACHEL and son THOMAS WHITEHEAD.
Wit: ARTHUR ARRINGTON, MARTHA ARRINGTON, ELIZABETH
ARRINGTON.

WHITEHEAD, NATHAN
   P. 222. Sept. 14, 1811 - Nov. Ct. 1811.   Wife
unnamed.   Son: NATHAN - whole estate at mother's
death.   If he dies before reaching maturity, his
Negroes shall be divided between ARTHUR WHITEHEAD,
MATTHEW WHITEHEAD, and THOMAS WHITEHEAD'S 3 children.
His land, if he dies before maturity, shall be divided
between ARTHUR WHITEHEAD, MATHEW WHITEHEAD, THOMAS
WHITEHEAD, JR., and JAMES BATTLE'S children he has had
by my sister, and the children of MOURNING BAYLEY.   Ex:
ARTHUR WHITEHEAD, GEORGE BODDIE.   Wit: WM. BODDIE,
TEMPERANCE BODDIE.   Codicil, with same witnesses, made
Sept. 16, 1811 provides for possible unborn child.

WHITEHEAD, THOMAS
   P. 180. May 21, 1798 - Nov. Ct. 1800.   Wife:
ELIZABETH.   Sons: 1. NATHAN, 2. THOMAS, 3. MATTHEW,
4. ARTHUR - 550 A. whereon I live.   Daus: 1. ABIAH
CULPEPPER, 2. MOURNING WHITEHEAD.   Gr. son: THOMAS
BATTLE.   Ex: Sons NATHAN and ARTHUR WHITEHEAD.   Wit:
RICHARD ARRINGTON, WILLIAM ANDERSON, RACHAL WHITEHEAD.

WHITEHOUSE, JOHN
   P. 209. Aug. 31, 1809 - Nov. Ct. 1810.   Wife:
PATSEY.   Son: JOHN LAMON WHITEHOUSE.   Ex: DAVID
RICKS.   Wit: JOHN RICKS, WILLIAM RICKS.

WHITFIELD, BENJAMIN

P. 181. Oct. 17, 1807 - Feb. Ct. 1808. Wife:
DELILAH. Sons: 1. WILLIE WHITFIELD, 2. GUILFORD
GRIFFIN WHITFIELD, 3. ARCHIBALD WHITFIELD, 4. BENJAMIN
GRIFFIN WHITFIELD, 5. JOHN THOMAS GRIFFIN WHITFIELD -
my land on east side Lassiter's Branch, also tract
bought of DAVID STRICKLAND, including the grist mill.
Daus: 1. ELIZABETH WHITFIELD, child of my second wife
ELIZABETH, 2. DREWSY BUNN, child of my now wife - land
bought of THOMAS HART and THOMAS W. WHITE, 3. _____?
TISDAL and her husband PHILANDER TISDAL - land bought
of WILLIAM WILLIAMS. Gr. dau: MARTHA MATILDA
WHITFIELD - land bought of THOMAS. Ex: Wife DELILAH,
NATHAN GILBERT, JOHN ATKINSON. Wit: JAMES WILLIAMS,
DREW HUNTER, JOSEPH STRICKLAND.

WHITFIELD, CHARITY

P. 540. Jan. 4, 1852 - Aug. Ct. 1854. Niece:
PENELOPE PRICE and her chil. - my whole estate. Ex:
JOHN E. THORN. Wit: EDWIN EDWARDS, THEOPHILUS T.
THORNE.

WHITFIELD, DELILAH

P. 300. Mar. 26, 1818 - Nov. Ct. 1818. Sons:
1. HARDY G. WHITFIELD, 2. WILLIE G. WHITFIELD,
3. GUILFORD G. WHITFIELD, 4. ARCHIBALD G. WHITFIELD,
5. BENJAMIN G. WHITFIELD, 6. JOHN T. G. WHITFIELD.
Daus: 1. PRISCILLA TISDALE, 2. DRUCILLA DORTCH. Ex:
Son HARDY G. WHITFIELD. Wit: BATSON SMITH, ASA SNEED.

WHITFIELD, ISAAC

P. 238. Jan. 6, 1796 - no prob. date. Wife:
EASTER. Father and Ex: SOLOMON WHITFIELD. Wit:
JOHN HAYS, HENRY BUNN, DREW HUNTER.

WHITFIELD, MARY

P. 239. Feb. 19, 1792 - no prob. date. Son:
ELISHA WHITFIELD. Legatee - no relationship given:
SOOKEY WHITFIELD LONG. Ex: ARCHIBALD GRIFFIN. Wit:
LUCY GRIFFIN, SOOKEY WHITFIELD.

WHITFIELD, MARY

P. 468. Apr. 26, 1843 - May Ct. 1844. Sis: CHARITY

WHITFIELD - 60 A. whereon I live. No Ex. Wit: JOHN
RICKS, MOURNING STRICKLAND.

WHITFIELD, PENELOPE
    P. 576. Oct. 20, 1858 - Nov. Ct. 1861. Mother:
PENELOPE NICHOLSON. Daus: 1. MARY J. WHITFIELD,
2. MATILDA JOYNER, 3. ELIZA WHITFIELD. Gr. dau: MARTHA
FRANCES JOYNER. Ex: REDMUN BUNN. Wit: JAMES F.
ODUM, ELIAS BUNN. Codicil, April 5, 1859, wit. by:
JAMES F. ODUM, EDWIN EDWARDS.

WHITFIELD, REUBEN
    P. 273. Feb. 5, 1816 - Feb. Ct. 1816. Daus:
1. MOURNING WHELESS, 2. CATHERINE WHITLEY. Ex: RICHARD
HOLLAND. Wit: ISAAC SESSUMS.

WHITFIELD, SARAH
    P. 413. Dec. 16, 1835 - Aug. Ct. 1836. Sis:
MARY WHITFIELD, CHARITY WHITFIELD. Niece: TEMPERANCE
MELTON. Ex: JOHN RICKS. Wit: RICHARD RICKS,
DREWSEY DORTCH.

WHITFIELD, SOLOMON
    P. 194. Dec. 8, 1807 - Nov. Ct. 1808. Wife: ANN.
Son: JACOB - all land. Daus: 1. SARAH, 2. MILLY
MELTON, 3. MARY, 4. NANCY, 5. CHARITY, 6. WINNIE
NOLLEJOY. Mentions furniture bought of J. MELTON.
Ex: Son JACOB WHITFIELD, JOHN VICK. Wit: SAM WESTRAY,
WM. SHORT, SALLIE B. WESTRAY.

WHITFIELD, THOMAS
    P. 224. July 6, 1781 - Jan. Ct. 1782. Wife: MARY.
Sons: 1. THOMAS, 2. REUBEN, 3. SOLOMON, 4. JOHN,
5. WILLIAM, 6. BENJAMIN, 7. ELISHA, 8. ISRAEL - 115 A.
part of land where I live, on lines of RICHARD THOMAS
and Peachtree Crk., 9. HARDY - 150 A., the remainder of
land where I live. Daus: 1. MARY, 2. SARAH, 3. MILDRED,
4. ELIZABETH. Ex: Sons SOLOMON and HARDY WHITFIELD.
Wit: JACOB DICKINSON, WILLIS WHITFIELD, CHLOE WHITFIELD.

WHITFIELD, THOMAS
    P. 229. May 21, 1798 - Nov. Ct. 1800. Wife and

Ex: ELIZABETH. Sons: 1. WILLIS, 2. MATHEW - the 2
sons to have all land. Daus: 1. MARY WILLIS, 2. SARAH
BRYANT, 3. CHLOE STOKE (?), 4. NANCY MASSENGILL. Ex:
Friend SAM WESTRAY. Wit: MARY VICK, SOPHIA VICK.

WHITFIELD, WILLIAM
    P. 335. May 12, 1826 - Aug. Ct. 1826. Sons:
1. WILLIAM, 2. ELISHA. Gr. dau: WILLEY WHITFIELD.
Old friend: CHARITY RAY "for her good conduct, her
industry and careful services rendered to me for the
space of 40 years" - remainder of estate. Ex: WILLIAM
WHITFIELD, JR. Wit: A. B. BAINS (ABSALOM), JAMES B.
BAINES.

WHITFIELD, WILLIAM JR.
    P. 356. April 27, 1826 - May Ct. 1828. Wife:
EDY - 200 A. 3 sons unnamed - 348 A. No Ex. Wit:
WILLIAM JOHNSTON, ANDREW JOHNSTON.

WHITLEY, JOSIAH
    P. 372. Mar. 12, 1821 - May Ct. 1831. Sons:
1. WILLIE, 2. SION W. - my land, 3. JOEL. Dau:
MOURNING BATCHELOR. Ex: TIMOTHY FERRELL. Wit:
EXUM L. CURL, JNO. S. BUNN.

WHITLEY, MILLS
    P. 450. June 20, 1834 - Nov. Ct. 1836. Wife:
MARTHA. Sons: 1. JOSIAH, 2. HENRY, 3. WILLIAM. Gr.
dau: ELIZABETH JOHNSON. Ex: JOSHUA WATSON. Wit:
BYTHEL BRYANT, BLOUNT COOPER. Ordered recorded Nov.
Ct. 1840.

WHITLEY, SION
    P. 436. June 13, 1839 - May Ct. 1840. Wife:
PRUDENCE. Sons: 1. JOHN - reversion of 227 A. adjoin-
ing JOHN JONES, DAVID JONES, and DANIEL A. DUGGINS,
2. JOSIAH, 3. SION, 4. WIATT, 5. DAVID, 6. LITTLEBERRY,
7. LAWRENCE. Gr. son: ISAAC WHITLEY. Gr. dau: MARY
JANE WHITLEY, dau. of SUSAN WHITLEY. Daus: 1. SUSAN
WHITLEY, 2. CHARLOTTE WHITLEY, 3. CHARITY BECKWITH.
Wit: WILLIAM DOZIER, THOMAS GRIFFIN.

WHITLEY, THOMAS
    P. 240. Dec. 2, 1800 - no prob. date. Son: THOMAS.
Daus: 1. EDITH LANGLEY, 2. ELIZABETH MARSHALL. Friend:
MARTHA THOMAS. Ex: SOLOMON WHITFIELD. Wit: JOHN
ATKINSON, HOWELL UNDERWOOD, PENELOPE CLARK.

WHITLEY, WILLIE
    P. 575. April 24, 1861 - Nov. Ct. 1861. Sons:
1. JOHN D. - 100 A., 2. JAMES D., 3. WILLIE D., 4. JOEL
B. - 100 A., 5. ARTHUR A. - land where he lives with
reversion to son JOHN D., also part of land where I
live. Daus: 1. ELIZABETH RACKLEY, 2. MARTHA ANN
RACKLEY, 3. KATHERINE P. WHITLEY. Gr. chil: YANCEY
M. RACKLEY, MATILDA J. RACKLEY, WILLIE F. M. RACKLEY,
WILLIAM J. RACKLEY. The above named appear to be the
children of FRANCIS and ELIZABETH RACKLEY. SARAH E.
RACKLEY, CELESTIA ANN D. RACKLEY, MARTHA AN F. RACKLEY.
Ex: Son JOHN D. WHITLEY. Wit: R. H. MARRIOTT,
REDMUN BUNN.

WILDER, MATHEW
    P. 576. Dec. 22, 1857 - Nov. Ct. 1861. Wife:
MARTHA. "All my heirs". Ex: Sons MATHEW WILDER,
JOHN W. WILDER. Wit: BENNETT GAY, SHERWOOD GAY.

WILLIAMS, BENJAMIN
    P. 298. June 15, 1818 - Aug. Ct. 1818. Wife:
CHARITY. Sons: 1. LAWRENCE, 2. BENJAMIN, 3. THOMAS,
4. LUNFORD (LUNSFORD?) - 4 sons to have all land. Daus:
1. SARAH, 2. CHARITY ALFORD. Ex: GEORGE WILLIAMS,
HENRY WILLIAMS, JESSE HAMMOND. Wit: JOSEPH EARP,
JESSE HAMMOND, HENRY WILLIAMS.

WILLIAMS, BENJAMIN
    P. 451. Apr. 22, 1841 - May Ct. 1841. Wife:
MARSILLA. Ex: BENJAMIN W. AVENT. Wit: JAMES
DOZIER, FRANCIS AVENT.

WILLIAMS, BILLEY
    P. 148. April 10, 1804 - May Ct. 1804. Wife and
Extx: CHARITY. Sons: 1. SAMUEL - 2 tracts on Toisnot
Swamp, called the old place and Mirey Branch place,

2. DRURY - 3 tracts, one called CAULSON place, one on
Beaver Dam, one on Juniper, 3. WILLIAM M. - plantation
whereon I live adjoining JOHN EATMAN. Daus: 1. TRECEY
KENT, 2. LUCY WILLIAMS, 3. NANCY WILLIAMS, 4. MORNING
WILLIAMS, 5. CHRISEY WILLIAMS, 6. BUNCH WILLIAMS -
100 A. on Beaver Dam. Ex: Bro. DRURY WILLIAMS, NOEL
EATMAN. Wit: JAMES BROWN, BIDY EATMAN, BURWELL KENT.

WILLIAMS, CHRISTIAN
    P. 274. Apr. 15, 1815 - Feb. Ct. 1816. Sons:
1. KINCHEN, 2. BURRELL, 3. ELIAS, 4. MATHEW, 5. JAMES.
Daus: 1. ZILPHEY, 2. MARY, 3. ELIZABETH, 4. LUCY,
5. SALLEY. Wit: WILLIAM WHELESS, LEMUEL WALKER,
E. (EDWIN) EDWARDS.

WILLIAMS, JOHN W.
    P. 617. Nov. 18, 1872 - Dec. 19, 1872. Legatee:
1. ESAKIAH (HEZEKIAH) E. FLOWERS, son of LOUISA FLOWERS,
afterwards LOUISA ROE - 150 A., 2. JAMES HOWARD, son
of SALLY HOWARD - 97½ A. adjoining the home tract, and
WILLIE FARMER, 3. JOSEPH J. WILLIAMS, son of my sister,
4. VIRGINIA FLOWERS, wid. of BENNET FLOWERS, 5. ROENA
STRICKLAND, wife of HENRY STRICKLAND - $120 for her
great kindness, attention and services to me while
affected, 6. JOSEPH J. WILLIAMS. Ex: A. B. BAINES.
Wit: JOHN W. RICE, HENDERSON RICE.

WILLIAMS, PHILLANDER
    P. 242. May 3, 1794 - no prob. date. Wife:
ELIZABETH. Sons: 1. SAMUEL - 690 A. on north side
Tar R., 105 A. adjoining LEWIS JOINER and DREWRY
JOINER, also 180 A. which is part of tract bought of
BRITTON SMITH, also 100 A., formerly owned by THOMAS
PRIDGEN, also 270 A. purchased of JOSEPH CROWELL, in
all 1350 A. when he arrives at 18 yrs., 2. PRIDE -
650 A. on south side Tar R. when he arrives at 18 yrs.
Daus: 1. POLLY, 2. NANCY, 3. ELIZABETH, 4. JEAN.
Ex: LEWIS LAMKIN, DAVID PRIDGEN. Wit: JOHN LAMON,
ARTHUR ALLEN, ROLAND WILLIAMS.

WILLIAMS, ROLLEN (ROLAND)
    P. 279. Dec. 30, 1813 - Feb. Ct. 1816. Wife:

MARTHA. Son: PILGRIM S. WILLIAMS - all land. Daus:
1. DINAH, 2. CHARITY, 3. ELIZABETH, 4. PRISCILLA (her
heirs). THOMAS RICKS (no relationship given - but
appears to be gr. son), son of URBAN RICKS; TEALE
RICKS, son of URBIN RICKS (ERVIN?). All money paid
in discharge of debts against estate of THOMAS RICKS
desc. to be deducted from legacy bequeathed to sons of
URBAN RICKS. (Could URBAN be dau. of ROLAND WILLIAMS,
having married THOMAS RICKS?) Ex: Son PILGRIM S.
WILLIAMS, WILSON TAYLOR, JR. Wit: WILLIAM HORN,
THOMAS HORN, THOMAS CARTER.

WILLIAMS, SAMUEL of St. Mary's Parish, Edgecombe Co.
    P. 17. Feb. 18, 1773 - Oct. Ct. 1781. Wife:
ANNE - land on north side Tar R., adjoining ARTHUR
ALLEN and CANADAY. Son and Ex: PHILANDER. Daus:
1. DELILAH POPE, 2. SARAH, 3. CHARITY, 4. ZELPAH,
5. SISLY. Legatee: BETTY CONE. Ex: ROWLAND
WILLIAMS. Wit: EDWARD MOORE, SOLOMON POPE, HARDY
STRICKLAND.

WILLIAMS, SAMUEL
    P. 547. Dec. 14, 1854 - Aug. Ct. 1855. Sons:
1. NATHAN C. - part of land on west side Mirey Br. on
lines of WM. McWILLIAMS and Toisnot Bridge - to be
held for his son, RICHARD S. WILLIAMS, until he come
of age. Dau: 1. AQUILLA GRIFFIN - land where she
lives, to be held for her son, FLETCHER GRIFFIN.
Property to be divided between 9 lawful heirs. Ex:
Son NATHAN. Wit: PETER EATMAN, ALEXANDER EATMAN.

WILLIAMS, SARAH
    P. 190. June 14, 1808 - Aug. Ct. 1808. Sons:
1. ROWLAND, 2. JONAS, 3. JOEL, 4. DRURY. Dau:
MORNING TISDALE. Gr. sons: DRURY and SAMUEL, sons
of BILLEY WILLIAMS, desc'd., KEDDICK DRIVER, son of
NANNIE DRIVER, desc'd., NATHAN, son of NATHAN WILLIAMS,
desc'd. Gr. son? NATHAN PERSON. Ex: Sons JONAS
and DRURY WILLIAMS. Wit: WM. MOORE, JOHN WILLIAMS.

WILLIAMSON, JOSEPH SR.
    P. 113. June 25, 1797 - May Ct. 1797. Wife and
Ex: ANN. Sons: 1. JOSEPH - land northeast side of
Marsh Swamp where he lives, 2. THOMAS - land where I
live, 3. HARDY. Daus: 1. SARAH, 2. ANN, 3. PENELOPE.
Ex: Son HARDY WILLIAMSON. Wit: J. NICHOLS, JOSEPH
WILLIAMSON, JR., JOHN NICHOLS.

WILLIFORD, MEEDY H.
    P. 490. Aug. 23, 1846 - Nov. Ct. 1846. Wife:
PENELOPE. Sons: 1. GRANBERRY V., 2. ELIJAH L.,
3. DR. S. THOMPSON - these 3 sons to have remaining
land, 4. MEEDY B. - 200 A. where I live, 5. BLAKE.
Daus: 1. ELIZABETH, 2. DELLA, 3. MARTHA, dec'd. "All
my living children." Gr. chil: CAROLINE, ANDREW J.,
MARY ANN and TIMOTHY WILLIFORD. Ex: Son BLAKE,
WILLIAM H. HINES. Wit: H. WILLIFORD, WM. T. DORTCH.

WILLIS, THOMAS of Edgecombe Co., N. C.
    P. 237. July 2, 1777 - no probate date. Wife:
ELIZABETH. Sons: 1. WILLIAM - plantation where I
formerly lived, in Edgecombe Co., 2. WILSON - 150 A.
whereon I now live, also 200 A. in Pitt Co. Daus:
1. MARY, 2. ELIZABETH, 3. ESTER, 4. SARAH, 5. ALICE.
Ex: Friends WILLIAM HORN, JACOB DICKINSON. Wit:
THOMAS HUNTER, JEREMIAH THOMAS, BENJAMIN RICKS.

WILSON, EDWARD SR.
    P. 241. Nov. 3, 1799 - No prob. date. Gr. daus,
children of son ROBERT: ELIZABETH and ANNE WILSON.
Ex: JAMES WILLIAMS. Wit: WILLIAM POWELL, LODRICK
ELLEN, POLLY ELLEN.

WILSON, JAMES
    P. 116. May 5, 1797 - Aug. Ct. 1797. Wife:
SARAH - 320 A. whereon I live. Sons: 1. THOMAS -
land on south side Turkey Crk., adjoining WILLIAM
PASMORE, 2. RICHARD CHRISTIAN WILSON - land on south
side Turkey Crk. and Mirey Branch, 3. ZACHARIAH and
4. JAMES - to share land on north side Turkey Crk.
Daus: 1. ELIZABETH WILSON, 2. SARAH CLIFTON, 3. MARY

WILSON, 4. NANCY WILSON.   Ex: Young WILLIAM ANDREWS,
MICAJAH BRIDGERS.   Wit: WILLIAM PASSMORE, MARY
WILLIAMS.

WINBORNE, DAVID
    P. 511. Dec. 8, 1847 - Feb. Ct. 1848.   Wife:
ISLY - land bought of HARDY PRIDGEN.   Sons provided
for in advance: 1. JAMES, 2. JOSIAH, 3. IVEY F.,
4. DAVID, 5. WILLIAM, 6. JOHN I. - reversion of his
mother's land.   Daus: 1. MELANY BEZZELL, 2. NANCY
WILLIAMS, 3. MARY WINBORNE, 4. ELIZA C. WINBORNE,
5. MARTHA A. WINBORNE, 6. ISLY JANE WINBORNE.   Ex:
Son JOSIAH WINBORNE.   Wit: WILLIAM HARE, HINTON M.
GODWIN.

WINBORN, JOSEPH
    P. 121. Sept. 6, 1794 - Nov. Ct. 1798.   Wife:
FERIBY.   Chil: 1. ABRAHAM and 2. SARAH - share 300 A.
on lines of Crain Pond, Beaver Dam Branch and Kent,
3. JOHN - 150 A. on Beaver Dam and Cattail Branch,
4. DAVID - land whereon I live, also 300 A. on lines
of JOHNSON, 5. ELIZABETH, 6. JOSIAH, 7. FEREBY.   Ex:
Sons ABRAHAM, JOHN and DAVID.   Wit: WILSON TAYLOR,
MARTHEW JOHNSON, WILEY HOPKINS, PRISILLA JOHNSTON.

WINSTEAD, DAVID
    P. 513. Aug. 26, 1848 - Nov. Ct. 1848.   Wife:
BETSEY - 532 A. adjoining JOHN FARMER on south side
Tar R., whereon I live, with reversion to sons JAMES
W. and DAVID W. WINSTEAD.   Daus: 1. HARRIET HESTER
ANN EDWARDS, 2. MARY ANN TAYLOR.   Gr. chil: WRIGHT
BARNES, EDY DEW, WEALTHY BARNES, MAHALA I. WINSTEAD,
BETSEY ANN WINSTEAD, JOHN A. WINSTEAD.   Ex: Sons
JAMES W. WINSTEAD, DAVID W. WINSTEAD.   Wit: B. B.
SMITH, E. B. HART, JOHN B. DEANS.

WINSTEAD, ELIZABETH
    P. 523. Mar. 24, 1849 - Nov. Ct. 1850.   Sons and
Ex: 1. JAMES W. WINSTEAD, 2. DAVID W. WINSTEAD.   Gr.
chil: JAMES L. WINSTEAD, NANCY W. WINSTEAD.   Wit:
B. B. SMITH, CALVIN COOPER, DEMPSEY WINSTEAD.

WINSTEAD, JOSEPH

P. 88. April 15, 1788 - Feb. Ct. 1794. Wife: ANN. Son and Ex: JOSEPH WINSTEAD. Dau: SUZANNA WINSTEAD - 150 A. whereon I live, at death of her mother. Relationship unnamed, but apparently daus: ELIZABETH BOON, NANCE (NANCY) COCKRELL, SARAH POLING. Gr. son: SAMMIE WINSTEAD - 100 A. Ex: JORDAN SHERROD. Wit: DAVID PRIDGEN, ROGENNE (ROGER?) WINSTEAD, SARAH WINSTEAD.

WINSTEAD, THOMAS

P. 526. Jan. 7, 1847 - Feb. Ct. 1852. Wife: PENNY - land and mill, with reversion to Gr. son: HARRIS ATKINSON WINSTEAD; GEORGE WASHINGTON WINSTEAD- 100 A. Gr. dau: HESTER WINSTEAD. "All my children" unnamed. Ex: DAVID W. WINSTEAD. Wit: DAVID WINSTEAD, C. I. PARKER, HAYWOOD HARDY.

WITHERINGTON, JAMES

P. 364. April 25, 1829 - May Ct. 1829. Wife: MARY. Wit: JAMES SOLOMAN, WILSON GAY.

WOODARD, C. W. W.

P. 606. Dec. 17, 1864 - no prob. date. Wife: VIRGINIA - 510 A. Father: COLEMAN WOODARD. Ex: Wife VIRGINIA WOODARD. In case my wife shall have an heir by me, son or dau., she shall have 1/3 estate and the heir 2/3 estate. No wit. Paper exhibited and proved by oath of JAMES H. CHAPMAN, next of friend to the only heir of sd. deceased. Handwriting proved by R. B. GRIFFIN, W. T. GRIFFIN and C. W. WARD.

WOODARD, JAMES

P. 233. Feb. 13, 1808? - no probate date. Wife: MARY. Sons: 1. AARON, 2. DAVID, 3. DANIEL. Daus: 1. ELIZABETH HOLLAND, 2. KEZIAH MASINGALE, 3. SARAH DANCE, 4. MOURNING JACKSON, 5. MARY HUNT BRASWELL. Gr. sons: COLEMAN WOODARD, son of AARON; HENRY WOODARD, son of DAVID; JAMES DANCE. Ex: JAMES WILLIAMS, son AARON. Wit: WILLIAM BODDIE, BURWELL WOODARD, DAVID WOODARD. Codicil attached dated Feb. 18, 1808. Wit. to codicil: WM. BODDIE, SARAH DANCE.

WORTHINGTON, MARY
   P. 557. Nov. 14, 1850 - Feb. Ct. 1858. Dau:
ELIZABETH DAVIS. Whole estate left in hands of:
ARCHIBALD DAVIS, NEVERSON ALDEN DAVIS, JULIA ANN DAVIS,
and ISABEL DAVIS for the benefit of dau., ELIZABETH
DAVIS, during her life and divided between the four of
them at the death of dau. ELIZABETH. Note: It
appears that all five are her chil. M.G.G. Ex: JOS.
B. MANN. Wit: BOLEN MELTON, ALLISON STRICKLAND.

WRIGHT, CLOE
   P. 296. Jan. 31, 1816 - May Ct. 1818. Sons:
1. MATHEW CULPEPPER, 2. OSBORN CULPEPPER, 3. NATHAN
CULPEPPER, 4. ERASMUS CULPEPPER, 5. JOHN CULPEPPER,
6. WILLIAM WRIGHT. Daus: 1. MARY DANIEL, 2. HULDY
POWELL (apparently desc.), 3. ELIZABETH TAYLOR. Ex:
Sons MATHEW and ERASMUS CULPEPPER. Wit: ARTHUR
WHITEHEAD, ELIZA B. HILLIARD, TEMPERANCE G. WHITEHEAD.

WRIGHT, WILLIAM
   P. 258. Apr. 7, 1812 - Feb. Ct. 1814. Wife: CLOEY.
Sons: 1. JOHN WRIGHT, 2. WILLIAM WRIGHT. Gr. sons:
ALPHEUS WRIGHT POWELL, WILLIAM WRIGHT POWELL, sons of
LAZARUS POWELL. Daus: 1. ELIZABETH (youngest), wife
of JESSE TAYLOR - manor plantation including lands
purchased of ABSALOM and ABRAHAM SAULS, the WYATT and
COOPER tracts, also 1 A. purchased of HENRY FREEMAN
for a mill seat; 2. BARSHEBA, wife of JOHN CULPEPPER -
569 A. purchased of HENRY WHITEHEAD. Ex: Friend
WILLIAM ARRINGTON, son WILLIAM WRIGHT. Wit: JOHN
HILLIARD, JAMES MANNING.

YORK, EDWARD
   P. 295. Mar. 17, 1816 - Feb. Ct. 1818. Wife:
JUDITH - land whereon she formerly lived, also the
following: bond against HENRY FLOWERS for $175, debt
against EDWARD FLOWERS for $30. Sons: 1. JOHN,
2. LAMON, 3. EDWIN, 4. DUNCAN. Daus: 1. ZANEY LEWIS,
wife of JOHN LEWIS, 2. NANCY LAMON. Ex: Sons LAMON,
EDWIN and DUNCAN YORK. Wit: WILLIE TAYLOR, JOHN
TAYLOR.

YOUELL, HENRY

P. 248. Mar. 6, 1798 - no probate date. Legatee:
HENRY TURLINGTON, son of ELIZABETH TURLINGTON - 100 A.
on Maple Crk., purchased of REUBEN HARRELL. If HENRY
TURLINGTON die without heirs, estate to be divided
between: THOMAS TURLINGTON and MARY YOUNG, wife of
JOHN YOUNG. Ex: JOHN LAMON. Wit: DUNCAN LAMON,
JR., J. S. GLAMON.

YOUNG, ROBERT

P. 9. Oct. 15, 1780 - July Ct. 1781. Sons:
1. STEPHEN - all land, 2. WILLIAM. Dau: ELIZABETH
WHITFIELD. Gr. dau: MARY ANN YOUNG. Ex: NATHAN
BODDIE, WILLIAM ANDREWS. Wit: DENNIS LINEHAN, SAMUEL
BRYANT, JACOB CARTER.

UNRECORDED WILLS

OF

NASH COUNTY,

NORTH CAROLINA

1790 - 1922

Filmed by the Genealogical Society

of Utah.

North Carolina Department of

Archives and History,

Raleigh, N. C.

Film #C.069 - 80006

ARMSTRONG, THOMAS J.
Aug. 30, 1808. Estate to be divided between all brothers and sisters. Bro: LEWELLIN ARRINGTON - the Negro left me by the will of LEWELLIN JONES. Ex: Father-in-law (step-father?): PETER ARRINGTON, bro: ARTHUR ARRINGTON. Wit: WYATT (?) HINES, JOHN ARRINGTON.

ARRINGTON, CAROLINE
Feb. 20, 1895. Legatees: JOHN P. ARRINGTON (colored) - horse, buggy, harness, and gold watch. To JOHN P. ARRINGTON (colored), CARRIE ARRINGTON, DREW ARRINGTON, and WILLIAM ARRINGTON (the last named a son of my sister ELLEN) - one feather bed and fixtures each. Also 100 A. on north side Swift Creek and on both sides of road from Arrington's Mill to Hilliardston, divided equally among them. Ex: Friend SHERIFF JOHN P. ARRINGTON. Wit: W. T. SPRUILL, W. M. Y____?

ARRINGTON, CONNAR
Aug. 28, 1920. Wife: HARRIETT - all real estate including home place in Griffin's Township for her natural life with reversion to my gr. son OPIE ARRINGTON. Ex: Wife HARRIETT. Wit: W. W. WARD, J. H. MATTHEWS.

BALLARD, EDWARD
Oct. 22, 1819. Daus: 1. CHARITY LINDSEY, 2. PATSEY VANLANDANHAM (VANLANDINGHAM), 3. NANCY TUCKER, 4. MOURNING BONE - the property I bring to NELSON BONE'S. Gr. dau: PHERIBA BALLARD. Son: EDWARD BALLARD. Ex: NELSON BONE. Wit: W. W. COOPER, BEN TISDELL.

BATCHELOR, JAMES
April 20, 1820. Wife: ANN. Sons: 1. CULLEN - the TUCKER tract, 2. JAMES M. - land, 3. JOSEPH - plantation where JAMES lives, 4. SAMUEL. Daus: 1. CHERRY, 2. LIZEY ANN, 3. JERUSHA WHITLEY, 4. RHODA MATTHIS. Ex: Wife ANN, RICHARD HOLLAND. Wit: ABIJAH PRIDGEN, JOSEPH BATCHELOR, DAVID PRIDGEN.

BATTLE, CONSTANCE
     April 20, 1907.   Dau: OLIVIA CRISP - the lot in
Rocky Mount on which I live (the same being the premises
conveyed to me by THOMAS H. BATTLE), with reversion to
her son SPENCER CRISP.   Ex: FRED SIMPSON.   Wit: JACOB
BATTLE, W. E. McLEMORE.

BONE, WILLIE
     Feb. 20, 1848.   Wife: MOURNING - tract of land
adjoining Jacob's Swamp, MATTHEW JONES, and DAVID BONE.
Sons: 1. PHILLAMON B. BONE - tract on east side Jacob's
Swamp, 2. HARDY - 215 A. on west side Jacob's Swamp.
Dau: NANCY W. BONE.   Ex: WM. JOINER.   Wit: ? BONE.

BOTTOMS, JOHN L.
     Oct. 19, 1816.   Wife: MARY L. - 75 A. where I live
with reversion to TEMPY OLVY (OLIVE?) WILLIAMS.   Niece:
TEMPY OLVY WILLIAMS - 123 A.   Friend: HARDY FLOD (FLOOD
or FLYOD?).   Ex: ELIJAH ATKINSON.   Wit: JESSE JOINER,
DAVIS JOINER.

COOPER, GEORGE
     Oct. 8, 1845.   Wife: TEMPERANCE - land where I
live on Sappony Swamp, and lines of SALLY EVANS and
ISAAC EVANS, with reversion to my four sons.   Sons:
1. THOMAS J. A. COOPER, 2. WILLIAM A. COOPER, 3. NEVERSON
W. COOPER, 4. GEORGE W. COOPER.   Dau: ANN JACKSON BUNN.
Ex: Sons THOMAS J. A. COOPER and WILLIAM A. COOPER.
Wit: JOHN H. DRAKE, JR., ELISHA H. COCKRELL.   This will
was offered for probate at the Nov. Term, 1845, but was
not admitted for probate because the witnesses believed
the Testator was not in a proper state of mind to make a
will, at the time of signing.   F. W. TAYLOR, C. C. C.

CURL, ELIZABETH
     Dec. 19, 1820 - Aug. Ct. 1821.   Dau: MOURNING CURL-
all estate.   Ex: ALFRED BUNN.   Wit: JAMES C. B.
ATKINSON, WILLIE BUNN.

DAVIS, JOHN
     Mar. 11, 1817.   Wife: WINNEFRED.   Sons: 1. JOHN -

100 A. where I live, 2. ARTHUR - 150 A., 3. DRURY,
4. BENJAMIN - sell Halifax land and divide between DRURY
and BENJAMIN.   Daus: 1. SALLY HARPER, 2. ELIZABETH
DAVIS, 3. NANCY BENNET, 4. PRISCILLA HARPER, 5. MARTHA
HILL.   Ex: JOSEPH ARRINGTON, ISAAC PORTIS.   Wit:
EDW'D SMITH, MARTHA HARRISON, MARY HARRISON.

ETHERIDGE, PETER
     Wife: ANN - 150 A.   Son: JOHN.   Dau: MARTHA.
Gr. dau: EDY ROSE.   Ex: GEORGE BODDIE.   Wit: JOS.
HOPKINS, JESSE BASS.

EVANS, SUSAN CATHERINE
     Feb. 25, 1903.   Friend: GEORGE WOMBLE.   Dau:
MINNIE ESTELLE COLLINS - whole estate with reversion to
her heirs.   No Ex.   Wit: L. M. CONYERS, ? DACIA
JOHNSON.   R. U. BROOKS and J. W. BLOUNT swore that
L. M. CONYERS was dead 22 Feb., 1910 when paper was
offered for probate.

FOX, MARY K.
     Jan. 13, 1873.   I bequeath to my step-son REDEN P.
FOX my estate for his kindness and attention to me for
the last year or two.   Wit: N. W. COOPER, J. R.
SAUNDERS.

GAY, MARTHA
     Aug. 15, 1883.   Bro: JOHN GAY - all estate.   Ex:
THOMAS M. ARRINGTON.   Wit: A. G. DAVIS, B. F. PROCTOR.

GLOVER, JOHN
     July 31, 1834 - May Ct. 1836.   Wife: BARSHABA.
Sons: 1. KELLY, 2. THOMAS, 3. JOHN, JR., 4. CASWELL,
5. HILLIARD, 6. PEYTON, 7. HILLERY.   Daus: 1. SINTHY
(CYNTHIA?) MATTHEWS, 2. ANEY (ONEY or ANNIE?) YOUNG,
3. MARY JOINER, 4. SARAH ROSE, 5. JINSY GLOVER.   Ex:
WILLIAM B. BRYANT, JAMES F. DOZIER.   Wit: JOHN DEANS,
DANIEL BATCHELOR.

GRIFFIN, NATHAN
     Feb. 28, 1888.   W. G. GRIFFIN states he believes he
is Executor to the last will of NATHAN GRIFFIN, dec'd...

that he examined the private papers of said deceased
which are in possession of MARGARETT GRIFFIN, and after
such search, did not find said will. Wherefore, he asks
that she be called before the Clerk of Superior Court
and produce such will or tell what disposition she made
of same. Signed, W. G. GRIFFIN, JOHN T. MORGAN,
GIDEON COGGIN was ordered to appear before the Clerk of
Superior Court on March 1, 1888 at 12 o'clock to give
evidence in relation to the will of NATHAN GRIFFIN,
deceased. 28 Feb. 1888.

HAMMONS, CHARITY
Jan. 12, 1869. Gr. chil: WILLIAM GRIFFIN; CENORAH
(SENORA?), dau. of MARGARET GRIFFIN; CORNELIA, dau. of
MARGARET GRIFFIN; LEONIDAS, son of MARGARET GRIFFIN.
Dau: MARGARET GRIFFIN. Ex: PRESLEY GRIFFIN. Wit:
M. C. BRANTLEY, J. S. DENTON.

HAMMONS, EATON
Feb. 27, 1821 - May Ct. 1821. Sis: ELIZABETH
HAMMONS. Legatee: MADDERSON TUCKER. Ex: JOHN YORK.
Wit: DUNCAN YORK, EDWIN YORK.

HARRIS, JACKY E.
April 7, 1871. Niece: MARY JANE HARRIS, dau. of
my bro. MOSES C. HARRIS. Friend: SARAH W. WARD, dau.
of G. W. WARD. Bro: MOSES HARRIS, residue of all
property, with reversion to his heirs. Ex: G. W.
WARD. Wit: ROENY COLLINS, C. W. WARD.

HARRISON, EMILIUS
June 3, 1853 - April 14, 1855. Wife: RHODA - land
where I live, also the DRAKE and WELDON tracts adjoining
it. Son and Ex: WILLIAM H. HARRISON. Dau: MARTHA
E. SIMS - reversion of land where I live, and the adjoining tracts. Gr. daus: MARY ELIZA HARRISON, JOHN CORA
HARRISON. Gr. son: NATHANIEL HARRISON. Wit: JOHN
G. F. DRAKE, THOS. W. WRIGHT. Codicil, Aug. 3, 1854 -
Wit: NICHOLAS W. ARRINGTON, JOSEPH A. DRAKE, "bequeathing to son WM. HARRISON any property or money which may
come to me from estate of my brother, HENRY HARRISON,
dec'd.

HARPER, REBECCA

May 17, 1883 - 1891. Daus: 1. SALLIE HARPER - 32 A., all cleared land, including houses, adj. N. W. COOPER and E. B. DRAKE, 2. PATTY GAY - 50 A. adjoining home place, 3. MARY WHELESS. Ex: SALLIE HARPER. Wit: N. W. COOPER, N. K. COOPER.

HENDRICK, SIMON

Dec. 25, 1868. Wife: MORNING - all personal property, provided she does not take her son F. M. RACKLEY to live with her. Son: SAMUEL - whole estate when he comes of age. Ex: W. E. MANNING. Wit: B. H. VESTER, W. E. MANNING.

HILLIARD, NELSON

May 31, 1911. Wife: SALLIE ANN - all land, with reversion to all my children. Ex: H. B. MARRIOTT. Wit: JAMES T. TAYLOR, GRACE J. TAYLOR.

HINTON, HATTIE BEULAH

No date. Son: ROBERT LEON HINTON. Dau: MARTHA ELIZABETH HINTON. These two minor chil. to share equally all property. Ex and Guardian: S. M. TAYLOR. Wit: LIDAY L. STRICKLAND, A. F. MOORE.

HORN, GRANTHAM

May 20, 1820 - Aug. Ct. 1820. Legatee: LEAH EDWARDS, dau. of MATILDA EDWARDS. Bro: MERIT HORN of Hartford (?), Georgia, County of Pulasky. If LEAH EDWARDS dies without issue, property to be divided among my brothers and sister. Neph: THOMAS HORN, son of my bro. MARTIN HORN - 150 A. Sis: ELIZABETH TAYLOR - 100 A. Bro: JOEL HORN - 100 A. Ex: CUTTON (?) SAMUEL WILLIAMS. Wit: ISLEY HORN, RHODA HORN, HILLIARD HORN. Very difficult to read.

Certified copy of will of O. L. JACKSON, dec'd. of
    Edgecombe County
JACKSON, O. L.

June 9, 1890. Wife and Ex: CATHERINE JACKSON - all houses and lots in Edgecombe and Nash Counties, with

reversion to my children or gr. children. Sons:
1. O. L. JACKSON, JR., 2. WILLIAM, younger son. Wit:
W. R. JACKSON, L. BOON. Clerk's copy dated Aug. 5,
1890.

JOHNSON, ELIZABETH
    Jan. 16, 1850. Dau: SALLY ANN JOHNSON. Ex:
EDWIN ROSE. Wit: J. READ (?).

JOINER, HARDY
    Nov. 7, 1819. Wife: ELIZABETH - land where I live,
with reversion to my heirs. Ex: Bro. MOSES JOINER.
Wit: DRURY JOINER, CALEB DAVIS.

KITTRELL, THOMAS G.
    Nov. 14, 1893. Son: S. W. KITTRELL - all estate.
No Ex. Wit: W. O. DUNN, S. J. BARTHOLOMEW.

LANDING, MARTHA
    Nov. 7, 1899 - Dec. 23, 1911. Sons: 1. WILLIAM
A. LANDING, Ex., 2. JOHN. Daus: 1. FANNIE LANDING,
2. LAURA ANN, wife of GEORGE WEAVER, 3. MARY JANE, wife
of JOE WORRELL. Wit: JOHN W. WALKER, R. V. BATCHELOR.

MACKLIN, JANE L.
    Feb. 11, 1889. Son and Ex: JOHN MACKLIN. Daus:
1. FRANCIS WALLACE, 2. SARAH MACKLIN. Wit: MILES
BOBBITT, W. D. AVENT.

MOORE, EDWARD
    Oct. 5, 1785 - Nov. Ct. 1785. Wife unnamed -
plantation and mill where I live. Sons-in-law: JOHN
TANNER, JAMES LEE - land where he lives, it being land
I purchased of ? SANDERS, also another tract adjoining
it,purchased of WILLIAM HORN. Dau: ZILPHIA. Gr.
chil: HENRY HORN and wife AMEY - land purchased of NATHAN
WEST; CHRISTOPHER MOORE CLINCH - land where WILLIAM FINCH
lives; MOORE LEE, dau. of MILLEY TAYLOR. Ex: WILSON
TAYLOR may sell land in Johnston Co. to help with care of
family. Wit: JOHN BONDS, ETHELDRED DANER ?

MORGAN, LUCY J.
Dec. 29, 1893 - 1897. Chil: 1. PATSY MEDORA
MORGAN, 2. WILLIAM GAY MORGAN, Ex., 3. JAMES HENDERSON
MORGAN. Chil. to share whole estate. PATSEY and
WILLIAM to have the house tract, and JAMES to have the
RACKLEY tract. Wit: H. H. MATTHEWS, W. D. WESTER.

MORGAN, WILLIAM B.
Nov. 7, 1851. "For the love and affection and
good will which I have for POLLY EARP.....who has lived
in my service for seven or eight years.....she has done
a dutiful part as a hireling and waited on my sister
and my mother on the bed of affliction.....I give and
grant for good attendance my colt, etc., bed, and so
long as she lives I want her to have twenty gallons of
brandy per year and a home her lifetime under good
quality, not to make destruction nor havoc of the
plantation." Part of this will is illegible, but it
appears that after the death of POLLY EARP, a nephew
of WILLIAM B. MORGAN named WILLIAM ALSTON (or ALFORD)
is to have $125, and the heirs of HENRY MORGAN are to
have $10 each, and E. H. MORGAN is to have a legacy -
all this from the sale of the devisor. Ex: JOHN B.
RICE. Wit: WILLIAM EARP, WILLIAM D. STRICKLAND.
The records show that a suit was brought by JOHN MORGAN
and LAMON WHITLEY, objecting through their attorney,
WILLIAM T. DORTCH, to the probate of the will of WILLIAM
B. MORGAN. However, following proper investigation,
etc., the will was admitted to probate. No date. JOHN
B. RICE refused to serve as executor and E. H. MORGAN
was named administrator.

NORFLEET, BETSY
May 18, 1922. Gr. dau: CORNELIA PITT - house and
lot in Rocky Mount, on "Happy Hill." Guardian for
CORNELIA PITT, a minor: THADDEUS LYON. Wit: ELLA
M. PARKER, JOSEPHINE BATTLE.
                X   X

PITTS, WALTER
Feb. 8, 1849. Sons: 1. WILLIAM - 500 A. where I
live, 2. FREDERICK. Daus: 1. ELIZA WHITAKER - land

143

where they now live, 2. REBECCA TATE - wife of JOHN B.
TATE of Alabama, 3. MARY FOX, 4. MARTHA HILLIARD,
5. LUCY HUNT.   Ex: JOSHUA WATSON.   Wit: THOS. C.
ARRINGTON, CARY WHITAKER.   Very difficult to read.

PUGH, WILLIAM
     July 23, 1796 - Feb. Ct. 1798.   Wife unnamed.
Daus: 1. PASHANTS (PATIENCE) STRICKLAND, 2. PERNELERPER
(PENELOPE) ELVETANT (?) (SILLIVENT?), 3. ORPAY
ELVETANT (?) (SILLIVENT?), 4. SENATH PUGH.   Sons:
1. TIGNAL PUGH, 2. ARNAL (ARNOLD?) PUGH, 3. LABORN
PUGH - reversion of wife's land.   Ex: Sons ARNOLD and
LABORN PUGH.   Wit: WM. MOORE, OWEN SILLIVENT.

ROSE, TEMPIE
     June 4, 1884.   Dau: CASANNA ? E. J. ROSE - all
estate.   Ex: ISAAC WOMBLE.   Wit: W. T. GRIFFIN,
JAMES M. EARL.

SHERMAN, H. G. of Henderson, Vance County, North Carolina
     July 24, 1914.   Wife and Ex: NANNIE.   Dau: RUTH
GRAHAM SHERMAN.   Wit: W. O. BURWELL, W. W. PARKER.
Certified copy almost entirely illegible.

SMITH, CHARITY
     Aug. 20, 1836.   Bro: ARCHIBALD SMITH.   Sis:
MORNING SMITH.   Sis-in-law: BARSHABA SMITH.   Ex:
ALFRED JOINER.   Wit: EXUM L. CURL, MARY WESTRAY.

TAYLOR, ROSAMAN
     April 19, 1827 - Aug. Ct. 1829.   I have by deed
this day and date given the land where I live to GEORGE
COOPER, my Ex.   All remaining property to be equally
divided between GEORGE COOPER, WILLIAM COOPER and JOHN
DEANS.   The lawsuit now pending between myself and
Heirs of SAM'L WINSTEAD in the Superior Court of Law
and Equity shall be carried on by my Ex.   Wit: H.
BLOUNT, ABRAHAM EVANS.

THOMSON, JOHN B.
     July 28, 1923.   Sons: 1. J. B. THOMSON and

2. ALFRED REDING THOMSON - to share my home tract of
18 A., 3. D. F., 4. H. E., 5. CHARLIE A., 6. BILLY.
Daus: 1. ANNIE LEE THOMSON, 2. MIRIA LEE THOMSON,
3. CLEAO, 4. LOUISE, 5. ANNEWERT ?. These nine chil.
to share 77 A. No Ex. Wit: W. G. HEDGEPETH, J. O.
LEONARD.

Copy of Will of
TISDALE, RENISON of Edgecombe Co.
   Sept. 26, 1808. Wife unnamed - 850 A. where I
reside. Sons: 1. HENRY, 2. WILLIAM, 3. EDWARD,
4. PHILANDER. Dau: ELIZABETH PIERCE. Gr. sons:
JOEL, JOSIAH. This will is incomplete - no Ex., no
Wit., no signature.

TUCKER, WRIGHT
   Feb. 18, 1890. Wife: NANCY. Dau: MARTHA ANN
E. TUCKER. Gr. dau: LULA MAY TUCKER. The following were probably his children, but are not designated
as such: 1. JOHN D. TUCKER, 2. WILLIAM W. TUCKER,
3. ROSELLA TUCKER. No Ex. Wit: JOHN J. DRAKE, M.
W. DRAKE.

TURNER, TEMPERANCE
   Nov. 7, 1880. Gr. dau: MARY ELIZA TEMPERANCE
COLEY. Ex: A. H. RICKS. Wit: SAMUEL (?) R.
HILLIARD, C. M. MANN.

VICK, HUDSON
   Feb. 18, 1884. Nephew: RANSOM WHITLEY - 77½ A.,
part of the WYATT land. Niece: LOURANY VICK - 77½ A.,
the other half of my land. Ex: NOAH BISSETT. Wit:
J. G. SILLS, R. A. P. COOLEY.

WARD, JOHN
   Aug. 1, 1870. Wife: LYDIA - 170 A. where I live,
which is the remainder of my land, after I gave land to
my three oldest children: 1. HENRIETTA HAWKINS, 2. J. L.
WARD, 3. G. W. WARD - two youngest chil. to have
reversion of mother's land: 4. EMILY A., wife of JOHN
BARFOOT, 5. JOHN L. WARD. Ex: JOHN W. DAVIS. Wit:
T. P. BRASWELL, JOS. U. PRICE.

WHITEHEAD, ARTHUR
     May 8, 1874.   It is my desire that all my crops
shall be finished, and as soon as that is done, the
crops, all stock, household and kitchen furniture,
plantation utensils, except what part of the horses my
executor may think proper to reserve for the purpose
of moving my family to the Western Country. I also
wish all my lands sold on the same credit, all just
debts paid, and all my Negroes shall be carried to the
Western Country. My mother's lifetime estate shall be
reserved.   My wife and children, Negroes, and horses
shall be in the care of ELISHA LOT, who shall be
guardian for my children.   Ex: Bro-in-law WILLIS W.
BODDIE.   Wit: JOSEPH ARRINGTON, JAMES R. BATTLE,
RICH'D ARRINGTON.   On Sept. 2, 1824 JAMES R. BATTLE
made a sworn statement to the effect that he was called
upon by ARTHUR WHITEHEAD the day before he died to witness his will, which he did, with JOSEPH ARRINGTON, the
other witness. RICHARD ARRINGTON was present also, but
did not sign his name. The deponant further saith and
believes that the said ARTHUR WHITEHEAD was not in his
right mind at the time nor had been for ten days before.
Wit: J. H. DRAKE, N. J. DRAKE.

Nash County
     Nov. Session 1823.   The petition of BENNETT
WHITEHEAD and wife MARY, formerly MARY BECKWITH,
BENJAMIN BECKWITH, MAHALA T. BECKWITH, NANCY BECKWITH,
DAWSON BECKWITH, THOMAS W. BECKWITH and CLINTON BECKWITH,
which five last named are infants under age of twenty one
years, and petition by their guardian, FRANCIS DRAKE.....
they are children and heirs of SION BECKWITH dec'd, late
of this County.....who died in the month of April 1821...
he was possessed of 1600 A. adjoining the lands of WILLIAM
BRASWELL, PHILANDER TISDALE and others......petition for
division of said land.

WHITLEY, J. L. R.
     Jan. 23, 1886.   Wife: ELIZA MAY - 180 A. on lines
of LARKIN TAYBORN, Pott's Branch, A. M. CONE, and BURRELL
TAYBORN.   Dau: SHELLEY MARY, wife of LATTAMORE MORGAN -
40 A. on lines of HENRY MORGAN and JOHN IZZARD.   Sons:

1. M. R. WHITLEY - 60 A., part of land purchased of the
late JOHN RICKS, also 40 A. where I live; 2. HENRY R.
WHITLEY - remainder of the JOHN RICKS land. Ex: JOHN
T. MORGAN. Wit: J. G. SILLS, BENJ. F. COLLINS, JOHN
T. MORGAN.

WHITLEY, RICHARD R.
     Aug. 8, 1862. Sis: MARY A. B. WHITLEY. The
following are apparently brothers and sisters of the
testator: HENRY A. WHITLEY, JOLBY (JOLLEY?) B. WHITLEY,
MARY A. B. WHITLEY, ELISA A. B. WHITLEY, SALLY A. E.
WHITFIELD. Ex: JOEL ? B. WHITLEY. Wit: E. L. CURL,
REDMUN BUNN.

WILLIAMS, JOEL
     Nov. 9, 1809. Wife: PENNY. Sons: 1. HENRY,
2. ROWLAND, 3. DRURY, 4. HERBERT or ROBERT - land adjoining WILEY TAYLOR and MARK STRICKLAND, 5. WILSON, 6. WILEY,
7. NATHAN - 100 A. of the LEE land and the mill. Daus:
1. ZILPHIA CROWELL, 2. SEALAH WILLIAMS - plantation where
I live, 3. PENNY APRIL WILLIAMS - all land on south side
Whiteoak Swamp. Gr. chil: REDDEN SMITH WILLIAMS, son
of ROBERT WILLIAMS - 100 A. near THOMAS HAMILTON and
DEMPSEY TAYLOR; MILBREY, dau. of WILLIAM WILLIAMS - the
CAULSON land; HENRY, son of WILSON WILLIAMS - the land
joining where I live; JOEL, son of HENRY WILLIAMS - the
land lying above where I live, joining the _____?
land and the BIRD land; SEALAH WILLIAMS, dau. of ZILPHIA
CROWELL - the BIRD land; REDMON WILLIAMS, son of WILEY
WILLIAMS; and EDMOND WILLIAMS, son of WILEY WILLIAMS -
all land not given away. Dau: NANCY HENRY - her son
WILLIAM HENRY - 100 A. joining the LEE land. NANCY is
now wife of NATHAN WILLIAMS. (Note: She must have
been dau-in-law, as she was eventually wife of NATHAN
WILLIAMS.) M.G.G. Ex: Sons ROWLAND, HENRY, and DRURY
WILLIAMS. Wit: BRYAN WILLIAMS, WILLIAM NAIRN, HARDY
BRYAN, JOHN PRICE. Very difficult to read.

WILLIAMSON, ANN
     Nov. 8, 1807. Legatees: SAMUEL HOLEMAN, JAMES
HINNANT. Sons: 1. JOSEPH, 2. HARDY, 3. THOMAS.
Daus: 1. ANN WILLIAMSON, 2. SARAH WILLIAMSON, 3. MARTHA

HINNANT, 4. PENELOPE BOYKIN. Ex: Sons HARDY and
JOSEPH WILLIAMSON. Wit: BRATLEY (BARTLEY) DEANS,
THOMAS WILLIAMSON, SARAH WILLIAMSON. In a court
action - the executors vs. JACOB BOYKIN et al, the jury
found that this will was no will. H. G. BLOUNT, C.C.C.

WINSTEAD, DUNCAN H.
     Chil: 1. MARY BRASWELL, wife of COLUMBUS BRASWELL
of Nash Co.; 2. WM. H. WINSTEAD, of Pitt Co.;
3. HAYWOOD H. WINSTEAD, of Wilson Co., 4. GERMAN A.
WINSTEAD, of Wilson Co.; 5. FRANKLIN P. WINSTEAD, of
Nash; 6. JOHN H. WINSTEAD, of Nash Co.; 7. ROBERT P.
WINSTEAD, of Nash; 8. JOSEPH LAWRENCE WINSTEAD, of Nash
Co.; 9. LUCY ELLA WINSTEAD, of Nash Co. No Ex. or
Guardian for two minor chil. Wit: J. T. HOLLINGSWORTH,
A. S. BAINES.

WOODARD, THOMAS
     Dec. 27, 1790. Wife unnamed. Sons: 1. THOS.,
2. LUKE - 250 A., 3. JESSE - land on Turkey Crk. Daus:
1. ELIZ., 2. ABB ? This will just impossible to read.

YORK, LAMON
     Dec. 1, 1820. Sis: NANCY LAMON. Ex: EDWARD
YORK, DUNCAN YORK. Wit: M. A. CARTER, ZEALOUS TAYLOR.

Averett, Hardy, 8; Jedutham, 8; Nancy, 8; Rebecca, 8

- B -

Babb, Fanny, 9
Baggett, Granberry, 62
Bailey, Celia, 8; Chrischaney, 8; Daniel, 87; Henry, 8; John, 8, 95; Judith, 8; Kinchen, 9; Levy, 8; Milley, 87; Nancy, 95; Ruth, 8; Samuel, 8; Unity, 8; Wilson, 9
Baily, Levi, 103
Baines, A. B., 43, 89, 129
Baines, A. B., Jr., 26, 68, 88, 89, 98, 116
Baines, A. B. B., 37, 101
Baines, A. B. B., Sr., 78, 101
Baines, Absalom B., 20
Baines, Absalom B., Jr., 96
Baines, A. S., 148
Baines, James B., 127
Bains, A. B. (Absalom), 127
Bains, A. B. B., 102
Bains, A. B. B., Sr., 102
Baker, Adalina, 9; Alexander, 9; Allen, 9; Archibald, 9; Calvin, 9; Duncan, 9; Elisah (Elisha?), 9; Fereba, 22; John, 9; Josiah, 9; Nancy, 1; Nanney, 9; Salley, 9; William, Jr., 9; William, Sr., 9; W. M., 8; Zelphia, 84; Zilpha, 9
Baley, David, 8; Evalina F., 123; Lavina Mourning, 123; Mourning, 123;
Baley (Bailey), Richard, 123
Baley, Richard Thomas, 123; Robert Williamson, 123
Baley (Bailey), Salley, 123
Ball, Milly, 9; William, 9; William Kinchen, 9
Ballard, Anna, 9; Devx., 84; Edward, 71, 137;Phereby, 9; Pheriba, 137; William, 9
Ballentine, John 9; Linny, 9; William, 9, 100
Bandes, Henry, 123
Bandy, Henry, 123
Barbee, Frances Jane, 33; Susan, 33
Barfoot, Emily A., 145; John, 145
Baril (?), Elias, 28
Barnes, Barsheba, 10; Basheba, 68; Benjamin, 10, 11, 66; Bennett, 10, 11, 75, 88, 121; Bersheba, 11; Binel (?), 10; Burrell, 11;

Burwell, 12; Caswell H., 11; Charity, 10; Delilah, 10; Dempsey, 10, 61; Edwin, 10; Eliza, 12; Eliza C., 12; Eliza D., 11; Elizabeth, 10, 11, 12; Jacob, 10, 11, 12, 85, 120; Jacob H., 67; James, 11, 33; James, Sr., 11; James T., 11, 12, 62, 88, 92; J. D., 14; Jesse, 81; Jodin, 11; Joel, 11; John, 11, 12, 75; Jordan, 11; Joseph, 35; Joseph J., 12; Joseph James, 11; Joseph T., 11; Joshua B., 12; Louisa, 12; Louisa C., 12; Martha Ann, 12; Martha J., 13; Mary, 11, 12, 68; Mary E. T., 12; Molly, 12; Morning, 10, 11; Nancy, 11, 12; O. D., 86; Orren D., 11; Orrin D., 12; Piety, 12; Polley, 11; Polly, 11, 12; Primmy, 11; Rachel, 10; Rhoda, 10; Robert, 10, 12; Rosa, 32; Samuel, 12; Sarah, 35, 69; Thaddeus, 108; Theophilus, 11; Vincent, 10; Vinson, 11; Wealthy, 132; William, 10, 11, 12; Wright, 132; W. T., 86;
Barr, J. D., 107
Barrett, Davis G., 12, 13; Elias, 44, 91, 112; Elizabeth, 90; H. B., 12; Jane, 13; J. E., 12; Nancy, 13, 44
Barron, Barnaby, 13; James, 13; Onediance, 93
Barrot (Barrett?), Thomas, 76
Barrott, Jacob, 109
Barrow, Edmund, 114
Bartholomew, S. J., 142
Bass, Abraham, 13; Aldin, 13; Ann, 64; Aquilla, 14; Augustin, 13, 14, 89, 97; Betey (Beedie or Betsey?), 93; Cader, 70; Coffield, 14; Councel, 14; Cynthia, 97; Edmon, 14; Edwin, 14; Elias, 24; Elizabeth, 14; Embro, 14; Frances, 14; G., 122; Gideon, 14, 23, 26, 31, 89; Gideon R., 14; Goodman, 14; Isaac, 13, 14, 23; Jacob, 97; Jesse, 13, 14, 89, 108, 139; Jethro, 13, 113; John, 13; Jordan, 13, 14, 34; Julian, 97; Kinchen, 13; Louzany, 14; Lucy, 14, 92; Margaret, 122; Mary, 23; Mildred, 14; Nancy, 13, 14; Quinne, 13; Sion, 13, 14; William T., 14

Batchelor, Abel, 17; Ann, 110, 137;
Annanipas, 17; B., 80; Berry,
15; Berryman, 89, 90; Charity,
17, 45, 115; Charlotte, 15, 16,
121; Cherry, 137; Cullen, 15,
137; Cynthia, 15; Daniel, 16,
110, 139; Drewry, 15; Drury, 15;
Elizabeth, 15, 31, 87, 121;
George Washington, 31; Hardy
Davis, 17; Henry I., 15; James,
15, 17, 44, 137; James M., 137;
James S., 16; Joel, 45; John,
15, 87; Jordan E., 16; Joseph,
16, 72, 137; Leitha Ann, 16;
Lizey Ann, 137; Margaret, 16;
Mariah, 15; Mary, 15; Merritt,
15; Mourning, 127; Nathan, 32;
Nathan Wright, 17; Quilly, 16;
Quilly Lamon, 16; Rebecca, 15;
R. V., 142; Sallie Ann, 118;
Samuel, 15, 16, 137; Samuel Mc.,
16; Solomon, 16, 25; Starling
Jones, 15; Stephen, 16; Van B.,
14; William, 15, 16; William J.
B., 16; William John, 16; Willis,
15; Wilson, 15; Wright, 15;
Wright Stephen, 15, 17; Zelby-
ann, 85
Battle, Abiah, 17; A. J., 17; A. L.,
6; Alex W., 17; Alford, 5; Amos
J., 17; Angelina, 97; Benjamin
D., 17; Constance, 138; Curan,
17, 18; David, 97; Elisha, 28,
61; Elisha, Sr., 27; Elizabeth,
2, 5, 17; Fed, 6, 104; Fred,
50, 54; Frederick, 5; Henrietta
T., 17; Henrietta T. H., 17;
Jacob, 138; James, 17, 51, 124;
James P., 92, 98; James R., 146;
James S., 120; Dr. Jeremiah, 28;
Jesse, 28, 52, 57; Joel; 28;
John, 2, 17, 39; Josephine, 143;
Joseph J., 73; Joseph S., 9, 61;
Lark, 69; Larkin, 5; Lawrence,
5, 51; Lawrence F., 17; L. F.,
5; L. H. B., 55; L. N. B., 5;
Lovey, 17; Margaret, 27; Martha,
5; Mary, 2, 5, 17; Mary Ann, 5;
Mitty, 17; N. L. B., 17; Polly,
28; Richard H., 17; Sarah, 27;
Sarah Harriett, 120; Susan, 97;
Tempe, 17; Thomas, 5, 17, 124;
Thomas H., 138; William, 5;
William H., 17; William L., 17;
Wm. S., 10, 92

Bayley, Mourning, 124
Beal, Jesse, 44, 91
Beck, Sarah, 18
Beckwith, Amos, 18; Benjamin, 18,
146; Bollen, 18; Charity, 113,
116, 127; Clinton, 18, 146;
Dawson, 18, 146; Dempsey, 18;
Henry, 18; James, 18; Mahala T.,
146; Martha, 18; Mary, 146;
Nancy, 18, 146; Rodah, 18; Sion,
18, 40, 64, 90, 146; Thomas, 18,
25, 90; Thomas, Sr., 18; Thomas
W., 146; Thomas Wright, 18;
Willis, 18
Bedgood, John, 40
Bell, Arthur, 18; Benjamin, 18;
Catharine, 20; Elias, 18;
Elizabeth, 18, 31; George, 60;
Green, 18, 37; Isabel, 124;
James, 18, 57; Jo, 103; John,
82; Thomas, 18; William, 18
Bellamy, Alexander A., 19; Edward
C., 19; John F., 9, 19, 106;
John T. N., 19; Joseph C., 19;
Joseph Clinch, 19; Mary, 94;
Samuel C., 19; William, 19, 30;
William E., 105; Wm., 94
Bennet, Nancy, 139
Bennett, H. G., 109; H. T., 109;
Phil, 7; Salley, 38
Benson, Jethro, 52
Benton, Absalom, 80; Sarah, 94
Bergeron, Charity, 103; Demaris, 19;
Elias, 103; Wm. B., 19
Bevan, John, 55
Bezzell, Melany, 132
Biggs, John, Sr., 98
Bilbro, Benjamin, 19, 32, 75, 82,
111, 118; Berry, 19; Berryman,
19; Betty, 19; Bryant, 106;
Joseph, 19; Mariah, 111; Meriah,
19; Nathaniel, 19; Rebecca, 19;
Salley, 19; Thomas, 19; William,
19, 123; Z. B., 29
Bird, James, 20, 25; Kisiah, 20;
Patsey, 20; Wiley, 20
Bissett, David, 13, 20; Delia, 20;
John, 20, 71; John Henderson,
20; Joseph, 20; Judith, 20;
Lodrick, 20; Noah, 145
Blackwell, Asberry, 20; Hardy, 8,
36; Josiah, 20; Nathan, 20
Blanton, Chloe, 39
Blount, Benj., 118; Benjamin, 5,
37, 91, 100; Benjamin A., 49

G. M., 99; H., 20, 120, 144;
Henry, 38, 80; H. G., 29, 148;
John G., 29; J. W., 139; Mary,
100; Mildred, 53, 54
Blumery, Nathan Cobbs, 36
Blunt (Blount), Benjamin, 117, 123
Bobbitt, G., 107; Miles, 142
Boddie, Bennett, 8, 21, 107, 108;
Bettey, 21; Elijah, 4, 21, 105;
Elizabeth, 21, 105; Elvira
Cornelia, 21; George, 13, 14,
20, 21, 23, 33, 34, 57, 70, 73,
78, 91, 96, 99, 107, 108, 113,
124, 139; George, J.P., 45;
George, Sr., 90; James B. H.,
21; J. B. H., 76; John L., 21;
John S., 21; J. S., 21; Lucy,
13, 20; Martha Ann, 21; Mary,
21; Mourning, 21; Nathan, 8,
20, 34, 39, 96, 98, 107, 108, 135;
Nicholas, 45; Nicholas W., 45;
N. W., 45; Pattie, 21; Patty,
21; Penelope Jones, 21; Sarah
T., 21; Temperance, 21, 34, 124;
Thomas Jefferson, 21; T. I.,
118; Vanvan Salair, 20; William,
14, 21, 23, 108, 133; William
W., 7, 14, 21, 33, 57, 58, 76;
William Willis, 21; Willie W.,
20; Willis, 21; Willis W., 146;
W. N., 45; Wm., 124; Wm. W.,
44, 74; W. W., 7, 21, 37, 56,
58, 89, 97, 112
Bonds (Barnes?), Duncan, 36; John,
100, 142; Larry, 36; Lucreasia,
79
Bone, David, 16, 138; Elizabeth,
21; Hardy, 138; John, 9, 21, 67;
Mourning, 85, 137, 138; Nancy
W., 138; Nelson, 21, 22, 71,
83, 120, 137; Nicey, 15; Philla-
mon B., 138; Willie, 21, 138;
Boon, B., 81; Benjamin, 39; Cornelia,
45; Elizabeth, 133; L., 142;
Martha, 22; Martha L., 64; Mary,
22; Philimon, 22; Raiford, 22;
Rebecca, 76; Robert R., 45;
Roeny, 9; Susan, 32, 118
Borland, John, 5
Bottoms, Allaminta S., 22; Allevene
S., 22; Brittain H., 68; John
H.,68; John L., 138; John S.,
7; Lucy E., 22; Lucy L., 22;
Mary L., 138; Micajah S., 22;
Milly, 68; Nancy B., 85; Samuel
L., 22; Sarah Long, 22; William
H., 68; William Long, 23; Wm.
S., 22

Bowden, Arthur, 105; Delany, 15;
Harry, 22; Hiram, 22; J. J.,
14; Malcus, 22; Martha, 22
Bowen, Nancy, 35
Bowens, William, 35
Bowers, J. B., 85; William, 75
Boykin, Alfred, 22; Alsey, 22;
Betsey, 103; Blessing, 47;
Carolina, 43; Council, 22;
Counsel, 47; Eady, 23; Hardy,
22; Hardy W., 22, 47; Hilliard,
22, 23, 47; H. M., 43; Irvin,
22, 23; Jacob, 148; Jonathan,
23; Linsey, 22; Penelope, 148;
Polly, 22; Richmond, 22;
Stephen, 23, 76; Steven, 23;
Tempy, 23; Thomas, 23; Weighty,
47; Willie, 43, 47; Wright, 47
Braddy, Eliza, 106
Bradey, Jas., 1
Bradley, James, 23, 105; Virginia,
111
Brady, Elizabeth (Miss), 37; Thomas
J., 56
Brake, Daniel, 80; Elizabeth, 80
Brantley, Elizabeth, 23; Green B.,
19; Jacob, 23; John, 23; Joshua,
98; Martha, 98; M. C., 140;
Rosanna, 54; Zilpha, 104
Braswell, Addie, 24; Archibald, 47;
Benjamin, 23, 24, 25; Bersheby,
25; Brittain, 23; Celia, 82;
Charity, 24; Cloe, 23, 25;
Columbus, 148; Dawson, 23; Dem-
sey, 47; Dempsey, 4, 24; Deny,
23; Dinah, 82; Edward, 24;
Elizabeth, 25; Harriett, 24;
Jacob, 23; Jefferson, 24; Jere-
miah, 12, 24; Jesse, 4, 23, 24,
80; Joe, 24; John, 24, 25, 44;
John T., 16, 24, 46; Jno., 28;
Leah, 25; Lucy, 24; Louisiana
N. B., 24; Madison, 24; Margaret,
24; Martha, 24; Mary, 4, 148;
Mary Ann, 24; Mary Hunt, 133;
Micajah, 24; Mildred, 80; Milley,
25; Milly, 25; Mourning, 24;
Nathan, 23; Nicholas, 24; Nicho-
las C., 24; Norfleet, 23; Orren
D. (Orrendatus), 23; Penelopy,
25; Phereby, 25; Piety, 25;
Polly, 18, 116; Quinny, 24;
Reuben, 23; Rhoda, 25; Robert,
108; Robin, 24; Roeany, 23;
Sally, 24; Sampson, 24; Samuel,
24; Sarah, 24, 25, 61; Susan,
23; William, 23, 24, 25, 108,
146; William, Jr., 24; William,

Sr., 61; Susan Linch, 23; T. P.,
145; Weldon, 97; Wilson, 24
Bridgers, A. W., 69; Benjamin, 25,
121; Elizabeth, 13, 25; Henry,
25, 70; John, 25; Mica (Micajah),
25; Micajah, 25, 105, 132; Sam,
25; Sarah, 39; William, 13, 25,
39; Wm., 4; Wm. B., 30
Britton, Charles, 25; Jesse, 25;
Martha, 25; Nanny, 25
Brogden, Edward T., 69
Brooks, R. U., 139
Brown, Elizabeth, 25; Hardy, 108;
James, 129; Jeremiah, 25; John,
25; Joseph, 25; Martha, 25;
Mary, 25; Rebecca, 25; Sam, 20;
William, 25
Bruce, Cornealias (?), 113
Bruice, James, 34
Bryan, Bythel, 58; Hardy, 147; James
S., 3; William D., 106
Bryant, Aley?, 26; Benjamin, 71;
Betsey, 63; Bythel, 127; Delany,
26; Ellen, 27; Elizabeth, 26;
Elizabeth M. or C., 71; Evan
N., 26, 27; Evans, 26; G. B.,
26; Gideon, 26; Gideon B., 27;
Guston, 30; Harriet, 96; Henry
H., 26, 27; James, 51, 63, 70;
Jency (Jeney, Jiny), 26; John,
27; John W., 26, 27, 32, 102;
Martha, 30; Mary, 26, 70; Mil-
berry, 26; Penny, 30; Polly,
26; Robert, 26, 27; Samuel,
26, 100, 108, 135; Sarah, 26,
127; Simon, 30; Susan, 26;
Thomas, 23, 26, 103; Thomas N.,
26, 27; William, 26, 27; William, Sr., 26; William B., 26,
56, 139; William Jane, 26, 27;
William T., 26, 27; Wm. F.,
26; Wm. T., 71; W. T., 26;
William W., 30
Bunn, Alford, 28; Alfred, 12, 138;
Alfred (Alford?), 28; Amanda,
11; Ann, 27; Ann Jackson, 138;
Benjamin, 27, 36; Benjamin, Sr.,
27; Bennett, 27, 28, 60, 88;
Bennet H., 28, 110; B. H., 73;
Burwell, 27, 63; Charity, 10,
28; Creasy, 27; David, 27, 28,
90; David L., 114; David, Sr.,
27; Drewsy, 125; Drucilla, 28;
Elias, 126; Elizabeth, 27; Harriett C., 29; Henry, 27, 109,

125; H. S., 73; Jeremiah, 27;
Jno. S., 127; Joel, 27, 63, 119;
Joel D., 28; Joel Davis, 28;
John, 11, 27; John I., 28; John
J., 28, 67; John Jolly, 28;
Josiah, 27; Milley, 27; Nancy,
6, 109; Piety, 27; Priscilla,
27; R., 90; Rachel, 27, 28;
Rebecca, 76; Redmun, 10, 12,
27, 28, 60, 61, 88, 112, 126,
128, 147; Redmund, 49; Sally,
27; Sarah, 27; Sarah E. A., 98;
Seleter, 27; William B., 98;
Willie, 10, 11, 12, 27, 28, 58,
63, 107, 138; Willie, Jr., 28;
Wm., 27
Bunten, William, 73
Buntin, B. B. (Benjamin), 28; Jere-
miah, 82; Peggy, 82; William,
82, 102
Bunting, Annalizar, 92; Caroline,
29; David, 29; Elizabeth, 44,
123; Frances, 92; James, 29,
89, 91, 92; John W. B., 29;
Millaney, 92; Penelope, 29;
Sally, 29; Sally E., 29; Sarah,
28; Susan, 28; Thos. B. B., 29;
Vincent, 29; William, 29; Willie,
28, 29, 30
Burden (or Byrd), William, 101
Burge, Elizabeth, 99; Elizabeth B.,
100
Burnett, Calvin, 76; John N., 118;
Martha, 85
Burns, Jesse, 60
Burt, Ann L., 29; Cassandra, 29;
Cuffy (?), 29; Elizabeth, 29;
Lane, 29; Lucinda, 29; Lucy, 29;
Mary A., 29; Salumith, 29; Solo-
mon, 29; William, 29, 38, 58;
William, Sr., 41; Wm., 3, 41
Burton, Henry H., 42
Burwell, W. O., 144
Butler, Ann, 81
Butts, Jacob, 108
Byrd (or Burden), William, 101

- C -

Cain, Baldy, 106; Duncan, 106; James,
95, 117
Cammel (Campbell?), Sarah, 77
Capbell (Campbell?), Drucillia, 49
Capehart, Harriet, 52; John, 52;
William, 52

Carlisle, Elizabeth, 50; Hilliard, 48
Carpenter, Nancy, 88
Carr, Elias, 59
Carrell, Chasey, 27
Carrill, Elizabeth, 74
Carter, Adkins, 102; Charles, 25;
    Jacob, 135; M. A., 148; Mathew,
    102; Matt, 107; Mary, 29, 86;
    Nancy, 100; Polley, 52; Priscilla,
    8; Thomas, 71, 75, 77, 79, 82,
    102, 130; W. R., 115
Cauthon, John D., 84
Chadwick, Frances, 29; Martha, 29;
    Noah, 29
Chapman, Ann, 93; James H., 133
Clanton, Geo., 3
Clark, Herod, 61; J. W., 120;
    Penelope, 111, 128; Robert, 1
Clibon, Sarah, 118
Clifton, Sarah, 131
Clinch, Christopher Moore, 29, 142;
    Duncan Lamon, 30; Edward, 29,
    30, 93, 102; Elizabeth, 30, 94;
    Hannah, 29; Horation G., 30;
    Horatio Gates, 29; Joseph D.,
    30; Joseph John, 29, 30, 94;
    Mary, 30
Cobb, ?, 118
Cockrell, Anne, 30; Baldy, 30; Bet-
    sey, 30; Elisha H., 138; Eliza-
    beth, 85; Elizabeth H., 11;
    Jacob, 30; John, 30; Jonathan,
    30; Joseph, 30, 120; Nance
    (Nancy), 133; Nancy, 30; Nathan,
    30; Piety, 85; Samuel, 30; Sarah,
    85; Vincent, 30; William Hay-
    wood, 30
Coffield, Elizabeth W., 19; Martha
    C., 19; Sarah S., 19
Coggin, C. C. Gideon, 140
Coleman, Charles, 54
Coley, Guilford, 104; Mary Eliza
    Temperance, 145
Collins, Benj. F., 147; Clifton,
    116; Elizabeth, 39, 40; George,
    75; Irene, 116; J. J., 5, J. J.
    M., 41; John, 71; Josiah, 15;
    Michael, 5, 39, 40; Minnie
    Estelle, 139; Mrs. Patsey, 53;
    Peggy, 21; Roeny, 140; Sallie,
    116; Solomon, 34; Temperance,
    15; Viny, 4; Wilson, 21
Cone, Alsey May, 30; A. M., 146;
    Beedy, 30; Betty, 130; Burkely,
    78; Burtis, 28; Catherine, 30;
    Elizabeth, 37; Guilford, 30;
    Harriet, 30; Henry Richardson,
    30; James, 30; John Turner, 30;

Penelope, 30; Polly, 17; Susan,
    30; William, 30
Connigland, Edward, 41
Conyers, L. M., 41, 139; W. M., 5
Cook, Andrew G., 31; Celia, 31; Ed-
    win, 31; Lavinia, 31; Lazarus,
    31, 77; Lucy, 31; Martha, 31;
    Marthenia, 31; Mary, 31; Nancy,
    31; Salley, 50; Sally, 31
Cooley, R. A. P., 145
Cooper, Alfred, 31; Amy, 31; Ash-
    ley G. H., 32; Benj., 36;
    Blount, 127; Calvin, 32, 66,
    132; Cannon, 31; David, 31, 32;
    Edward, 31, 48; Elizabeth, 6,
    31, 74; George, 6, 28, 31, 32,
    138, 144; George H., 32; George
    W., 9, 32, 46, 138; Hardy, 31;
    Isabel, 36; Isham, 31; James,
    31, 36; Joel, 31, 123; John,
    31, 32; John D., 62; Little I.
    B., 32; Lucy, 31; Lucy M., 71;
    Marcom, 110, 122; Marcum, 31;
    Margaret, 32; Mark, 31; Mary,
    31, 32, 36; Masee, 36; Mathew,
    36; Mourning, 31; Nancy, 31,
    80; Neverson, 6; Neverson W.,
    113, 138; N. K., 141; N. W.,
    3, 32, 53, 111, 139, 141; N. W.
    Sheriff, 74; Peggy, 123;
    Penelope, 31; Rebecca, 36; Reu-
    ben, 31; Sarah, 31, 62; Temper-
    ance, 138; Tempy, 32; Thos. A.,
    20; Thomas I. A., 6; Thos. J.
    A., 2, 24, 35, 138; Vincent,
    32, 80; Vinson, 31; William, 6,
    28, 31, 32, 75, 85, 144; William
    A., 138; Willie H., 32; Willie
    H. (Wiley?), 32; W. W., 137
Coppedge, ?, 15; Anna Eliza, 15;
    Jesse, 32; Jordan, 32; William
    B., 32
Cotten, Samuel, 107; Solomon, 108
Counsel, Clarissa, 32
Courts, James, 63
Craig, Adam, 40
Crawford, Elizabeth, 107; Henry,
    57; Mary, 107
Creekmore, Annas, 33; Ballentine,
    110; Barsheba, 16; David, 102;
    Elizabeth, 16; Frances, 32;
    Nancy D., 33; Nanna, 33; Nanny,
    16; Robert, 35, 72, 73, 102,
    110, 112; Robert E., 110; Sally,
    33; Solomon C., 33; Thomas, 27,
    32, 118, Thomas F., 33; Timothy,
    33, 73; Timothy Terry, 33; Uriah,
    75, 118

Derring, Emelius, 36; James, 36; John, 7, 36, 54; John Randolph, 36; Josiah, 36; Josiah Nicholas, 36; Margaret, 36; Mary, 36; Sophonia, 36

Dew, Duncan, 36; Dunkin, 37; Dunkin (Duncan), 36; Edy, 132; Elizabeth, 36; Frances, 99; John, 36, 83; John, Sr., 36; Larry, 36; Nancy, 36; Patsey, 36; William, 37

Dickinson, Jacob, 126, 131

Dixon, Henry, 67; Keziah, 67; Martha, 67; Randolph, 67; Thomas G., 67;

Dortch, Drewsey, 126; Drucilla, 125; Isaac, 57; Janney, 37; Lewis, 37, 73, 77, 99; W. D., 45; William, 71, 116; William T., 17, 49, 62, 84, 143; Wm. T., 131; W. T., 67

Dozier, Ann, 37; Averilah (Averilla?), 37; Benjamin A., 1, 37; Charlotte T., 37; Elizabeth, 37, 77; Frederick, 41; James, 37, 44, 100, 128; James F., 139; James T., 26; John, 37, 43; John, Jr., 50; Julius, 37; Leonard, 37; Martha, 37; Martha Susan, 37; Mary, 37; Nancy, 37, 118; Peggy, 37; Richmond, 26, 28, 37, 70; Sarah, 37; Thomas, 37; William, 37, 56, 65, 70, 88, 105, 127; William S., 77; Wm., 106; Zachariah, 37

Drake, Albritton, 39; Allen, 36, 41, 81; Ann, 3, 50; Augustin, 37; Augustine, 38; B., 99; Benjamin, 39, 72; Benjamin F., 51; Caswell, 38, 40, 72, 81; Charity, 40; Chloe, 38; Delilah, 41, 81; Dorothy, 38, 40, 41; E. B., 141; Edmund, 38, 122; Edwin, 38; Elizabeth, 38, 41; Elizabeth D., 39; Elizabeth W., 38; Frances, 81; Francis, 38, 40, 41, 146; George W., 41; Green W., 38, 41; Harriett Adeline, 6, 39; Harriet Eliza, 120; Hartwell, 39; Henry, 38, 72; Hines, 39, 45, 47; Isaac, 51; (Dr.) J. A., 38, 61, 90; James, 39, 41; James W., 41; Jesse, 38, 40, 51; Jesse H., 32, 38, 39, 41, 44, 55, 62, 63, 92, 96; J. H., 146; John, 25, 39; Dr. John A., 61; Dr. John C., 98;

John G. F., 51, 77, 90, 140; Dr. John G. F., 98; John H., 38, 39, 40, 78; Dr. John H., 15, 98; John H., Jr., 15, 138; John Hodges, 39; John J., 38, 77, 98, 145; John Q. A., 1, 97; John William Wallace, 98; Jonas, 40; Dr. Joseph, 120; Joseph A., 21, 22, 44, 54, 140; Joseph John, 41; Louisa, 38; Louiza, 41; Luraney, 51; Margaret, 41; Martha, 40, 51, 59; Martha Emily, 1; Mary, 51, 54, 72; Mary Elizabeth, 41; Mary T., 6; Mathew, 17, 40, 64, 81; Mathew Bolivar, 41; Matthew, 108; Mourning, 32, 39, 40, 109, 110; M. W., 145; Nancy, 38, 81; Nathaniel, 41, 81; N. J., 146; Patsy, 38; Penelope, 72; Penny, 38; Polley, 38, 81; Richard, 41; Richard Armstrong, 6; Richard F., 24; Salley, 38; Sarah, 72; Selah, 105; Silas, 39; Sion, 51; Susannah, 8; Temperance, 39, 40, 53, 54; William, 18, 38, 41, 58; William F., 3, 38, 41; William Green, 41; Wm., 3

Draper, Robert E., 37

Drewry, Elizabeth, 3; James, 40, 81; John, 81; Lucy, 81; Mathew, 56; Samuel, 81

Driver, John, 70; Jonathan, 70; Keddick, 130; Nannie, 130; Rhoda, 51

Druery, Henry, 56

Druery (Drewry), James, 40

Druery, William, 56

Due (Dew), Duncan, 79; Patsey, 79

Duggins, Daniel A., 127

Dunn, Benjamin, 41; Elizabeth, 93; Francis Wilkinson, 41; Lamon S., 41; Margaret A., 41; Martha Susan, 41; William, 93; William Orris, 41; W. O., 142

- E -

Earl, James M., 144

Earls, John, 4

Earp, Haney, 42; Joseph, 42, 128; Lize, 42; Polley, 42; Polly, 78, 143; Richard, 42; Silvey (Sylvia?), 42; Tempy, 42; William, 42, 143

Earppe, William, 88
Eason, Allis, 42; Ann, 42; Dempsey,
    42; Dinah, 35; Edith, 42; Ely
    Everett, 42; Eunice, 42; Isaias,
    42; John, 42; John Smith, 42;
    Margaret, 42; Milley, 42; Nancy,
    42; Ruth, 42; Sam, Jr., 42;
    Samuel, 42; William, 42
Eatman, Aggathy, 43; Alex, 80;
    Alexander, 130; Beedy, 43;
    Bidy, 129; Elisha, 43; Eliza-
    beth Jane, 43; Everard, 30;
    Exum, 103; German, 43; Gincy,
    43; Greer, 43; Grimer (Grimmer?),
    43; Hayman, 43; Henry, 43;
    Jensey, 43; John, 30, 43, 61,
    129; Leonard, 43; Martha, 43;
    Mashel, 43; Nancy Mariah, 43;
    Noel, 43, 129; Peter, 60, 80,
    100, 130; Robert, 22; Ruffin,
    42, 60; Tempy, 43; Theophilus,
    43; Wiley, 43; Will Mc., 43;
    Willie, 43; Zilla, 47
Eatmon, Nicy, 43
Eden, Polley, 44
Edens, Ann, 43, 44; Mary, 43, 96;
    Nancy, 44; Polley, 43; Richard,
    35, 44; Sallie, 44; Siley
    (Cealey?), 44
Edwards, Benj., 13; Betsey, 44;
    Betsey H., 44; Catherine, 22;
    Chrissey Bennett, 84; Cullen,
    84; Dread, 44; E., 34, 75;
    Eaton, 20; Eaton H., 14; Edwin,
    22, 44, 45, 69, 84, 125, 126;
    Edwin Francis, 84; E. (Edwin),
    129; E. Edwin, 69; Elizabeth,
    14, 45; Eliza H., 120; Ethel-
    dred, 44, 60, 84; Eunice, 48;
    George, 44; Harriet Hester Ann,
    132; Henderson Battle, 84;
    Henry, 18, 44, 57, 91; James R.
    Clinton, 84; Jas. H., 45; John,
    34; Leah, 141; Lucy, 44; Martha,
    44; Matilda, 141; Mary, 44;
    Milley, 44; Nancy, 44; Philan-
    der Tisdale, 44; Salley, 84;
    Sally, 44; Sarah Ann Elizabeth,
    84; Sarah E., 13; Solomon, 45;
    Weldon N., 72; W. F., 27; W. H.,
    25, 97, 116; William, 84;
    William F., 32; William H., 45;
    Wm. L., 44, 64
Ellen, Howell, 18, 24
Ellen (Flewellen), Howell F., 90;
    Lod. F., 18

Ellen, Loderick F., 115; Lodrick,
    131; Polly, 131; Thos. F., 90
Ellin, Betty, 122; Cordal N. F.,
    121; Elizabeth F., 47; Howell,
    122; James B., 18
Ellin (Flewellen), James F., 91
Ellin, Loderick F., 47; Nancy F.,
    47; Temperance F., 47
Ellis, Elisah (Elisha?), 9; Reddick,
    77; Susanna, 77
Elvetant(?) (Sillivent?), Orpay,
    144; Pernelerper (Penelope), 144
Ely, Bearsheba, 79
Etheridge, Ann, 139; Courtney, 45;
    John, 139; Martha, 45, 139;
    Sarah, 87
Ethridge, Dinah, 113; Jeremiah, 45,
    86; Peter, 113, 139
Evans, Abraham, 144; Ann, 45; David,
    108; Dolly, 45; Elizabeth
    Warren, 45; George, 45, 98;
    Isaac, 45, 46, 138; Isaac B.,
    45, 46; James, 55; Lucinda, 118;
    Sally, 45, 138; Selah, 23;
    Sherrod, 45; Sherwood, 44;
    Susan, 45; Susan Catherine, 139;
    William, 45, 46
Evins, Abraham, 45
Evins (Evans), Ann, 45
Evins, George, 45; Isaac, 45
Evins (Evans), John, 45
Evins, Selah, 68; Sherrod, 45
Exum, Arkaddar (Arcadia?), 33; Char-
    lotte, 45; Joseph, 25; Pris-
    cilla, 24
Ezele, Thomas, 30

- F -

Farmer, John, 28, 132; Willie, 129
F. Ellin (Flewellin), Cordal N.,
    63; Howell, 47
Ferrell, A., 52; Ancel, 48; Benja-
    min, 46; Birton (Burton?), 46;
    Bry, 46; Burton, 46; Elizabeth,
    46; Harry, 101, 102; Henry, 46;
    Hutchens, 78; Iesley, 46; James,
    46, 48; John M., 46; Rollen
    (Roland), 46; Sela, 78; Temper-
    ance, 12; Timothy, 12, 28, 32,
    53, 60, 88, 114, 127; William,
    46; William Joel Tolliver, 12
Finch, C. H., 80; Claborn, 78;
    Ellen Jane, 95; H., 78; Henry,
    8; Irvin, 78; Irwin, 95; Isham,

8; John, 78; Kinchen, 95; Primmy,
32; Rahab, 95; Susanna, 78;
Temperance, 95, 100; William,
142
Fleetwood, William, 52
Fleming, James, 33; John, 33
Fletcher, John, 104, 112
Fletmore, William, 74
Flewellin, Mrs. E., 18
Flod (Flood or Flyod?), Hardy, 138
Flowers, Adam, 47; Benjamin, 46,
47, 70, 85; Benjamin, Sr., 47;
Bennet, 47, 129; Dycea (Dicia),
47; Edward, 134; Esakiah
(Hezekiah) B., 129; Guy, 47;
Henry, 134; Jacob, 47; John,
35, 47; Judah, 77; Louisa,
129; Martha, 47; Mary, 47;
Mason, 52; Nancy, 47; Nealy,
23; Rachel, 47; Virginia, 129;
William, 47
Floyd, Amos, 47; Diocletian Drake,
41; Duncan, 116; Fed, 13;
Frederick, 47; Mourning, 13;
Pennel (Penuel), 64; Penuel,
41; Penwell (Penuel), 122;
Salley, 18
Folks, Ann, 123
Forehand, David, 48; Lettie, 48
Foreman, Benjamin, 52; Cornelius,
48
Fort, Cresey, 28; Jacob G., 111;
Mary A. E., 111
Foster, Benjamin F., 87; Mary T.,
87; Rebecca, 21; Sally Ann, 87
Fountain, Penelope, 83; William H.,
83
Fowler, Burrell, 60
Fox, Isham, 48; Jacob, 48; Lucy,
48; Mary, 48, 144; Mary K.,
139; Readin, 48; Reden P., 139
Frazier, Alexander, 48; Sally, 48
Freeman, Amanda, 49; Amanda G., 49;
Amariah, 17, Amariah ?, 49;
Betsey, 23; Harriet, 49; Henry,
36, 134; John, 48; Mathew, 36,
48; William G., 49
Fulghum, Edwin, 43; James, 82
Fulgum, Edwin, 22; Elizabeth, 70;
Jesse, 22
Fuller, Bartholomew, 48
Futral (Futrell), William, 61

Gainer, Lucy, 34
Gandy, Amos, 20; Brinkley, 49;
Brinkly, 122; Brinly (Brink-
ley?), 31; Edward, 49, 95;
Elizabeth, 49; Foster, 9, 83;
Griffin, 49; Isham, 122; Tamsey,
49; Temperance, 7
Gant, Charles, 121; William, 121
Gardener, George, 49; Holman, 49;
Sarah, 49; Sophrona, 49
Gardner, George, 117; Hoalman, 7;
Mary, 76; Pryor, 117
Garner, Thomas H., 111
Garrett, John W. B., 29; L. A., 29;
Lucretia A., 29; Samuel B., 29
Gatlin, William, 48
Gay, Bennet, 26, 75; Bennett, 116,
128; Bethany, 49; Charles, 18;
Eaton, 11, 28; Elias, 49; John,
13, 49, 75, 139; Josiah, 49;
Martha, 49, 139; Mills, 49;
Patty, 141; Sherwood, 128;
Thomas, 111; William S., 75;
Wilson, 133
Gilbert, Charity, 49; John, 49;
Nathan, 28, 49, 88, 125; Phebe,
49; Rowena, 49; Salley, 49
Gilliam, Ephraim, 49
Glamon, J. S., 135
Glanden, Elizabeth, 38; Major, 80;
Patience, 38; Robert S., 38;
Sally, 38; Temperance, 38;
William Jackson, 38
Glover, Barshaba, 139; Caswell, 139;
Elizabeth, 15; Hillery, 139;
Hilliard, 139; Jinsy, 139; John,
139; John, Jr., 139; Kelly, 139;
Peyton, 139; Thomas, 105, 139
Godwin, Hinton M., 132
Good, Mary, 99
Goodrich, Constance, 39
Goodwin, James, 117
Gordon, John, 11
Green, Ann, 50; Arthur, 50; Eliza-
beth, 30; Hardy, 50; John, 1,
50; Joseph, 50; Mary, 31, 50;
Sally, 50
Gregor, William H., 79
Grice, Bartley Deans, 50; Elizabeth,
50; Garry, 50; Jacob, 50; James,
50; John, 50; Liddy, 50; Milley,
50; Penney, 50; Polley, 50, 53;
Rodey, 50; Sherrod, 50; Stephen,
50; Tempey, 50; Theophilus, 50;
Thomas, 50; Zilphey, 50

Griffin, Absalom, 51; Andrew I., 68; Ann, 65, 81; Appy, 51; Aquilla, 130; Arch'd, 45; Archibald, 31, 40, 76, 98, 107, 113, 125; Benjamin, 68; Bersheba, 65; Cenorah (Senora?), 140; Charity, 98, 107; Christian, 51; Cornelia, 140; Dolphin, 51; Drury, 51; Elisah (Eliza?), 51; Eliza, 51; Elizabeth, 41; E. Willie, 112; Fletcher, 130; Guilford, 110; Guliema ?, 122; Hardy, 18, 31, 69, 76; Jacob, 50; James, 51, 57; John, 50; Joseph, 51; Leonidas, 140; Lucy, 125; Margaret, 68, 140; Margarett, 140; Mariah, 51; Martha, 64, 76, 112; Mary, 51, 68; Micajah, 51; Nathan, 139; Newell (Penuel), 50; Pearce, 51; Presley, 140; R. B., 16, 99, 133; Roburty (Roberta), 68; Ruffin, 115; Sarah, 51; Temperance, 50; Thomas, 64, 127; Vilett (Violet), 115; W. G., 139; William, 51, 68, 82, 140; William T., 29, 99; William Thomas, 68; W. T., 133, 144; Zilpha, 51
Grizzell, Arthur, 51; Bonster (?), 51; Daniel, 51; Hardy, 51; Herrod, 51; Isabel, 51; Nancy, 51; Priscilla, 51; William, 51
Guilbert, James, 55

- H -

Hackney, Betsy, 51; Elizabeth, 52, 62; Jennens (Jennings), 52; Jennons (Jennings), 51; Massee, 36; Milley, 51; Penelope, 52; Penny, 51; Rachel, 51; William, 51
Hadley, Lyda, 39
Hales, Enoch, 60
Hall, Ann, 122; William, 61
Hall, (Hale?), William H., 18
Hall, Wm., 3, 122; Wm. H., 115
Hamilton, Dorothy, 118; Thomas, 13, 102, 147
Hammon, Charles, 73
Hammond, Charity, 103; Jesse, 42, 78, 128; Margarett, 103
Hammonds, Mildred, 122; William, 105, 122; William M., 93

Hammons, Burrell, 52; Charity, 52, 140; Eaton, 140; James, 52; Jesse, 52; John, 52; William, 52; Willie, 52; Willis, 52
Hamons, Elizabeth, 140
Hanes (Harris?), Malvina, 56
Haney, Elizabeth, 52; Frances, 52; Mary, 52; Thomas, 52
Hanks, John H., 91; Thomas, 37
Harden, Nancy, 52
Hardy, Haywood, 133
Hare, William, 132
Harper, Ateshia, 85; George, 89; James, 86; John F., 86; John H. B., 89; Priscilla, 139; Rebecca, 141; Sallie, 141; Sally, 139; Sidney S. B., 90, 91; William B., 92; William J. B., 89, 90, 91, 92; William John Batchelor, 16; Williamson, 53
Harrell, Ben, 63; Lucretia, 12, 53; Reuben, 114, 135; William, 53
Harris, Amos, 6; Anselma, 61; Canfield, 53; Charles H., 9; Coffield, 68; Eliza, 6, 39; Hardy, 61; Harty, 56; Jacky E., 140; James, 48, 49; James I., 18; J. H., 41; Joel, 53; John H., 29; Mary Jane, 140; Moses C., 140; Nancy, 100; N. M., 5, 55; Phebe, 109; Randolph, 53; Tempy Ann, 5
Harrison, Ann, 53, 54; Ann Eliza, 65; Benjamin D., 54; Betty, 54; Celestia E., 54; Charles, 103; Dempsey, 53; Demsey, 48; D. Y., 81; Elizabeth, 53; Emelius, 53, 54; Emelus, 50; Emilius, 53, 140; Emillius, 50; Hannah, 74; Henry, 53, 140; James, 25, 53, 54, 56, 97, 118; Jethro, 53, 94; John, 1, 36, 53, 54, 71, 117; John A., 56; John C. (?), 55; John Cora, 140; John F., 54; John H., 7, 54, 64; John, Sr., 118; Margaret, 54, 64; Martha, 139; Mary, 54, 109, 139; Mary Eliza, 55, 140; Milbray, 53; Nancy, 54; Nathaniel, 36, 53, 54, 64, 65, 90, 140; Nathaniel L., 55; N. C., 54; Nicholas C., 53, 90; Rhoda, 50, 140; Rhody, 55; Temperance, 8; W. D., 41; William, 8, 48, 53, 54, 84; William D., 86; William H., 54, 55, 140

Harrwood, Joseph, 85; Sarah, 85
Hart, E. B., 132; Elisha B., 55;
    Hartwell, 115; Mary, 76; Nancy
    W., 55; Robert D., 6; Rob't.
    C., 6; Susan E., 55; Thomas,
    55, 115, 125; Thomas, Sr., 55;
    Vandelia C., 55
Harte, Sarah, 69
Harwood, Joseph, 1
Haskins, Benjamin L., 55; Maria C.,
    55
Hatcher, Uriah, 104
Hatfield, Sarah, 73
Hattin (Hatton?), Sally, 112
Hawkins, Benjamin, 108; Henrietta,
    145; Mary, 50; Philemon, 107
Hawks, John H., 68
Hayes, Susana, 1
Hays, John, 125
Hearp (Earp?), Joseph, 81
Hedgepeth, Abraham, 34, 56, 117;
    Abram, 55, 97; Archibald, 55,
    56; Cealy, 56; Charity, 23;
    Elias, 55; Elias Green, 56;
    Francis, 24; Henry, 55, 56, 74;
    Henry W., 56; Jemima, 117;
    Jesse, 55; M. C., 56; Penelopy,
    55; Roena Mary Ann, 56; Taylor,
    55, 56; W. G., 145; William T.,
    56
Height, Francis, 3
Henderson, James M., 107
Hendrick, Clowey (Chloe), 56; Gran-
    berry, 56; Henderson W., 56;
    Morning, 141; Redding, 56;
    Samuel, 141; Simon, 141; Temper-
    ance, 56; William, Sr., 56;
    Wright B., 56
Hendricks, Eliza, 95; John H., 95;
    William, 37
Henry, Charity, 48; Nancy, 147
Hickman, Creesy, 101; Sarah, 101;
    Theophilus, 93
Higby, Emeline, 63
Higgs, Archilous, 37; John, 56;
    Jonathan, 56; Nathan, 37, 56;
    Philip, 56; Samuel, 56
Hill, Gilly, 100; Martha, 139; Mary,
    21; Polly, 60; Samuel S., 71;
    Thomas, 108
Hilliard, Alice, 57; Ammerylis W.,
    59; Ann, 57; Betsey, 57; Betsey
    M., 59; Caroline, 58; Carter,
    58; E. B., 24, 41, 44, 48; E.
    (Elijah) B., 56; Elijah B., 57,
    59; Eliza B., 134; Elizabeth J.,
    58; Elizabeth M., 58; E. W., 64;
    George W. B., 58; Henry, 57;

Isaac, 57, 58; Jake, 109; James,
    57, 58, 59, 65, 72, 78, 99, 109;
    James C., 57, 58, 64; James
    Carey, 58; Jeremiah, 61; Jesse
    P., 57; John, 57, 134; John H.,
    59; John T., 58; Jonas, 59;
    Jonas J. C., 58; Leah, 57, 58;
    Leah C., 59; Leah M., 58; Lucy
    E., 58; Martha, 57, 58, 144;
    Mary B., 59; Mary Eliza, 58;
    Mary S. M. A. E. J., 59; Mary
    T., 58; Mourning, 57, 59;
    Mourning B., 58; Nelson, 141;
    Rebecca, 57; Rebecca E., 59;
    Rebeccah, 106; R. C., 58;
    Robert, 58, 59; Robert C., 58,
    59; Robert Carter, 57; Robert
    C. T., 59; Sallie Ann, 141;
    Samuel, 59; Samuel (?) R., 145;
    Samuel R., 58; Sidney P., 57;
    Walter, 58; William, 57, 58,
    59; William H., 54, 59
Hilsmon (Hillman?), Betty, 19
Hilsmon, Nancy, 19; William, 19
Hindriot (?), Willie, 123
Hines, Alex, 59; Alexander, 57, 61;
    Alexander W., 59; Alex W., 31,
    95, 99; Allen, 97; C. A., 61;
    David D., 82; Eliza (Elizabeth),
    59; Elizabeth, 59, 114; Eliza-
    beth A., 59; Ella, 59; Francis,
    59; Frederick, 24, 59; Fred-
    erick B., 99; Hartwell, Sr.,
    59, 64, 95; John C., 59, 114;
    Joseph, 59; Kinchen, 82; Lewis,
    53, 110; Lewis H., 82; Little-
    berry, 64; Little Bray (Berry),
    65; Lucy B., 59; L. V., 59;
    Mary, 59; Mary Ann, 114; Nancy,
    59, 114; Patsey, 59; Peter R.,
    110; Richard, 110; Temperance,
    59; William H., 131; Wyatt (?),
    137
Hinnant, James, 147; Martha, 148
Hinton, Hattie Beulah, 141; Hilliard,
    80; Martha Elizabeth, 141; Nancy,
    63; Robert Leon, 141; William,
    70
Hobs, Mary, 26
Hocut, Henderson, 75
Hodges, Benjamin, 39; Hartwell, 39
Hogg, Charles, 20
Holden, Temperance, 53
Holeman, Samuel, 147
Holladay, Mary, 51

Holland, Elizabeth, 78, 133; Mourning, 14; Richard, 14, 44, 45,
71, 108, 126, 137
Hollingsworth, J. T., 148
Hollman, Benj. A., 1
Holman, Frederick, 109
Hooks, Will, 40
Hopkins, Alsey, 60; Betsey Polly,
52; Crofford, 60; David, 46,
60; Harriet, 52; Hilliard N.,
60; John, 60; Jos., 139;
Joseph, 60; J. W., 113; Martha,
116; Mary, 60; Milley, 46;
Milly, 60; Peter, 60; Susan,
60; Susannah, 60; Whitmel, 71,
116; Wiley, 60, 132; William,
60; Wilmoth, 60
Horn, Abishai, 60; Amey, 142; Amy,
70; Catherine, 61; Etheldred,
61; Frances, 109; Grantham,
141; Guilford, 67; Hannah, 61;
Hardy, 54, 61; Harris, 61;
Henry, 61, 142; Hilliard, 43,
141; Howell, 61; Isley, 141;
Jacob, 68, 118, 119; Jacob, Jr.,
61; Joel, 61, 141; Joshua, 61;
Josiah, 60, 109; Martin, 141;
Mathew, 61; Merit, 141; Michael,
47, 61; Milbrie, 61; Nancy, 53;
Polly, 67; Rebecca, 61; Rhoda,
141; Richard, 61; Thomas, 57,
61, 94, 119, 130, 141; Thomas,
Sr., 61; William, 30, 54, 61,
130, 131, 142; Wilson, 61; W.
R., 36
Horne, Henry, 60; Mary, 61; Patsey,
61
House, Polly, 106
Howard, James, 129; Sally, 129
Howell, Charles, 94; Mary, 74
Howerton, George Thomas, 61; Henri-
etta, 61; Sally Betty, 61;
Wiley Francis, 61; William
Baker, 61
Hunt, Alexander, 25; Ansle, 10;
Benjamin, 10; Brittain, 10;
Dicey, 61; Jesse, 24, 61; John,
31; Judah, 24; Judith, 61; Lucy,
144; Mary, 123; Morning, 61;
Nancy, 25; Rhoda, 10; Rodah,
18; Sarah, 61; W. L., 59; Wm.,
116
Hunter, Ann W. S. N., 19; Archi-
bald, 61, 108, 112; Benjamin,
19; Cordal, 45, 62; Cordal N.,

62; Cordal Norfleet, 62; David,
32; Delilah, 113; Drew, 87, 118,
125; Elizabeth, 59; Henry D.,
62; Henry Drew, 62; Isaac B.,
62; Isaac Blount, 62; James, 60,
88; Joanna, 62; John H., 62;
John Hodge, 62; Martha, 62;
Mary, 5, 61; Peter H., 32; Polley,
94; Polly, 2; Richard, 32; Sally
Ann, 62; Susannah, 32; Thomas,
61, 62, 131; Thos., 35; Weldon
S., 62; Weldon Smith, 62; Dr.
William, 19

- I -

Ing, Christopher, 51; Jacob, 37, 38,
59, 62, 65, 83, 84, 104, 106;
Sarah, 26
Izzard, John, 146

- J -

Jackson, Ann, 107; Catherine, 141;
George, 62; Joseph, 62; Lewis,
62, 119; Margaret Thomas, 107,
108; Mary, 62; Mourning, 133;
Mourning Thomas, 107; Newman,
62; O. L., 141; O. L., Jr., 142;
Reuben, 21; Simon, 22; Temper-
ance, 89; Temperance Thomas,
107, 108; William, 142; W. R.,
142
Jarratt (Jarrett), Betsey, 117
Jeffries, Simon, 57
Jelks, Etheldred, 100; Mellecan
(Milliken?), 62; Millican
(Milliken?), 57; Polley, 80
Jenkins, Jesse, 83; Rogers, 83
Johnson, Bery, 70; Catherine, 62;
Charles C., 75; Dacia, 139; D.
M., 27; Elizabeth, 62, 127,
142; Elizabeth H., 22; Emmy,
62; Harriet, 62; Henry, 62;
Jesse, 51, 83; Josiah, 108;
Littlebury, 62; Lucy, 75; Mar-
thew, 132; Mary, 62; Mathew,
62, 63; Moses, 62; Pattie, 63;
Polly, 62; Sally, 62; Sally Ann,
142; Stephen, 62; T. A., 27;
Timothy A., 32; Trecy, 63;
William, 62, 79

Keff (?), Mary, 78
Keith, Elizabeth, 42
Kemp, Catherine, 100; McBrantley,
   100
Kent, Burwell, 129; Mourning, 68;
   Trecey, 129
Keth, Bennet, 68; Elizabeth, 68;
   James, 68; William, 68
King, Azariah, 122; Julian, 108;
   Lucy, 70; Rebecca, 111; Rhoda,
   50; Sally, 68
Kitchen, Jesse, 109
Kittle, Polly, 117
Kittrell, S. W., 142; Thomas G.,
   142
Knight, Ann, 69; Benjamin F., 110;
   Caroline, 106; Elisha, 69;
   George, 68; James C., 48; John,
   69; Kiddey, 69; Kinsmere, 69;
   Sarah, 68; W. H. T., 48; Wm. H.,
   106
Knowlton, Asel J., 64

- L -

Lamb, Everett, 69; Jackson, 69;
   Nanney, 69; Penelope, 69; Thomas,
   69
Lamkin, Lewis, 129; Lewis Ablewis,
   33; Primmy, 85; Samuel L., 119
Lamon, Arch., 11, 101; Archibald,
   48; Dun., 33, 101; Duncan, 11,
   98, 109; Duncan, Jr., 135;
   Dunkin, 29; J. G., 27; John,
   30, 129, 135; Margaret, 27;
   Mary, 101; Nancy, 134, 148;
   Orrendatus, 27
Lampkin, Samuel, 85
Lancaster, Harte, 36; Robert, 36;
   William, 26
Landford, Mary, 122
Landing, Fannie, 142; John, 142;
   Martha, 142; William A., 142
Landman, Artimesia, 92; Charlotte,
   103; Nelson, 103; Owen, 103
Lane, Lamon, 38; Lemon, 62; Martha
   A., 62
Langley, Edith, 128; Elizabeth, 9,
   56, 66; German D., 20; G. D.,
   34; Joiner, 9, 96, 114; Joyner,
   43; Mary, 72; W. A. J., 34;
   William, 66
Lanier, R. H., 25
Lassiter, Wm., 69
Lawrence, Elizabeth, 69; Isaac, 70;
   Jesse, 69; Levecy, 14; Levicy,
   13, 70; Nicey, 69; Sealah, 74;
   Thomas, 69; Vicey, 69; William,
   69, 70, 74

Lee, Barnaby, 13; Bersheba, 70;
   Bud, 13; Clayton, 70; Eliza-
   beth, 13; James, 70, 142;
   Larry, 70; Moore, 70; Nancy,
   13; Talton, 13; William, 13
Legon, James, 63
Leigh, Didomy, 70; Jackson, 70;
   James, 70; Lindon, 70; Lind-
   sey, 70; Linford, 70; Loam-
   ma, 70; Moore, 70; Nancy, 70
Leonard, Henry G., 30; J. O., 145;
   John, 88; William, 48
Lewis, Abner, 70; A. F., 9;
   Catherine, 71; E. C., 22, 71;
   Elizabeth, 56; Emeriah, 71;
   Francis, 56; Geo. N., 22;
   George, 70; George N., 24, 27,
   49; G. N., 22; Harriett M. C.,
   29; H. D., 9; Henry, 70; John,
   19, 70, 107, 134; L., 95; Lucy
   S., 59; Lyda (Lydia?), 70; Lydia,
   79; Martha, 70; Mary, 35, 70;
   Nancy, 70; Nicholson, 70; Omey,
   103; Patsey, 56; Polly, 71;
Lewis (Luis), Robert, 80
Lewis, Salley, 43; Sparling B., 22;
   Thomas, 70, 71; Titus, 123;
   Tressa, 79; William, 2; Winney,
   70; Zaney, 134
Lindsey, Asbury, 71; Betsey Mary
   Fletcher, 71; Charity, 137;
   Chrischaney, 96; Edward Buxton,
   71; Jeptha, 71; Jerusha, 71;
   John E., 59, 92, 119; John W.,
   93; John Wesley, 71; Nancy, 85;
   Nathan, 71; Polly, 71; Polly
   Mintz, 71; Una, 111; William,
   9, 22, 67, 71, 108; William
   Ray, 71; Zany, 93
Linehan, Dennis, 135
Lipford, William A., 71
Long, Betty, 37; Joshua, 104; Mit-
   chell, 99; Sookey Whitfield,
   125
Lot, Elisha, 146
Louis, Omey, 103
Lyon, Thaddeus, 143
Lyons, John L., 50

- M -

Mack, Lenor, 94
Macklin, Jane L., 142; John, 142;
   Sarah, 142
Macom (?), Ellen, 62
Mallard, Alla, 74
Malone, Celah, 87; Dr., 97; Faith-
   ful, 87

Maning, Catey, 72; James, 73; Michal, 73; Mourning, 72; Nancy, 73; Phoebe, 72; Richard, 73; Samuel, 73; Thomas, 73

Mann, Allen, 72; B. D., 85; Benj., 4; Benjamin, 105; Benjamin D., 54; C. M., 145; Denton, 72, 121; Elizabeth, 72; James N., 71, 72; John, 4, 72; Jos. B., 26, 96, 134; Mary, 105, 106; Thomas, 39, 72; Thomas L., 55; Thomas N., 72; William, 72; Wm., 4

Mannen, Benjamin, 25

Manning, Aby (Abby), 73; Alexander, 92; Allen, 44; Argen, 73; Benjamin, 73; Betsy Ann, 15; Brittain, 44; Charity Ann, 14; David, 73; Drucilla, 73; Eli, 73; Elizabeth, 73, 121; Frances B., 32; James, 134; J. D., 14; John, 72, 73; John Batchelor, 16; John Wright, 73; Joseph, 72; Levy, 72; Margaret, 72, 121; Martha, 33, 121; Mary, 16, 121; Mathias, 72, 73; Matthew, 72; Merritt, 17; Michael, 44; Mourning, 73; Mourning Frances, 14; Nancy, 32, 118; Nathan, 83; Penelope, 21; Polly, 73; Pridgen, 16, 17, 71, 73, 96; Rahab, 73; Rich'd, 94; Sally, 91, 92; Samuel, 100; Susannah, 29; Thomas, 37; Warren ?, 32; W. E., 75, 89, 141; William, 73; Willibough (Willoughby?), 73; Willibough Lane, 73; Willis E., 32; Willoughby, 74

Marcus, Mary, 37

Mares (Mears), Joseph, 80

Marriott, H. B., 141; R. H., 128; R. H. (Dr.), 90; Robert H., 73, 82; Rob't H., 99; Tempie A., 73

Marsburn, G. R., 100

Marshall, Elizabeth, 128

Masingale, Keziah, 133; Walker, 37

Mason, Abner, 73, 74; Benjamin, 74; Catharine, 74; Elizabeth, 73, 74; Foster, 73, 74; Henry, 74; Isabel, 123; M., 68; M. (Marmaduke), 119; Mark, 73, 74; Mark, Sr., 74; Marmaduke, 88, 101, 118; Martha, 54; Milbury (Milbry), 123; Nathaniel, 4; Ralph, 101; Rebecca, 53; Richard, 60, 80; Temperance, 4, 54; William, 73, 74

Massenburg, N. B., 64

Massengail, Kessiah, 74

Massengale, Goodman, 100; Kiza, 74; Mary, 74; Massy, 74; Reddick, 74; Warren, 74

Massengill, Annis, 74, 75; Elizabeth, 74; James, 70, 74; Nancy, 127; Walker, 74

Massey, Matthew, 46; Milley, 46; Oscar K., 46

Massingale, Ann Arrabella, 74; Elizabeth, 74; George, 74; James, 74; James, Sr., 74; Matthew, 74; Walker, 74

Mathes, Arminda, 75; Elizabeth, 75

Mathes (Matthews), Evert (Everett?), 96

Mathes, Francis, 75; Isley, 75

Mathes (Matthews), John, 68

Mathes, Lecy, 75; Penelope, 75; William H., 96

Mathews, A., 86; J. D., 75; Jno. E., 38; Joel, 75; John, 68; John E., 86; John G., 15, 75; Joseph, 57;

Mathews (Matthews?), Josiah, 75

Mathews, Lucy H., 75; Lucy R., 75; William, 76; William H., 75

Mathis, John S., 110

Maths (Matthews?), John, 48

Matthews, H. H., 143; J. H., 137; Seleter R., 86; Sinthy (Cynthia?), 139

Matthis, Rhoda, 137

Mayfield, Thomas, 4

McBatchelor, Samuel, 121

McDade, Drewsilla, 75; Drucilla, 11; John, 75; John J., 75; Mary, 75; Nancy, 75; Salony, 75; William, 75

McDonald, William, 108

McFarland, Diana, 19

McGregor, William, 36

McLemore, W. E., 138

McWilliams, Wm., 130

Mearns, William S., 31, 57; William Skipwith, 37, 39; W. S., 18, 31, 51, 64

Mears, W. J., 72

Mecom, Betsey P., 75; Ellen, 75

Medlin, George A. G., 100; H. H., 94; Hilsman H., 100; Lucy Marriott, 100

Melton, Andrew, 75; Ann, 55, 76;
Bolen, 75, 134; Christian, 75;
Cooper, 76; David, 18, 76, 78,
87; Elizabeth, 64, 76; Fereby,
76; J., 126; John, 49, 57, 76,
107, 122; Joseph, 76; Joseph
Drake, 76; Josiah, 15, 76, 110,
112; Martha, 76; Mary, 76;
Mathew, 76; Milly, 23; Nathan,
76; Priscillia, 76; Robert, 76,
92; Robert Bolden Timothy, 76;
Sarah, 76; Temperance, 126;
Thomas, 76; Zachariah, 76; Zil-
pha D., 75
Mendendol (Mendenhall?), Fereby, 65
Mercer, Abba, 76; Eli, 65, 76; James,
76; James F., 20, 31, 77; Jane,
77; John, 76; Margaret, 76; Nan-
cey, 76; Rhoda, 77; Tempe Ann,
77; Thomas, 20, 31, 76, 77
Meritt, Benjamin, 77
Merritt, Benj., 94; Benjamin, 77, 88;
Berry, 37; Elizabeth Vester,
113; Henry, 77; Sarah, 77;
William, 77
Merton, Frances J., 12; John 12
Mials, Nanney, 51; Norsworthy, 51;
Purity, 51
Miller, Lewis, 117; Samuel, 1, 117
Mitchell, Elizabeth, 37; Gilly, 70;
H., 33; Henry, 20, 37, 77, 97,
109; Henry C. D., 77; Henry C.
Drake, 37; John W., 37, 77; J.
W., 54; Leroy, 111, 123; Martha
Ann, 37; Penelope, 77; Penelopy,
37; Samuel, 117; Sylvanius, 37
Moonehan, Amy, 77; Ann, 77; Enoch, 77;
John, 77; Judey, 77; Mary, 77;
Shadrick, 77; Thomas, 77
Moore, A. F., 141; Afred, 3; Ann,
13, 93; Bat (Bartholomew F., 20;
Cullom, 123; Collum (Cullen?),
13, 93; C. W., 78; Dennis, 99;
Edward, 30, 77, 84, 130, 142;
Elizabeth, 77; E. W., 25;
Indes ?, 93; James, 3, 23, 25,
77; James Willie, 14; Judah,
25; Lee, 142; Lucy, 20; Mahalah,
18; Mary, 77; Mary Elizabeth,
99; Moses R., 92; Nancy, 99;
Susanna, 77; William, 51, 54,
77; Wm., 130, 144; Zilphia, 142
Morgain (Morgan), Elizabeth Selah,
77
Morgain, James, 77; William, 77

Morgan, Bette Cealle, 78; Delacay,
46; E. H., 22, 143; Elijah H.,
69; Elizabeth, 78; Evan H., 95,
102, 103; Hardy, 78, 81, 105;
Henderson, 46, 102; Henry, 78,
143, 146; James, 78; James Henderson, 143; Jimerson, 46; John,
78, 143; John, Sr., 78; John T.,
140, 147; Lacy, 46; Lattamore,
146; Lucy J., 143; Martha, 46;
Nancy, 30, 78, 79, 103; Patsy,
48; Patsy Medora, 143; Rutha,
78; Shelley Mary, 146; Stone,
78; Willey (Wiley?), 102;
William, 16, 78, 102; William B.,
143; William Gay, 143; Wm., 16;
Wm. B., 102
Morgin, Mason, 52
Moris, Morning, 48
Morphis (?), James, 25
Morris, Allen, 78; Asey Hill, 78;
Bathseba, 78; Betsey, 78; Cloah
(Chloe), 78; Demcy, 78; Demsey,
78; Hardy, 78; Jesse, 78; John
M., 75; Preston, 78; Silvah
(Sylvia), 78; Thomas, 74, 78,
111; Thos., 29; Willis, 54
Mullins, James, 10
Murphy, Nathaniel H., 112; Nath. H.,
1
Murray, Absalom, 78; Burnel, 78;
Elijah, 79; John, Jr., 78; John,
Sr., 78; Mornin, 79; Reuben, 30;
Vincent, 78; William, 79
Murry, Holley, 42; William, 42
Musaw ?, Martha, 110

- N -

Nairn, William, 147
Narron, Bashaby, 43
Necome, Betsey, 63; Ellen, 63
Neele, Jas. W., 94
Nelms, Eben, 97
Nevin, William, 51
Newby, Thomas, 17
Newly (Newby?), Thomas, 84
Newsom, Molley, 37; Prisyla (Pris-
cilla), 117
Newsome, Isaac, 77
Newton, Susanna, 83
Nichols, Arnol (Arnold), 79; Eliza-
beth, 79; J., 131; Jeremiah,
79; John, 79, 131; Lurana, 47;
Sarah, 79

Nicholson, Abbagil, 79; David, 79;
Edw., 22; Edward, 8, 30, 37,
70, 79, 92, 93, 101; Eliza Ann,
79; Elizabeth, 72, 80; Eliza-
beth Crafford, 4; George, 79;
Gilford, 72; Guilford, 79; James
M., 79; James Mann, 72; John, 4,
17; Joseph, 79; Josiah, 79, 80,
95; Lettitia, 72; Lydia, 79, 80;
Malachi, 79; Martha, 80; Mary,
79; Matilda, 72; Nancy, 80;
Penelope, 72, 80, 126; Rhoda,
124; Sally, 80; Samuel, 74;
Thomas, 72, 79, 80; Timothy M.,
80; Timothy Mann, 72; Winifred,
93; Winneford, 79; Wright, 79
Nolleboy, Joseah, 55
Nollejoy, Winnie, 126
Norfleet, Betsy, 143
Norris, Mary, 74

- O -

Odom, Charity, 93; Christian, 116;
Theophilus,105
Odum, Christian, 80; David M., 80;
Exum, 80; Jacob, 80; Jacob
Richard, 80; James, 80; James
F., 126; John, 80; Louisa, 114;
Martha, 63; William, 80
O'Neal, Amy, 80; Arthur, 72, 76;
Axum (Exum), 80; Briant, 76;
Calvin Waton (Watson?), 80; Con-
dary, 80; Drewseller, 8; Jose-
phus, 80; Lucy, 80; Micajah, 80;
Nancy, 109; Polley, 51; Stephen,
80; Theophilus, 109; Trecy, 63;
Withy Ann, 80
Owen, Wm., 65
Owens, Daniel, 81; Elias, 77, 81;
Elizabeth, 81; Enoch, 81; John,
81; Malphusses, 108; Mary, 81;
William, 81

- P -

Paetrick, Elizabeth, 118
Paris, John, 19
Parker, Ann, 81; Cain, 51; Calvin,
81; C. I., 133; Ella M., 143;
Col. F. M., 41; Francis, 51, 81;
Henry, 58; Jesse, 94; John, 51;
73, 81; Josiah, 115; Kizzey Uers
(Eure?), 81; Martha Nailer, 40,
81; Mary, 81; Offe, 81; Pinkie,
90; Polly, 13; Polly Uers (Eure?),
81; Solomon, 81; Tempy, 115;
Unity, 51; Weeks, 81; William, 81;

William W., 111; W. W., 115, 144
Parrot, Anas, 110; William, 31
Parrott, Anna, 82; Austin, 82; Joseph,
25, 82; Mary, 82; William, 82
Pasmore, William, 131
Passmore, Elizabeth, 74; Joseph, 18;
William, 132
Peacock, Zadoc, 82
Peale, Jesse, 48; Joseph, 22
Pearce, Archibald, 97; Sally, 97
Pearson, Barney, 48
Peele, David, 82; Edith, 82; Jesse,
43; John, 79, 82; Martha, 82;
Nathan, 82; Patience, 82; Rebec-
ca Bell, 82; Sarah, 82
Peete (Peele?), Doctor, 57
Pender, Elizabeth H., 82
Perkins, James, 77
Permunter (Permenter?), James, 12
Perry, Dr. A. T., 57; Claborn, 46;
Claborne, 98; Eliza, 69; Hilli-
ard, 103; Jacob, 45; John W.,
103; Jonas, 69; Leah, 59; Lind-
sey, 69; Mark P., 29; Mary, 107;
Roenny, 103; Susan, 17; Sythoney,
69; Temperance, 107; Zilpha, 98
Person, Jesse, 4; Mary, 4; Nathan,
130; Presly C., 4
Petmond (Pitman?), Cloe, 79
Philips, Exum, 80; Frederick, 98;
James P., 98; Sally M., 80
Phillips, Jethro, 47, 53; Joseph, 47;
William, 53
Pierce, Clarkey, 82; Elizabeth, 82,
145; James, 60; Joshua, 82;
Richard, 82
Pillson, Thomas, 30
Pippin, Sel (?), B., 48
Pitman, Brinkley Gandy, 82; Duncan,
83; Jesse, 117; John, 22; Mary
White, 82; Olive, 22
Pitt, Cornelia, 143; Leah, 81; Mark,
117
Pittman, Dunking (Ducan), 67; Jesse,
83; Jno., 28; John, 82, 83;
Lucretia, 23; Mary, 67, 83;
Maryan, 83; Rhoda, 83; Robbin R.,
83; Saluda, 83; Susan, 83, 84;
William, 83; William B., 83
Pitts, Frederick, 143; Mark, 117;
Martha, 77; Walter, 143; William,
77, 143
Plummer, William, 72
Poland, Elizabeth, 115; Guilford, 28;
Joseph, 115; Polly, 33
Polen, Mary, 22
Poling, Sarah, 133
Poope (Pope?), Phereby, 73

Pope, Amanda, 63; Ann, 83; Archibald,
83; Arthur, 83; Arthur, Jr., 83;
Barbara, 62, 83, 119; Bedah
(Beady?), 83; Benjamin, 51; Deli-
lah, 120, 130; Dempsey, 83; Dem-
sey, 83; Elisha, 83; Hardyman, 83;
Jesse, 83; Joseph, 83, 84; Josiah,
83; Kindred, 84; Lazarus, 83;
Littleberry, 83, 106; Martin, 63;
Mary, 83; Mary Ann, 84; Penelope,
106; Priscilla, 119; Richard,
83; Sara, 83; Sarah, 51; Soloman,
130; Thomas, 119; William, 83;
William A., 84
Portis, George, 84; Ira, 84; Isaac,
139; Mary, 84; William, 84
Potter, Daniel B., 5
Poulan, Dinah, 104; Guilford, 84;
Henry W., 104; Henry W. H., 104;
John, 30, 84, 104; Joseph, 84;
Salley, 84; William, 84; William-
son, 84
Pouland, Elizabeth, 84; Jane, 96
Powell, Alansan, 1; Alanson, 112;
Alason, 40; Alpheus Wright, 134;
C., 106; Cherry, 33; Eliza, 7;
Elizabeth, 84; George W., 7;
Geo. W., 123; Huldy, 134; Jesse,
25; 69; John, 1, 53, 95; 112;
117; Lazarus, 134; Margaret, 85;
Martha, 85; Mary, 84; Mary Ann,
84; Mason, 50; N., 106; Nathan,
117; Nathaniel, 117; Patience,
74; Polly, 84; Rhoda, 24; Samp-
son, 21; Sarah Elizabeth, 85;
Susanna, 95; Tabitha, 50;
William, 75, 84, 131; William
Wright, 134; Willie, 41, 84, 85;
Willis, 69
Price, Charlotte, 110; Joel, 44;
John, 147; Jos. U., 145; Milley,
46; Penelope, 110, 125; William,
46
Pridgen, Abijah, 15, 16, 42, 85,
113, 137; Abijah Thomas, 85;
Achse, 16; Colen E. (Cullen?),
86; Dana, 85; David, 1, 16, 30,
42, 62, 73, 85, 129, 133, 137;
Drewery, 62, 85; Drewry, 9, 85,
86, 115, 120; Hardy, 8, 60, 62,
70, 85, 86, 132; Jesse, 16, 86;
Joel, 32; Mary, 16, 33, 42, 73,
86; Patrick, 86; Pinkey L., 85;
Polly Harriet, 85; Sarah, 16,
85; Thomas, 61, 129; William A.,
85, 86; William Asbury, 120

Prim, James, 85; Mary, 85
Privett, Elizabeth, 110; Luke, 110
Privette, Wesley, 19, 46, 95
Privitt, Israel, 60
Proctor, B. F., 139
Puckett, Hopne, 88
Pugh, Arnal (Arnold?), 144; Laborn,
144; Massey, 51; Senath, 144;
Tignal, 144; William, 77, 144
Pullen, Clarissa, 86; Elizabeth,
86; Emilus, 86; Ethelinda, 86;
John C., 86; Mary, 86; Willie,
86
Purcell, Edward, 86, 108; Elizabeth,
86; Hardy, 86; James, 86; Jane,
86; Jeremiah, 86; Sara, 86
Pyland, Robert

- R -

Rackley, Celestia Ann D., 128;
Cherry, 86; Cityvias?, 87;
Dinah, 72; Elizabeth, 128; F. M.,
141; Francis, 87, 128; Francis,
Jr., 86; Francis R., 86; Francis,
Sr., 86; Frederick, 87; John H.,
86; Joseph, 87; Lamon Dew, 86;
Lemon D., 86; Lucy, 87; Margaret
Cherry, 86, 87; Margarett, 87;
Martha Ann, 128; Martha Ann F.,
128; Mathew, 87; Matilda J.,
128; Molley, 87; Person, 87;
Persons, 87; Roeanna Ward, 87;
Sarah E., 128; Seleter Pansy, 87;
Silas, 87; William, 87; William
J., 128; William R., 17; Willie
F. M., 128; Yancey M., 128
Randolph, Beverly, 40
Ranson, James, 26; Sally, 26
Rawls, Cornelius, 87; David, 87;
Hardy, 87; Kelly, 87; Mary, 87;
Mary T., 39; Nancy, 87; Sally,
87; Sally Ann, 87
Ray, Charity, 127
Read (?), J., 142
Reading, Lurany, 12
Redding, Rhoda, 32
Reese, Roger, 19, 27, 28, 37, 120
Renfrow, Clarrey, 22; John H., 18
Respass, Isiah, 2; James, 2
Revel, Barnabas, 87; Delilah, 88;
Dolly, 87; Edith, 87; Elijah,
87; Elijah H., 88; Humphrey, 87,
88; Jonnathan (Jonathan), 87;
Mathew, 87, 88; Paul, 87; William
N., 88

Revell, Mary, 118
Revels, Edith, 87
Rice, B. D., 96; Benjamin, 26, 88,
102; Berry, 26; Boykin, 26, 88;
Bryant, 88; Bryant D., 89; Elizabeth, 26, 60, 88; Henderson, 26,
27, 88, 89, 129; Hopkins, 8, 88;
James M., 88; Jiney, 26; Jno. B.,
26, 101; John, 13, 26, 60, 88,
103, 104; John B., 26, 88, 95,
143; John, Esq., 81; John, Jr.,
33, 104; John, Sr., 88; John W.,
129; Martha, 88, 89; Mary, 88;
Mary M., 27; Mourning, 26, 27;
Nathaniel, 89; N. C., 56; Nicholas, 26; Nicholson, 26, 88; N.
N., 26, 27, 56; Patsey, 26;
Polly, 26; Richardson, 88;
William, 88
Richardson, Alsey, 89; George, 13,
89; Honour, 74; John, 13, 69,
70, 89; Numan (Newman), 89;
Reden, 88; Tempy, 89; William,
88, 89, 93; Winey (Winnie?)
Jackson, 83
Richerson, Sarah, 72
Richeson, Newman, 62
Ricks, Abraham, 52, 89, 92; Acksey,
89; Addison E., 93; A. H., 90,
145; Alsey, 91; Amos, 49, 68;
Ann, 68; Anna, 44, 90; Ann Ros-
ell, 90; Appy Ann, 91; Artimes-
ia, 92; Augustus H., 89; Benja-
min, 92, 131; Benton A., 92;
Buckanan, 90, 91; Burton A.,
93; Cary (Lary?), 90; Charity,
84; Charlotte, 92, 118; D. A. T.,
21, 65, 89; David, 49, 76, 87,
89, 90, 91, 114, 124; David A.
T., 90, 91; David B., 13, 119;
Delilah, 90; Dickerson, 91;
Dickeson, 92; Drusilla, 89;
Duncan, 52; Eli, 49; Elizabeth,
91, 92; Ellexander (Alexander)
Urban (?), 92; Exum, 89, 99;
Frances, 90, 91; Frances A., 54,
90; Frances Ann, 64; George, 21,
90, 91; Gideon, 90; Henry, 49;
Indiana, 91; Irvin, 50; Isaac,
28, 89, 90; Isaac W., 93; Isa-
bella, 89; Isbell (Isabel?), 90;
Jacob, 49, 90, 111; James, 54,
90, 98; James W., 93, 109;
Jerome, 90; Jesse, 90; Jethro,
54; Joel, 92; Johanna, 90; John,
21, 36, 68, 89, 90, 91, 92, 115,
118, 124, 126, 147; John A., 90,
91; Jonathan, 44; Lydia, 91, 92;
Marmaduke, 115; Martha, 90, 109;
Mary, 10, 90; Micajah, 91; Milberry, 92; Millicent, 92; Morning, 53, 54; Mourning, 98; Nancy
H., 92; Nero, 90, 91; Peninah,
92; Polly, 47; Priscilla, 92;
Rachel, 89; Redmun, 90; R. H.,
65; Rhoda, 91, 92, 98, 107;
Richard, 90, 126; Robert H.,
119; Ruffin, 92; Ruffin H., 10,
91; Salley, 119; Sarry, 118;
Spencer D., 115; Teachen, 48;
Teale, 130; Tempy, 44; Thomas,
92, 130; Urban, 130; Whitmill,
52; William, 49, 89, 90, 91, 92,
124; Willie, 28, 88, 89, 92;
Willie B., 93
Rickson, Jesse, 33
Ritcheson, Joseph, 25
Rives, Dr. John G., 98; Rev. Willis,
64
Robbins, Betsey D., 36; Cate, 36;
John, 37; John, Sr., 36; Nancy,
36; Obedience, 36; Rodah, 36;
Roland, 117; Susanna, 118
Robertson, Anna, 95; Henry, 116
Robins, Joanna, 119
Robinson, Elizabeth, 96
Roe, Louisa, 129
Rogers, Ann, 93; Charity, 13, 93;
Dinisha, 14; Frederick, 63;
Jacob, 93; James, 93; Jesse, 93;
John, 23, 93; Mary, 93; Moore,
93; Mourning, 13, 93; Nanny, 93;
Nise, 13; Patience, 93; Peleg
(Pealick), 93; Robert, 13, 23,
93, 105, 108; Thomas, 93; Uny,
93; Zany, 93; Zona, 13
Rooker, Presley, 103; Susan, 103
Roper, Joel, 93; Mary, 93
Rose, Alise (Alice?), 52; Ann, 13,
93, 94; Benjamin, 94; Burrel,
112; Casanna ? E. J., 144; Eady,
45; Edwin, 142; Edy, 139; Eliza-
beth, 83, 93; Fannie, 3; Francis,
52, 94; Lidy, 45; Mariah Eliza-
beth, 34; Martha, 94; Nancy, 110;
Patty, 94; Richard, 83; Sarah,
139; Tempie, 144; Thomas, 13;
Thompkins, 8; Tomkins, 94;
William, 25, 94
Ross, James D., 61
Rosser, Joel, 53; Wineford, 106; Wm.,
106

Rountree, Franky, 95; Jincy, 95;
   Sally, 95
Row, Christian, 50; Jacob, 50; Jane,
   47; Jean, 94; William, 94
Rowland, Dr., 111; Martha, 111; W.
   F., 113; W. H., 73; William H.,
   57
Ruffin, Betsey, 48; David, 48;
   Elizabeth Frances, 48; Fred-
   erick, 107; John, 48; Lamon, 117;
   Martha Ann, 48; Polly, 48; Sam-
   uel Henry, 48
Rutherford, Robert, 13
Rutland, Shadrack, 108

- S -

Sandeford, Benjamin, 117; Henry, 94;
   Nancy, 5; Wm., 18
Sanderford, Benjamin, 57; Henry, 94;
   James, 2, 94, 123; Mary, 94,
   124; Nathan, 94; Pheriby, 124;
   Tompkins, 94; William, Jr., 94
Sanders, Cally, 94, 95; Elizabeth,
   46, 95; John, 53; Lautory Susan
   Frances, 95; Lindy M., 95; Mary,
   94; Mazie, 46
Sanders (?), Nancy, 102
Sanders, Philander, 94; Polly, 62;
   Primmy, 94, 95; Rhoda, 118;
   Richard, 94; Robert, 94; Ruffin,
   46; Ruffin H., 95; Sion, 46, 52,
   94, 95, 103; Starling E., 95;
   William B., 95
Sargent, Martha, 59
Sary, Pininah, 92
Sauls, Abraham, 134; Absalom, 134
Saunders, Ellender, 101; John, 41;
   J. R., 139
Savage, Drewry, 110; Thomas, 19, 82,
   123; William, 82
Savedge (Savage?), Lucy, 15
Scarborough, Nancy, 118
Scott, Mary E., 17; T. H., 16, 32,
   35, 46; Dr. T. H., 17
Scoules, Valley, 29
Screws, Henry, 1, 95, 117; James,
   95; John, 95; Labon, 104; Little-
   ton, 95; Mourning, 6, 39; Polly,
   95; Salley, 95; Sally, 36; Sarah,
   95; Talton, 104; William, 95
Sealey, Katy, 34
Segraves, Sillear (Priscilla?), 96
Selah, Barsheba, 96; Benjamin, 95;
   Billey Baker, 96; Cordy, 96;
   Edward, 96; Elizabeth, 76, 95;
   Joseph, 96; Joseph, Jr., 85, 95;

Mourning, 95, 96; Rebecca, 96;
   Richard, 95; Rodah, 95
Seley, Cordal, 96
Sellars, Cloah (Chloe), 23; William,
   20
Sellers, John, 82; Lydda, 79
Sessums, David, 120; Isaac, 126;
   Dr. Isaac, 120; Mary Ann, 120;
   Solomon, 120
Seward, Edwin, 53
Shelley, Philip, 72
Shelton, Fereby, 80
Sheppard, John, 8; John, Sr., 42
Sherman, H. G., 144; Nannie, 144;
   Ruth Graham, 144
Sherrod, Anselina, 96; John, 20;
   John J., 96; Jordan, 22, 28,
   71, 96, 133; Leviney, 96; Nancy,
   43, 96; Penny, 20; Redmund, 96;
   Silas, 96; William G., 43
Shores, Ann, 64
Short, George C., 96; Jourdan Hill,
   120; Louisianna, 96; Mary, 96;
   Masora?, 96; Mathew?, 96;
   Richard, 96; Sarah B., 39, 120;
   Thomas, 120; William, 120; Wm.,
   126
Shrader, T., 29
Sikes, Edmon, 100; Edmond, 97;
   Edmund, 14; Jacob, 96; John, 96;
   Joseph, 96; Julian, 97; Madison,
   14, 15, 16, 45, 95, 97, 100;
   Margaret, 97; Martha, 16; Martha
   W., 15; Maryan, 97; Morning, 14;
   Mourning, 93, 96, 97; Sara, 97;
   William Jourding, 97
Sillant (?), Owen, 77
Sillivent, Owen, 144
Sills, Alexander, 69; D., 13; David,
   69, 75, 97, 121, 122; Elizabeth,
   97; Gray, 97; Isadore, 97; J. G.,
   145, 147; Lucy, 97; Virginia·
   Rebecca, 97
Simms, Leonard L., 29
Simpson, Clary, 23; Fred, 138; Jesse,
   50
Sims, Harriet W. B., 98; Henry, 29,
   98; L. S., 98; Martha E., 140;
   Dr. Richard S., 98; Swifton L.,
   55
Sircey, Equila (Aquilla), 37
Skinner, Nicholas, 69; Samuel, 10;
   William, 68, 90
Sledge, W. P., 53
Smedley, John, 33; Martha, 33;
   Patty, 74

Smith, Abraham, 16, 68; A. H., 46;
  Ailey, 35; Alexander, 40, 53;
  Amey, 98; Anna, 78; Archibald,
  144; A. W., 98; Barshaba, 68,
  144; Bathshera, 82; Batson, 125;
  B. B., 132; Benjamin, 97; Ben-
  jamin B., 55; Bennett, 78, 98;
  Brittain, 98; Britton, 129;
  Charity, 144; Chloe, 98; Edw'd,
  139; Elizabeth, 82; Esther, 122;
  James, 98; Jno. B., 4; John, 98;
  John Francis Merrilon, 82; Jor-
  dan, 98; Josiah, 98; Martha,
  120; Micajah, 98; Morning, 144;
  Mourning, 98; Sam, 11, 40, 45,
  109, 119; Samuel, 31, 53, 98;
  Simon, 98; Sion, 98; William
  H., 98; Wm., 34; Wm. H., 15; Wm.
  H. J., 15
Sneed, Asa, 125; Harriet, 90; Mourn-
  ing, 18; Serina, 90
Snipes, Martha, 69
Soloman, James, 133
Sorey, Dennis, 9; Gracy, 99; Jesse,
  99; Mary Eliza, 99; Robert, 28,
  99; Whitmael, 99; William, 99
Sorsby, Alex, 73, 80, 99; Alexander,
  99, 100; Ann, 99; Benja. H.,
  99; Benjamin, 99, 100; B. H.,
  16, 46, 118; B. H., Sr. (Benj.
  H.), 99; Charlie B., 99; Eliza-
  beth, 99, 100; Frances, 100;
  Frances M. E., 99; Henry, 99,
  100; Jeremah (?), 99; Lidda,
  99; Polley, 99; Samuel, 99;
  Samuel D., 100; Samuel S., 99;
  Susan, 99; William, 36, 99
Southall, Mary, 117
Speight, John F., 55; John H., 55
Spruill, W. T., 137
Stallings, Strickland, 105
Statter (Slatter?), Elvilah (Elvira?),
  18
Stephens, Merritt, 29; Nancy, 29
Stevens, Elizabeth, 100; Henry, 57;
  Jeremiah, 100; John, 100;
  Joseph, 100; Joshua, 108
Stewart, William, 49
Stoke, Chloe (?), 127
Stokes, Bathany, 122; Thomas, 62
Stone, Elizabeth Thaney, 23; Happy,
  100; Mary E., 100; McCullar,
  100; Wm., 103
Stott, Henry, 82; Nathan, 82

Strickland, Alerson, 75; Allison,
  103, 134; Alsey, 46; Arnold, 50,
  100; Bartley C., 46; Bartly C.,
  94; B. C., 75, 100; Bollin, 102;
  B. T., 100; Burrell, 60; Burwell,
  60, 101; Carrolus, 101; Charity,
  108; C. M. J., 69, 101; C. O.,
  103; David, 101, 125; Dinah,
  101; Edith, 42; Edward, 102;
  Elie, 101; Elisha, 101; Elizabeth, 101, 102; Elizabeth M.,
  56; Eunice, 42; F. K. W., 101,
  103; Gideon, 101; Hardy, 77,
  101, 102, 130; Henry, 101, 129;
  Isaac, 96, 101, 102; Ishamel,
  52; Ishmeal, 101; Ismel, 101;
  Jacob, 28, 101, 102, 103; Jasper G., 75; Jesse, 101; Jincy,
  88; Jinny, 101; Joseph, 88, 101;
  108, 116, 125; Liday L., 141;
  Lucy, 100; Madison, 103; Mahaly,
  101; Margaret, 101; Mark, 147;
  Marke, 101; Martha, 101; Mary,
  42, 101, 108; Mary Ann, 46;
  Mary W., 56; Mason, 46; Mathew,
  60; Matthew, 101; Millicent, 36;
  Mourning, 126; Nalby M., 101;
  Nancy, 56, 102; Noah, 102; Osbon,
  102; Osborn, 100, 101, 102;
  Pashants (Patience), 144;
  Patience, 101; Rebecca, 102,
  103; Redding, 103; Reuben, 28;
  Robert N., 75; Roena, 129;
  Roenny, 103; Sally, 26; Solomon,
  101; Susanney, 52; Theophilus,
  101; Walter R., 101; Warren, 46,
  101, 102; Waymore, 101; W. D.,
  95; William, 101; William D.,
  102, 143; William Dew, 102;
  Zadock, 103
Stricklin, Chrischaney Penelope
  Elizabeth Ann, 96
Styles, Edwin, 110; Hixsey, 110;
  John, 110; Kelly, 110
Sullavent, Owen, 22
Sullivant, Cornelius, 103; James,
  103; Lucy, 103; Martha, 103;
  Owen, 103; Tim, 103
Sumner, Daniel E., 4; D. E., 7; D.
  W., 40; Edwin, 103; John, 26;
  John Lewis, 103; Mary, 40; Mary
  E., 4; Sally, 103
Sutton, Catherine, 103; George, 103;
  John, 103; Lemwell, 103; Marget,
  103; Sebrina, 113; Thomas, 103;
  Vinson, 103

145; William Hutson, 85
Tisdall, Philip Andrew, 71
Tisdel, Anzada, 109; Elisha, 109
Tisdel (Tisdal), Henry, 109
Tisdel, Joel, 109; Mourning, 109;
    Philip Andrew, 71; Rennison,
    109
Tisdell, Ben, 137; Philip Andrew,
    71
Todd, Henry A., 63
Tomlinson, Isaac, 55, 64, 109
Tompkins, John Franklin, 110; Ros-
    anah, 110
Trevathan, D., 12; Elizabeth, 99;
    Mary, 110; Matthew, 110; Sally,
    110; Selah (or Lilah), 110;
    Williamson, 110; Willis, 110
Tucker, Amey, 110; Barna, 71; Barna-
    bus, 110; Benjamin, 110; Betty,
    111; Corban, 25; Cuziah (Kizziah),
    111; Dinah, 110; Ditson, 111;
    Easter, 110; Enos, 43; Fanney,
    111; Farabee, 110; Fracy (?),
    70; Frances, 111; George K.,
    111; James, 110; Joab, 110,
    111; Job, 34; John, 43; John D.,
    145; Lewis B., 111; Lula May,
    145; Madderson, 140; Margaret,
    111; Margret, 111; Martha, 111;
    Martha Ann E., 145; Nancy, 43,
    137, 145; Nicy, 111; Patsey, 87;
    Pharaby, 76; Rosella, 145; Taylor,
    111; Temperance, 145; Thomas, 110,
    111; Timothy, 79; William W., 145;
    Willoby, 111; Wood, 7, 99; Wright,
    111, 145
Tunnell, Byrd B., 28, 111; Drusilla,
    111; Massilon L., 111
Tunstall, Lucy, 114
Turlington, Elizabeth, 52, 111, 135;
    Henry, 135; John, 111; Mary, 111;
    Thomas, 111, 135; Timothy, 111
Turner, Ann, 112; David, 97; Edward,
    26; Elizabeth, 112; George, 112;
    Henry, 112; James, 65, 112;
    Julian, 112; Laza, 112; Lazarus,
    112; Milly, 74, 112; Nanny, 112;
    Rebecca, 36, 112; Robert, 39;
    Sion, 112; Una, 65; William, 112

- U -

Underwood, Dolly, 112; Fillitha
    (Falitha? Felicia?), 62; Hannah,
    112; Howell, 112, 128; Jacob,
    112; Levi, 112; Levi S., 45;

Malechi, 112; Selley (Sally),
    43; Temperance, 44; Zachariah,
    112
Upchurch, Albert, 110; Alfred, 113;
    R. (Richmond), 110; Richmond,
    15; Sion, 110; Susan, 26
Ures (Eure?), Alford, 81
Uzell, James, 107

- V -

Valentine, Jacob, 39; John, 112;
    Mary, 112
Vallentine, Ratchford, 84
Vanlandanham (Vanlandingham), Pat-
    sey, 137
Vasser, Martha, 35
Vaughan, Christopher, 112; Dempsy,
    112; Easter, 112; Efram, 112;
    Hulday, 112; J., 39; Molley,
    112; Patty, 112; Paty (Patty),
    112; Preston, 112; Rhoda, 78;
    Stephen, 112; Vinson, 112
Vester, Abisha, 113; Benjamin, 113;
    Benjamin H., 113; B. H., 141;
    Cherry, 113; Elijah, 113; Eliza,
    Elizabeth, 110, 113; Frances,
    113; Green, 113; Jordan, 113;
    Joseph, 113; Michael, 45; Nancy,
    113
Vester (Wester), Nancy, 43
Vester, Nathan, 113; Polly, 113;
    Solomon, 113; Suckey, 113;
    Temperance, 113; Wiley, 113;
    William 113
Vick, Achash, 113; Achrah (?), 115;
    Achrih, 76; Aquilla Ann, 91;
    Asael, 113, 116; Asel, 113;
    Ashael, 115; Benjamin, 113, 115;
    B. L., 115; B. S., 113; Charity,
    114; Ebeline (Eveline?), 115;
    Edy, 15; Elender, 115; Eli, 114,
    115, 116; Elijah, 115; Elizabeth,
    2, 5, 59, 114; Elizabeth W., 115;
    Granby, 116; Granberry, 70, 114;
    Harriet Jane, 115; Henry, 2, 10,
    15, 114; Howel R., 115; Hudson,
    145; Iredell, 91; Isaac, 114;
    Jacky C., 115; Jacob, 76, 115,
    116; Jincy, 115; Joel, 76, 107,
    114, 115; John, 8, 15, 30, 85,
    113, 114, 115, 116, 120, 126;
    John H., 65, 116; Jos., 30;
    Joseph, 15; Joseph John, 115;
    Jos(h)ua, 115; Josiah, 20, 26,
    85, 114, 115, 116; Lewis, 18,

55, 76, 115, 122; Little G. B.,
84; Little Grandberry, 114;
Louisa, 115; Lourany, 145;
Lucinda, 15; Ludenda, 115; Margaret, 115; Martha, 59, 114;
Mary, 98, 113, 114, 115, 116,
127; Mary M. V., 115; Matthew,
116; Nancy, 21, 89; Nancy K.,
113; Nathan, Jr., 116; Nathan,
Sr., 116; Orphaline, 115;
Patience, 113, 115; Peggy, 28;
Piety H., 11; Polly Harriet,
114; Rahab, 115; Rich., 119;
Richard, 113; Robert, 77, 102,
105, 116; Sally, 107, 114; Sam,
52; Samuel, 34, 118; Samuel W.
W., 66, 86, 91, 115; Sam. W. M.,
28; Sam. W. W., 86, 116; Sophia,
127; Susannah, 114, 116; Unity,
68; William, 115, 116; Wilson,
25, 36, 76, 108, 109, 111, 119
Vicks, John, 30; Josiah, 84
Vinson, David, 49; James, 116;
Sallie, 116
Viverett, Elizabeth, 116; Henry,
116; James, 117; Launcelot, 117;
Micajah, 117; Thomas, 35, 116

- W -

Walker, Arabella C., 114; Bolden,
114; Boldin, 59; Boling, 9;
Daniel, 120; Elick H., 9; Eliza-
beth, 79; Francis, 56; Jacob,
117; James, 59, 114; James Hart-
well, 114; Jesse, 117; Joel,
117; John B., 9; John W., 142;
Jonathan, 117; Jones, 89; Judah
K., 74; Lemuel, 69, 117, 129;
Mathew, 71; Micajah, 117; Milli-
cent, 92; Nancy, 69; Patsey,
117; Polley, 99; Priscilla Law-
rence, 9; Rebecca, 59; Rebecca
H., 9; Richmond, 74; Salathiel
R. D., 74; Sarah, 51; Silvia,
117; William, 93; Worrel P., 74;
W. P., 109
Wall, Betty, 117; James, 117; Sary
(Sarah), 117
Wallace, Francis, 142
Ward, Benjamin, 117; Calvin, 15, 118;
C. W., 24, 89, 133, 140; Eliza-
beth, 3; Fanny, 117; Francis,
117; German, 118; G. W., 6, 14,
91, 140, 145; James E., 32;
Jarman, 113; J. L., 145; Joe,

117; John, 3, 118, 145; John,
alias Mathews, 117; John (alias
Matthews), 118; John L., 145;
Lucy, 118; Lydia, 145; Marget,
16; Mary, 3; Nathan, 49, 117,
118; Rebecca, 3; Sally, 39;
Sarah, 117; Sarah W., 140;
William, 117; Willis, 80, 110,
118; W. W., 137
Warren, Fanny, 118; John, 108, Mary,
118; Willis, 32, 95, 118
Watkins, Ann, 90; Beveton, 118;
Charlotte, 119; Chloe, 116;
Delila, 118; Elizabeth, 118;
Henry, 118; Isaac, 118, 119;
James, 118; Jinney, 118; John,
118, 119; Joseph, 118; Mary,
118; Nancy, 118, 119; Rachel,
118; Stephen, 118; Thomas, 118
Watson, A., 29; John T., 87; Joshua,
36, 87, 123, 127, 144
Weaver, Elizabeth, 118; George, 142;
Laura Ann, 142; Wm., 14
Webb, John, 108; J. T., 32, 75, 89,
101, 116; Willis, 97
Weeks, Geo. A., 99
Weldon, Martha, 50; Mathew, 50
Wells, Absalom, 119; Bartley, 120;
Elizabeth, 119, 120; Frederick,
119; Jeremiah, 119, 120; Joel,
28, 99, 119; John, 86, 119, 120;
Joshua, 119, 120; Laura, 45;
Lewis, 81; Mary, 9, 120; Redman,
119; Redmon, 119; Redmond D.,
120; R. D., 115; Sally, 45;
Solomon, 85, 119; Stephen, 119,
120; Stephen, Jr., 120; Thomas,
117
West, Nathan, 142
Wester, A. D., 24; A. H., 15; Arthur,
36, 120; Benjamin, 120; Eli,
120; Hardy, 120; Kissiah, 120;
Mary, 25, 120; Mathew, 36
Wester (Vester), Nancy, 43
Wester, Polly, 120; Samuel, 61; W.
D., 143; William, 76, 120
Westray, Elizabeth, 22; Harriet, 22;
Kiziah, 34; Mary, 34, 144; Polly,
44; S., 49, 52; Sallie B., 126;
Sally, 120; Sally T., 34; Sam,
52, 95, 114, 119, 126, 127;
Samuel, 34, 108, 120; Sarah B.,
120; T. P., 10, 12, 114; Turner
P., 120; William, 44; Willis, 22

James D., 128; James R., 19;
Jerusha, 137; J. L. R., 146;
Joel, 127; Joel B., 128; Joel ?
B., 147; John, 127; John D.,
128; Jolby (Jolley) B., 147;
Jonas Barnes, 11; Josiah, 120,
127; Katherine P., 128; Lamon,
143; Lamon R., 91; Lawrence,
127; Littleberry, 127; Martha,
36, 127; Mary, 69; Mary A. B.,
147; Mary Jane, 127; Mills, 48,
79, 127; M. R., 147; Nancy, 63;
Perry, 69; Prudence, 127; Ransom,
145; Richard R., 147; Roena W.,
86; Sion, 18, 122, 127; Sion W.,
127; Susan, 127; Thomas, 128;
Wiatt, 127; William, 112, 127;
Willie, 111, 127, 128; Willie
D., 128; Willie (Willis?), 53
Wiggins, James, 67; John, 95
Wilder, John W., 128; Martha, 128;
Mathew, 106, 128; Sally, 15
Wilheight, Monford, 105
Wilhight, Penelope, 14
Wilhite, Elizabeth, 121; Rhody, 26;
Sally, 97; William, 97
Wilkinson, John D. P., 36
Williams, Anna P., 82; Ann E., 54;
Anne, 130; Archibald, 72;
Arthur, 102; Barbara S., 3;
Barshaba, 110; Benj., 94; Ben-
jamin, 25, 128; Billey, 128,
130; Bryan, 147; Bryant, 26, 51;
Bunch, 129; Burrell, 129;
Catherine, 96; Charity, 128,
130; Chrisey, 129; Christian,
129; Cooper, 121; Cutton (?)
Samuel, 141; Delilah Pope, 130;
Dinah, 130; Drucy, 51; Druery,
43; Drury, 35, 129, 130, 147;
Edmond, 147; Elias, 129; Eliza-
beth, 70, 71, 129, 130; Eliza-
beth A., 72; Elizabeth Ann, 3;
George, 128; Guilford H., 56;
Henry, 128, 147; Henry G., 3,
55, 57, 71; Herbert or Robert,
147; H. G., 7, 61; H. (Henry)
G., 113; Howell F. Ellin (Flewe-
ellin), 47; Isley, 33; Jacob,
115; James, 24, 32, 39, 47, 84,
115, 122, 125, 129, 131, 133;
James T., 74; Jas., 99, 113;
Jean, 84, 129; Jeremiah, 38, 93;
Joel, 130, 147; John, 40, 72,
130; John B., 57, 59; John W.,
129; Jonas, 35, 84, 130; Joseph
J., 129; Kearney, 6; Kinchen,

129; Lawrence, 128; Lucrecy, 24;
Lucy, 106, 129; Lunford (Luns-
ford?), 128; Marsilla, 128;
Martha, 130; Mary, 51, 56, 129,
132; Mathew, 129; Milbrey, 147;
Milly, 43; Morning, 129; Mourn-
ing, 15, 31; Nancy, 129, 132;
Nathan, 130, 147; Nathan C.,
130; P., 42; Penny, 15, 147;
Penny April, 147; Philander, 68,
83, 129, 130; Pilgrim L., 100;
Pilgrim S., 130; Polly, 129;
Pride, 129; Priscilla, 43, 130;
Redden Smith, 147; Redmon, 147;
Reuben, 108; Richard S., 130;
Robert, 100, 147; Roeny, 43;
Rolan, 102; Roland, 35, 92, 102,
129; Rollen (Roland), 129; Row-
land, 84, 130, 147; Salley, 129;
Sally, 47; Sam, 68; Samuel, 71,
128, 129, 130; Sarah, 65, 128,
130; Sealah, 147; Senath, 43;
Sherod, 7; Sherrod, 9, 114;
Simon, 23; Sisly, 130; Solomon,
71; Tempe, 59; Tempy Olvy
(Olive?), 138; Thomas, 72, 128;
W. B., 75; W. C., 69; Wiley,
147; William, 25, 65, 69, 125,
147; William K. A., 3; William
M., 129; William T., 72; Wilson,
107, 147; Wm. T., 7; Zelpah,
130; Zilpha, 4; Zilphey, 129
Williamson, Ann, 131, 147; Bluford,
115; Gilly, 47; Hardy, 82, 131,
147; Isaac, 76; Jos., 23; Joseph,
131, 147; Joseph, Jr., 131;
Joseph, Sr., 131; Morning, 88;
Mourning, 89; Penelope, 131;
Sally, 76; Sarah, 131, 147;
Thomas, 131, 147
Williford, Andrew J., 131; Blake,
131; Caroline, 131; Della, 131;
Elijah L., 131; Elizabeth, 59,
131; Granberry V., 131; H., 131;
Josiah B., 10; Martha, 131; Mary
Ann, 131; Mary Ann E., 10; Meedy
B., 131; Meedy H., 131; Penelope,
131; Dr. S. Thompson, 131; Timo-
thy, 131
Willis, Alice, 131; Elizabeth, 131;
Ester, 131; Mary, 127, 131;
Sarah, 131; Thomas, 131; William,
131; Wilson, 131
Wills, Absalom, 83

Westry, Bennett, 121; Bennett, Junior, 121; Elizabeth, 121; Nancy I., 121; Temperance, 121; William, 121; William S., 121; Willis, 121
Wheddon, Mary, 42
Wheeler, Jacob, 105, 109
Wheeles, Amos, 72
Wheeless, Amos, 122; Benjamin, 122; Elijah, 122; Elizabeth, 122; John, 122; Mildred, 72; Patsey, 122; William, 121; Wm., 72
Wheless, Ann Elizabeth, 1; Amos, 121; Archibald, 121; Benjamin, 97, 122; Charlotte, 121; Dolphin, 121; Drewery, 121; Edney, 121; Elizabeth, 122; Hardy, 121; Joel, 121; Lemuel, 1; Lemuel F., 48; L. F., 85; Martha, 123; Mary, 141; Milbrey, 39; Milbry, 121; Mourning, 126; Patsey, 121, 122; Polly, 121; Suffia (Sophia?), 121; William, 47, 97, 121, 129; William, Sr., 69; Wm., 121; Wm. B., 121
Whidden, Elizabeth, 122; James, 122; Lott, Sr., 122; Maxwell, 122; Sarah, 122; William, 122
Whiddon, Forten (Fortune), 22
Whitaker, Cary, 144; Eli B., 120; Eliza, 143; Henry, 1; H. W., 54; Jane, 56; J. B., 19; L. H. B., 55; Mary Eliza, 1; Richard M., 1
White, Abraham, 123; Appy, 69; Armeger, 122; Charles, 123; Edward, 123; Elizabeth, 14, 122, 123; Guelminus (?), 122; Gulielmus, 122; Harriet, 97; John, 123; Joseph, 122; Joseph H., 97, 123; Joseph Hartsfield, 123; Joseph, Jr., 122; Joseph, Sr., 122; Little B., 14, 31; Littleberry, 122, 123; Margaret, 122; Martha, 122; Mary, 122; Millicent, 122; Sarah, 122; Thomas, 64, 122; Thomas W., 125; T. W., 122; William, 54; William Heath, 123; Wortham, 123
Whitehead, Abiah, 33; Whitehead, Arthur, 17, 124, 134, 146; Benjamin, 123, 124; Bennett, 146; Burrell, 69; Charles, 123; Elizabeth, 33, 98, 106, 123, 124; Henry, 33, 123, 124, 134;

James, 4, 123; John A., 7, 21; Jonathan, 109, 123; Joseph, 123; Lazarus, 80; Martha, 123, 124; Mary, 3, 123, 146; Mathew, 124; Matthew, 124; Mourning, 124; Nathan, 17, 33, 47, 124; Patsey, 124; Pheraba, 114; Pherebe, 116; Portland C., 123; Rachal, 124; Rachel, 124; Rahab, 33; T. C., 87; Temperance G., 134; Thomas, 37, 124; Thomas, Jr., 124; William, 37, 59, 68, 98, 123; Col. Wm., 93
Whitehouse, John, 124; John Lamon, 124
Whiteone (?), Nancy, 19
Whitfield, Ann, 126; Archibald G., 74, 125; Benjamin, 57, 61, 87, 125, 126; Benjamin G., 125; Benjamin Griffin, 125; Charity, 125, 126; Chloe, 126; Delilah, 125; Dilly Ann, 74; Dilly P., 74; Easter, 125; Edith, 15; Edy, 127; Eli, 115; Elisha, 125, 126, 127; Eliza, 126; Elizabeth, 81, 125, 126, 127, 135; Emeldred, 91; Franklin, 74; Guilford, 44; Guilford G., 68, 125; Guilford Griffin, 125; Hardy, 126; Hardy G., 116, 125; Isaac, 79, 115, 125; Israel, 126; Jacob, 126; Joel, 79; John, 115, 126; John T. G., 125; John Thomas Griffin, 125; Martha Matilda, 125; Mary, 80, 125, 126; Mary J., 126; Mathew, 71, 127; Mildred, 126; Milly, 126; Nancy, 126; Patrick L., 74; Penelope, 80, 115, 126; Priscilla, 115; Reuben, 107, 108, 126; Sally A. E., 147; Sarah, 126; Solomon, 125, 126, 128; Sookey, 125; Tammen, 110; Thomas, 126; Willey, 127; William, 126, 127; William, Jr., 127; Willie, 125, 126, 127; Willie G., 125
Whitley, Alley, 69; Arthur A., 128; Bathseba, 76; Benjamin, 98; Britton, 1; Catherine, 126; Charlotte, 53, 127; David, 127; Elisa A. B., 147; Elizabeth, 8; Eliza May, 146; George H., 91; Henry, 112, 127; Henry A., 111, 147; Henry R., 147; Isaac, 127;

James D., 128; James R., 19;
Jerusha, 137; J. L. R., 146;
Joel, 127; Joel B., 128; Joel ?
B., 147; John, 127; John D.,
128; Jolby (Jolley) B., 147;
Jonas Barnes, 11; Josiah, 120,
127; Katherine P., 128; Lamon,
143; Lamon R., 91; Lawrence,
127; Littleberry, 127; Martha,
36, 127; Mary, 69; Mary A. B.,
147; Mary Jane, 127; Mills, 48,
79, 127; M. R., 147; Nancy, 63;
Perry, 69; Prudence, 127; Ransom,
145; Richard R., 147; Roena W.,
86; Sion, 18, 122, 127; Sion W.,
127; Susan, 127; Thomas, 128;
Wiatt, 127; William, 112, 127;
Willie, 111, 127, 128; Willie
D., 128; Willie (Willis?), 53
Wiggins, James, 67; John, 95
Wilder, John W., 128; Martha, 128;
Mathew, 106, 128; Sally, 15
Wilheight, Monford, 105
Wilhight, Penelope, 14
Wilhite, Elizabeth, 121; Rhody, 26;
Sally, 97; William, 97
Wilkinson, John D. P., 36
Williams, Anna P., 82; Ann E., 54;
Anne, 130; Archibald, 72;
Arthur, 102; Barbara S., 3;
Barshaba, 110; Benj., 94; Ben-
jamin, 25, 128; Billey, 128,
130; Bryan, 147; Bryant, 26, 51;
Bunch, 129; Burrell, 129;
Catherine, 96; Charity, 128,
130; Chrisey, 129; Christian,
129; Cooper, 121; Cutton (?)
Samuel, 141; Delilah Pope, 130;
Dinah, 130; Drucy, 51; Druery,
43; Drury, 35, 129, 130, 147;
Edmond, 147; Elias, 129; Eliza-
beth, 70, 71, 129, 130; Eliza-
beth A., 72; Elizabeth Ann, 3;
George, 128; Guilford H., 56;
Henry, 128, 147; Henry G., 3,
55, 57, 71; Herbert or Robert,
147; H. G., 7, 61; H. (Henry)
G., 113; Howell F. Ellin (Flewellin), 47; Isley, 33; Jacob,
115; James, 24, 32, 39, 47, 84,
115, 122, 125, 129, 131, 133;
James T., 74; Jas., 99, 113;
Jean, 84, 129; Jeremiah, 38, 93;
Joel, 130, 147; John, 40, 72,
130; John B., 57, 59; John W.,
129; Jonas, 35, 84, 130; Joseph
J., 129; Kearney, 6; Kinchen,

129; Lawrence, 128; Lucrecy, 24;
Lucy, 106, 129; Lunford (Luns-
ford?), 128; Marsilla, 128;
Martha, 130; Mary, 51, 56, 129,
132; Mathew, 129; Milbrey, 147;
Milly, 43; Morning, 129; Mourn-
ing, 15, 31; Nancy, 129, 132;
Nathan, 130, 147; Nathan C.,
130; P., 42; Penny, 15, 147;
Penny April, 147; Philander, 68,
83, 129, 130; Pilgrim L., 100;
Pilgrim S., 130; Polly, 129;
Pride, 129; Priscilla, 43, 130;
Redden Smith, 147; Redmon, 147;
Reuben, 108; Richard S., 130;
Robert, 100, 147; Roeny, 43;
Rolan, 102; Roland, 35, 92, 102,
129; Rollen (Roland), 129; Row-
land, 84, 130, 147; Salley, 129;
Sally, 47; Sam, 68; Samuel, 71,
128, 129, 130; Sarah, 65, 128,
130; Sealah, 147; Senath, 43;
Sherod, 7; Sherrod, 9, 114;
Simon, 23; Sisly, 130; Solomon,
71; Tempe, 59; Tempy Olvy
(Olive?), 138; Thomas, 72, 128;
W. B., 75; W. C., 69; Wiley,
147; William, 25, 65, 69, 125,
147; William K. A., 3; William
M., 129; William T., 72; Wilson,
107, 147; Wm. T., 7; Zelpah,
130; Zilpha, 4; Zilphey, 129
Williamson, Ann, 131, 147; Bluford,
115; Gilly, 47; Hardy, 82, 131,
147; Isaac, 76; Jos., 23; Joseph,
131, 147; Joseph, Jr., 131;
Joseph, Sr., 131; Morning, 88;
Mourning, 89; Penelope, 131;
Sally, 76; Sarah, 131, 147;
Thomas, 131, 147
Williford, Andrew J., 131; Blake,
131; Caroline, 131; Della, 131;
Elijah L., 131; Elizabeth, 59,
131; Granberry V., 131; H., 131;
Josiah B., 10; Martha, 131; Mary
Ann, 131; Mary Ann E., 10; Meedy
B., 131; Meedy H., 131; Penelope,
131; Dr. S. Thompson, 131; Timo-
thy, 131
Willis, Alice, 131; Elizabeth, 131;
Ester, 131; Mary, 127, 131;
Sarah, 131; Thomas, 131; William,
131; Wilson, 131
Wills, Absalom, 83

www.ingramcontent.com/pod-product-compliance
Lightning Source LLC
Chambersburg PA
CBHW020459030426

42337CB00011B/159